FINDING THE GAME

FINDING THE GAME

Three Years, Twenty-five Countries, and

the Search for Pickup Soccer

Gwendolyn Oxenham

St. Martin's Press

New York

www.stmartins.com

ISBN 978-1-250-00204-4 (hardcover)
ISBN 978-1-250-01088-9 (e-book)

First Edition: June 2012

10   9   8   7   6   5   4   3   2   1

To the players,
families, and friends
who helped us
find the game

CONTENTS

FINDING THE GAME

PROLOGUE

LUKE AND I were going eighty miles an hour when we hit the deer.

Two days earlier we had loaded our lives into my '96 Camry, moving to Los Angeles from North Carolina to turn three hundred hours of footage into a ninety minute feature-length film. While the Camry had 168,000 miles on it, there was no reason to believe we wouldn't make it.

It was the good kind of drive—rolling hills and cornfields, trees rising out of rivers, sideways light, and the feeling that so much was ahead.

It turned dark in North Dakota. The speed limit was seventy-five miles per hour, and there was something vaguely eerie about driving that fast through empty land. We passed a trucker about every twenty minutes. The Camry was humming and we were crossing off the hours—fourteen yesterday, twenty down so far today. Two more hours to go before we reached the cabin in Montana that Luke's friend had won for a week in a raffle. This was the land of Norman Maclean's *A River Runs Through It,* my favorite book and the reason why Luke was able to talk me into a thirteen-hour detour.

I'd scrunched up my pillow against the window and shut my eyes when I felt Luke come down hard on the brakes. It happened in a second but it felt slow: there it was—the deer—appearing suddenly out of the dark, beautiful and bright in our headlights. He was moving right so Luke swerved left as our brakes and tires screeched. I waited for the relief, the heart pound of nearly hitting something, but then I realized we weren't going to miss it. The deer, his instinct clashing against ours, made an about-face and ran in the same direction we swerved.

He came at me, his brown eyes staring into mine right before his face hit the windshield. His body thumped against the car, and I screamed. I felt surprised to hear myself scream.

Then it was quiet, except for the new rattle of the steering wheel and the thump of our bumper against tire. We turned on our hazard lights and limped to the nearest exit. Beneath the exit sign another sign read NO SERVICE HERE. There was one shed with a floodlight in a gravel parking lot, so we turned off the car there. Luke got out and I waited for him to come let me out. The inside door handle was missing, so this was always how it was: I was trapped in there until Luke made his way around to work on the outside door handle, which was also broken but could be pried open if it wasn't raining or humid.

Luke's fingers jimmied the door handle up, but the door still didn't open, dented inward from the body of the deer. I crawled across the driver's side and stood with Luke, staring at the shattered windshield and headlight. We tried to open the hood, but it was also too warped to get open.

I leaned up against the unwounded side of the bumper, feeling the clarity that comes with thirty-four hours staring at open road. In the past year, I'd slept in twenty-three countries. I'd played soccer in sand-swept streets in Togo, with felons in Bolivia, with fifteen-year-old rappers in France. Now I was stuck in Montana, on my way to L.A., with my entire life in my car and deer blood on my fingers.

AWAY FROM
THE BRIGHT LIGHTS

1.

FIVE YEARS EARLIER Luke and I had set up life in a downtown loft in Asheville, North Carolina. It was one large room with wooden floors, high ceilings, and a big old window that faced the morning sun. We bought a table for thirty dollars from a thrift store down the street and carried it over our heads on the walk home. We slept on a blow-up mattress on the floor. Below us, there was a French restaurant and a wine shop with a five-dollar discount table. We could walk to the two-screen theater, Izzy's Coffee Den, and Malaprop's Bookstore. Two tuba players, brothers simultaneously divorced by their wives, owned the loft across the hall; when they came up on weekends, we sat on their window ledge and drank single-malt scotch.

Luke worked an office job selling billboards. He woke up at seven, took a shower, and kissed me on the forehead as I slid deeper under the sheets. I woke up around nine and sat down at the desk Luke and I made together. I was on a writing grant to finish my first book. I had all the time in the world, all day long. I spent the mornings thinking. I tried to focus on my first-grade teacher, who told my mother on Parent-Teacher Conference Day, "Whatever you do, keep her away from sports. . . . She has the soul of an artist." We thought that teacher was an idiot for a long time. Now I hoped she wasn't.

At night we played in the parking lot of the social services building. Luke could only score by hitting the silver pole of the light post. I could score between the white lines of a parking space. We tried tricks. Luke did rainbows, shin juggles, snazzy things you see on YouTube videos. One side of the parking lot was bookended by a large mural painted by kids. We banged the ball off pastel handprints, trees, and outlined clouds. Bums occasionally stopped to watch, dangling their arms over the wall and whistling. When one of us kicked it over the wall, they didn't retrieve it for us; instead they watched as we sprinted to catch the ball that rolled faster and faster down the sloping street.

After our game was over, we sat along the curb, tired, nostalgic. Luke had been a Notre Dame center midfielder who scored big goals in big games. I'd been the youngest Division I athlete in NCAA history, a starter and leading scorer for Duke at sixteen. Now we made jokes about being twenty-four-year-old has-beens.

DURING THE DAY there was too much time. I tried to kill the hours: I read books, great books, but I felt guilty just laying there reading page after page while the rest of the world complained about a lack of time.

The writing wasn't going well. My book was about my brother, and the effect one kid has on the other, but it was hard to squeeze our lives into pages. He has a way of saying things that land—like the time after the hurricane, when twenty-two trees fell down in our backyard, and he said, "Damn, sis, looks like somebody used the sun as a wrecking ball." Or the time he described prison as "a lot like middle school, people trying to be cool." The story was important to me and I wanted to say it right. I spent all day sitting there, running my hand along the wood of the desk. Luke and I didn't know how to make a desk: we'd nailed down four planks of raw wood atop four skinny logs we'd found laying along-side a vacant lot. The wood was starting to warp and the trunks were splintering, but I loved that desk.

I kept a short stack of books on the left corner—my current favorites, books I could pick up and flip open, reading sentences and voices I hoped would influence my own. One of them was a planner my best friend, Leah, gave me when we were fourteen; in it there was a photograph and a quote from a famous author every month, and even though the dates were all wrong, I still read the quotes and stared at the photos.

On the tenth month of my yearlong writing grant, I was sitting at the desk once again looking through the planner. I thumbed past June, July, and August until I reached the black-and-white photo of Truman Capote and stared into his round eyes. Right beneath his portrait there were these words: "The test of whether or not a writer has divined the natural shape of his story is just this: After reading it, can you imagine it differently, or does it silence your imagination and seem to you absolute and final? As an orange is final. As an orange is something nature has made just right." When I sat and read my 240-page draft, I knew it wasn't an orange, and I had no idea how to make it one.

I lay down on our fake-suede couch and thought about my dad, who for the last several months had said things like, "You should join the FBI—fantastic benefits." He was worried because I had no health insurance. I told him I'd be the world's worst spy, but he took that as evidence I'd be a good one: "See, no one would ever guess." I started taking suggestions like this into consideration. I entertained the possibility of anything—law school, business school—things I'd ruled out from the very beginning. Suddenly I wondered about wearing pencil skirts and high heels, carrying a briefcase and spreading papers across a long conference table. Anything but writing.

Because of a large hole in our Camry's muffler, I could hear Luke get home from work. I'd pull on the chain that angled our window up and wave to him, grateful that my time to write was up. Watching him walk across the parking lot, wearing button-downs, tan slacks, and brown dress shoes, it looked like he was playing grown-up. He had wild blond curls that he wore in a big fro in college (opposing teams called him Brillo Pad), but now he had me cut the curls off so that he'd look "professional."

In the beginning he enjoyed having a pattern—brewing coffee and ironing down the collar of his shirt in the mornings. He liked trying on a profession. During his job interview, he'd taken an aptitude test. He lied through most of it, picking whatever answer he thought a true salesman would pick. If the question asked, "At a party, would you be in the center of the crowd or along the wall?" he of course said he'd be the guy in the center. Then when he failed the test and the results said he'd make a terrible salesman, he didn't know what to make of it. As they debated whether or not to hire him, he thought about telling them he lied, but that admission seemed worse than just failing. They ended up hiring him, and he was left to wonder in private what the test would have said if he'd answered honestly. *Maybe,* he thought, *I'm meant for sales.*

Six months in, one of the maintenance guys quit, so they started sending Luke—the most limber guy with a desk job—up to repair the billboards. He did not like going up there. He wouldn't admit he was unhappy, but I could tell from the way he curled up on the bed when the alarm went off, his whole body sweating. I guess up there, 150 feet above the highway, standing on a see-through iron grate, wind howling, vinyls flapping, he came to two realizations: one, he didn't like being up on billboards, and two, he didn't like selling billboards. His plan was to make it through the end of the year. After that, he didn't know. Neither of us did.

ON A SUNDAY afternoon, I drove to Durham to watch ninety minutes of my old life. I sat on the far side of the bleachers, away from everyone else. It embarrassed me to come back. I felt like the loser who graduates from high school but still hangs around the benches in the mornings before school.

I came primarily to watch Rebekah Fergusson, a freshman on the team when I was senior. In college, I'd made a twenty-minute documentary centered on identity through sports. Ferg was one of four characters. While the other three were standouts on the field who said things like, "I would do anything to win," she was the bench-warming counterpart who said, "You think you'll get here and run sprints and work hard and then one day you'll play and then one day you'll start—you know, Rudy and all that crap—but, well, it's not always that easy." When a professor watched footage of her green puppy-dog eyes looking earnestly at the camera, he said, "It's almost like you can see it—she's too nice to be good." But that Sunday she got her first start against Florida State, and in the rain, in the mess, she was playing with the effort of someone who'd spent three years pent up on the bench: she beat the FSU forward to the ball, stripped it off her when she tried to dribble, and won everything in the air. "That kid's playing her heart out," a gravelly voice said from behind me, mostly to himself. The man had bushy white hair and chewed on a cigar as he paced back and forth in the aisle. Most likely he was somebody's dad: dads always sought space by themselves, never wanting to risk anyone trying to engage them in conversation while they were trying to watch.

"Playing your heart out"—when I was a kid, it was my favorite expression. Even now, guiltily, I love it. "Heart" lost its power as we got older; too many coaches said it in too many pregame speeches. You stopped really hearing them. But you still knew what it meant when it happened, when nothing could touch you. It was the main thing I missed.

When my senior season ended, they handed us plaques that showed our span: 2000–2004. One of the underclassmen said, "It looks like you guys died." I would have tried out for the women's professional league, but it folded the year I graduated. Your whole life you're a soccer player, then suddenly you're not.

So I applied for graduate school in creative writing. I came up with my forty-page writing sample during a two-week tear in the athletes' computer cluster, drinking Mountain Dews and writing all night. I thought it could work: I'd just replace soccer with writing. I applied to two schools, Florida and Notre Dame. The Florida rejection came startlingly fast, like they emphatically didn't want me. It made me feel foolish for applying in the first place. It took me fifteen years to get good at soccer; what made me think I could just try something else? Several months went by and I assumed Notre Dame got so many applications they didn't have time to notify everyone who'd been rejected. But in March, I came home from a run and was standing in the doorway panting when Thora, my Icelandic roommate, said, "Some man named Villiam called." I had no idea who William was or why he was calling, but I called back and he said it was William O'Rourke, the director of the University of Notre Dame's creative writing program, and that he'd like to invite me to South Bend. I got off the phone as quickly as I could, afraid of saying something that would let him know they'd made a mistake. I looked at Thora, who was watching me. "Thora, Thora, THORA," I said. "They want me! Somebody wants me!"

There was an easiness for a while: I knew what I was going to do, who I was going to be. The end of the school year glided by, and I spent the summer before I left for South Bend working as a deckhand on a fifteen-million-dollar yacht in Mexico. I Windexed toilets, turned down high-thread-count sheets, and placed chocolates on pillows. I went bonefishing in the mangroves, kayaked through small inlets, and tried different tequilas in straw-hut bars on the tips of islands. During my shifts of night watch, I listened to the crew. Gary spent a few years in Alaska ice-fishing, got his degree in chemical engineering, studied astronomy in grad school, then became a boat captain. Alfredo owned a Mexican resort that went bankrupt; he gave me one of the teak rocking chairs he'd made by hand. Jody, a former pastry chef, told stories of working on boats across the world; she'd opened wine bottles for Jimmy Buffett, Mariah Carey, and *Forbes*'s second-richest man. They saw my devotion to soccer as unnatural and odd. For the first time, single-mindedness—dedication—was presented as limitation. As I sat in the swiveled captain's chair, bobbing softly with the waves while scanning the water for the lights of other boats, I too wanted to try everything and anything. I wanted to move past soccer.

This, I soon discovered, was a lie. We anchored far out in Ascension Bay, close to an island that served as an outpost for the Mexican army. It was a remote, buggy location, and as Alfredo and I skinned grouper on the back of the yacht, he pointed with his knife toward the island: "That's where the bad soldiers get sent." We could see them in uniform, sitting on the dock, machine guns strapped across their chests, machetes in hand. But right along the shoreline was a makeshift soccer field, and after weeks without ball or field, all I wanted was to play.

I dinghied over to the uniformed men and made kicking gestures until my intentions were clear. A half-hour later, in monsoonlike rain, I shared goal celebrations, drank beer, ate ceviche, and took Fun Shot photos in which I am sandwiched between Mexican soldiers, holding on to their guns.

I thought, *Who am I kidding? I want to play soccer until I die.* Well-roundedness seems disloyal: How can you move to a new world without betraying the first? How can you drop it if you love it?

As I scrubbed toilets all the next day, and then later, as I went to classes in the cold of South Bend and then wrote in the stillness of our apartment in Asheville, I kept thinking about that game. Now, sitting here in the bleachers, with my hands beneath my thighs, I thought about it again. I looked out at the field, at Ferg running up the sideline, at the dad violently combing his hands through his hair, but I was seeing Ascension Bay and the soldiers, and daydreaming about pickup.

THAT NIGHT I met Ferg on West Campus. Like me, Ferg had gone on to spend all her time in Documentary Studies. We were both the over-thinker sort who spent as much time wondering what the game meant as we did playing it. I wanted to go to the library, to sit at a table with an old-fashioned lamp while people all around us bent their heads over books. I wanted to hash out some sketch for the future, to sit there with coffee and a legal pad and spend two hours thinking about what we would do if we could do anything. I wanted that game in Mexico to be the start of something.

2.

BOTH MY PARENTS had adventure in them. My mom had worked as a secretary in downtown Los Angeles and saved up enough for a semester at West Liberty State College in West Virginia, a place she picked because she wanted to go somewhere with green rolling hills. She got there and discovered the school was in the middle of a coal-mining town. She thought if she made straight As, they'd give her a scholarship. She made the As but nothing happened, so she drove her Vega back to L.A., where she met my dad.

My dad had been a lifeguard in Laguna Beach and a Green Beret in Vietnam. Before he was shipped to the front lines, he flew to Hawaii and spent three months surfing, putting toilet seats on toilets, and sleeping on the beach. Even after kids and a job, he still seemed unquenched: when a dog bit my sister's face, he used the insurance money to buy his first sailboat. He studied a How-to-Sail pocket manual, and he and my mom spent the next ten years weekend racing. When we moved to Pensacola, Florida, the Catalina 38 wouldn't fit beneath the bridges, so we sold it, but he'd still watch the masts as we drove over the three-mile bridge. He kept his longboards, but eventually they got moved to the attic. When he needed the money, he sold one of them for $245 to a man named Ron. I remember him standing in the driveway with his arms folded across his chest, watching that guy walk away with his surfboard. He never sold another one.

Every year we watched *Endless Summer,* the documentary about two surfers who trekked around the world. As a teenager, I didn't want to watch a documentary, I didn't want to watch something from 1966, I didn't want to watch something I'd already seen before. "This is cool," my dad said matter-of-factly. "You don't know how cool this is." (He always tried to educate me: when I'd asked for the New Kids on the Block album, he gave me the Rolling Stones and told me I could thank him later.) So I sat there with my legs beneath the coffee table and I watched.

Now I called and told him the plan Ferg and I came up with in the library: we'd move from country to country and, instead of looking for waves, we'd go in search of pickup games. He was silent longer than I expected him to be. "Well, honey," he said, "where are you going to get the money? *How* are you going to do it?"

"We're going to apply for a grant."

"For how much?"

"Five thousand dollars."

He snorted. "That's not going to get you very far."

My dad is an interesting paradox of confidence and negativity; he believed each of his kids could do anything and constantly told us so, but as soon as you picked whatever that thing was, he nagged at you with all of the exhausting details you were going to have to think about in order to make it happen. And, of course, he was right. Five thousand dollars wouldn't get us far.

Luke was similarly negative. I told him the idea after he'd come home from the billboards and was sitting at our thrift-store table, loose with the release of being away from work. I hung my arm around his neck and told him. My excitement pounced on him. He didn't respond.

Luke was the only person I knew who loved the game more than I did. We'd walk down to the abandoned field in front of the projects and play for hours, and then I'd want to leave but he'd still be juggling the ball up and down while I sat in the grass and said, "I want to go home." Because now, there was nothing to train for, nothing to get better for. Luke loved it anyway.

So I didn't understand his blank face. I didn't get how I could say "want to go around the world playing in game after game" and get zero response. "So you don't want to do it?" I said, my voice accusing.

"I didn't say that," he said.

I sighed. Once, Luke told me a parable he liked: There were two sons, one who said he'd help his father in the field but then never did, and one who acted resistant but then did go to work in the field. As the girl trying to analyze the guy, I viewed the story as a clue. Now, whenever he acted unenthusiastic, I realized this was somehow linked in his mind to virtue: he was unwilling to promise anything. He didn't want to be the guy who talked and didn't do. Which—it dawned on me as I sat across from him at the kitchen table—might also mean he thought of me as son number one. The one who came up short on the follow-through. And maybe it was true. As a kid, I thought I was going to be the best player in the world. I made bets with boys who didn't think I could do it. I shook their hands and thought, *What fools!* But, of course, it never happened. And when I was older, I said I wanted to be a writer, that I wanted to write books, but the 240-page draft sitting on my desk said that wasn't looking too likely either.

Ferg and I were both afraid a decade from now we'd talk about the great idea we once had. Sometime that year her roommate had said to her, "You're just not a finisher." That bothered her. Now, like me, she had anxiety. After three weeks calling each other and saying, "Are you serious? I'm serious," we filled out the application for the Benenson Award in the Arts. A professor suggested we leave out the around-the-world part. It sounded too big, too impossible. So we wrote about South America and won the grant. When I told Luke, his face finally furrowed up with what looked like hope. "We're going to do this?" he asked, still afraid to let himself see it—billboards ending, game beginning. "We're really going to do it?" he said, voice rising, smile forming.

The three of us let ourselves sink into the idea. We got a big map, spread it out on the table, and stuck pushpins in all the places we wanted to go. We started tracking down places to stay, looking for couches and floors of friends of friends. We piled up all relevant books—*Travels with Charley, Fever Pitch, Soccer in Sun and Shadow, Among the Thugs, How Soccer Explains the World, On the Road, The Miracle of Castel di Sangro,* Simon

Kuper's Perfect Pitch series—and combed through the pages for hints. We walked to Malaprop's and bought the Lonely Planet guide, *South America on a Shoestring*. Listening to loud music, we made long lists on legal pads. At night, Luke and I lay there on our half-deflated mattress. There were the fun things to think about—where we would go, all that we would do—and the unfun thing: how we'd raise the money for the rest of it.

THE CENTER FOR Documentary Studies is an old Victorian house on the edge of Duke's East Campus. You have to walk up a small hill past the graffitied trestle in order to know it's there. Every year there were only a dozen or so students in the program, which meant you got as much time with your professors as you wanted. They had stories they cared about: Gary Hawkins made films about great southern authors; John Biewen recorded audio narratives of immigrant families; Charlie Thompson wrote ethnographies about Appalachian moonshine runners. If you had an idea, CDS was the place to take it.

On a Friday, Ferg and I went to see Tom Rankin, the director of the program and our favorite professor. Tom, a photographer who took black-and-white shots of rural southern churches, usually wore cowboy boots, faded Levis, and button-down shirts with the sleeves rolled up. His farm was thirty miles out of town, and his slow smile made it look like some part of him was still out there.

We knocked on his door. We hovered around his desk. We told him, "We have an idea."

"Going around the world," we said, "looking for pickup games."

He brushed his lip where his mustache used to be. You could tell he liked it—both our idea and our excitement.

"Have you called Ryan?" he asked, leaning back in his chair.

"I e-mailed him," I said.

"You need a fourth. He'd be good."

Ryan White was my camera partner in college, a guy with a great eye and strong instincts. He made three school documentaries: one about a lady who was a bank teller by day and a stripper by night, another about the Triangle Ferret Lovers club, and a third about the city mortician, a man who decorated his apartment with lava lamps and horror-film posters. Since school, Ryan had worked as a production assistant in D.C. for an Emmy-winning filmmaker. But I knew he'd just quit his job, and I hoped my e-mail would catch him during a gap. I hoped he'd be unable to turn down a chance to make a film while traveling around the world.

Tom tapped a pen against the top of his desk. "Draft out a proposal," he said. "Make it good. I'll take you to the provost."

SOCCER: IT'S INTERNATIONAL stars signing multimillion-dollar contracts. It's World Cup finals and Barcelona against AC Milan in the Champions League. But away from the professional stadiums, bright lights, and manicured fields, there's another side of the game.

This, we wrote in our proposal, is a story that hasn't been told: no one has focused on pickup soccer, the global phenomenon spanning gender, race, religion, and class. We found striking pictures on the Internet and clustered them together on our proposal cover page—old men playing on a beach in Tel Aviv, Afghan women playing in burkas, teenagers playing in front of what looked like a giant crumbling sand castle. We gleaned inspiration from Sean Wilsey's introduction to *The Thinking Fan's Guide to the World Cup*: "The joy of being one of the couple of billion people watching thirty-two nations abide by seventeen rules fills me with the conviction, perhaps ignorant, but like many ignorant convictions, fiercely held, that soccer can unite the world." Like Wilsey, we believed in the reach of the game. And pickup, the world at play, was the strand we thought had the most to offer, able to create intimacy between strangers.

In June, the four of us—Ryan, Ferg, Luke, and I—met Tom on West Campus, walking past gothic stone. In the Allen Building, a receptionist sat us down in a room that smelled like ancient books and tradition. We looked out two turret windows and waited for the provost.

"You've got fifteen minutes," a voice boomed out from the doorway.

Peter Lange, a short Jewish man with a big, intimidating presence, set our proposal down on the table in front of him, pushed the center of his horn-rimmed glasses, and glanced at his watch.

Our shaky voices regurgitated what we'd already written: "Away from the bright lights . . ."

He cut us off. "I know all that. For twenty years I played in pickup games with surgeons, drug smugglers, Mexicans, Nigerians. I get it," he said. "Tell me what you need from me."

"Equipment, cameras," Tom said, our representative of cool and calm.

Dr. Lange patted down his red silk tie and peered at Tom over the top of his glasses. "And you think they can do it?"

Tom nodded.

Dr. Lange leaned over a legal pad while he asked about the cost of a camera, a tripod, a lavalier microphone. He scribbled figures onto paper and flipped the notepad toward us. "Here's what I can do. Through the Duke Arts Initiative Fund, I'm granting the Center for Documentary Studies twenty-five-thousand-dollars' worth of equipment. You guys may use it."

He stood up, shook our hands, and walked out of the office.

Pickup around the world—it had been a farfetched idea. Now, incredibly, it was happening.

WE SPENT FOUR more months raising money, writing fund-raising letters to anyone from my grandma's eye doctor to friends of distant relatives. "So let me get this straight," Mr. Davis, my dad's friend, said into the phone. "You want me to give you money. So that you can travel around the world. Playing soccer."

Um, well . . . yeah. I tried to explain what the game had to offer: the connective quality, its ability to provide a window into the spectrum of culture. I told him about the Mennonites who play in the Bolivian jungle and the Peruvian women who play in traditional skirts way up in the mountains, but my heart pounded and I stuttered and mumbled and paced, until I just said bye and hung up the phone, sinking down into the couch. But some of those sweaty-palmed phone calls went a little better; people liked the idea of helping kids chase down a long shot.

"You're a con artist," my dad said, his voice disbelieving and proud as I gave him financial updates.

My brother, a short-order chef, also marveled. "I sweat my balls off every day. Ain't nobody giving me a thousand dollars," he said. "And, sis, soccer's no fun to watch—it's fun to play. Nobody in this country's going to watch a documentary about soccer."

Luke's aunt, who was waiting for him to get a "real" job, said, "Why you're going around the world to make a home video, I have no idea."

We moved out of our apartment during the Bele Chere music festival, carrying our desk above our heads as we stepped over beer cans and wove around bodies swaying to folk music. We scattered our belongings among our Asheville friends: Scotty took our desk, Pfister took our chair, Jarret took our kitchen table.

We pinged the soccer ball across the empty wood floor.

GROWING UP, MY club coach was a six-feet-two Trinidadian who once trained dogs for the Port of Spain police force. We revered him. He started with a team of eight-year-olds and got us scholarships to Division I programs across the country. Having spent ten years eating island-style roti and listening to Coach say at winter practices, "One day I'm going to buy myself a plot of Tobago land—me and Debi going to retire beneath a palm tree," T&T is the first country I think of when we make our list.

Coach had that combo of toughness and jokes; he never smiled until he was making fun of you. In the decade he taught me how to play, he delivered only one outright compliment. We were riding the elevator after a team camp all-star game. As he got off on the sixth floor, he hitched the bag of balls up on his shoulder, turning back toward me. "Child, you were smooth like butter tonight," he said, running one hand through the air as if he were spreading Land O'Lakes on bread. He turned and walked down the hall, elevator doors closing behind his praise. From the sixth floor to the tenth floor, I leaned against the handrail, looking for some kind of internal nook to lodge his words so that I'd be able to put his yelling and grimacing into context. For the next four years, whenever he jumped up from the bag of balls he sat on, addressing me in a tone that dropped toward the ground, I knew he thought I could be great.

He made sure we loved the game, but he also made sure we knew we played in order to get somewhere. "Use the ability to kick a ball to open the world for you," he'd said. At first that meant college. Now it meant Trinidad.

ON SEPTEMBER 7, 2007, in Ryan's mother's living room in Atlanta, we folded up maps, made lists of phone numbers, Xeroxed passports, assembled camera bags, and mashed our clothes into space-maximizing Ziplocks. At 3:30 the next morning, we finished packing, I lost my passport, and Ryan thought he went blind. By 4:15 I found my passport, Ryan discovered he'd stuck two sets of contacts in his eyes, and Luke and Ferg waited by the car, worried about time. At 6:30 we took off, watching Atlanta retreat from our plane window.

Ryan, Luke, Gwendolyn, and Rebekah on the night before setting out
(courtesy: JB Reed)

TAKING A SWEAT

PORT OF SPAIN, Trinidad: I imagined the Caribbean—cool breezes and palm trees—but it is a city and it is hot. There's some evidence of an island: gray water peeking out from behind the port, men cutting coconuts with machetes, venders selling oysters and snow cones. But mainly there is hustle—traffic and car horns and smog, people with unsmiling faces crowding broken sidewalks.

On the car radio, two men argue about Trinidad's embarrassing result against Australia. I cling to this. The game, the thing I expected. "Soccer," I say, sitting up straight in the backseat and looking to Ian, our host, brother of my coach's wife, the man who will help us navigate the country.

"No," Ian says, catching my eyes through the rearview mirror. "Cricket. Our national sport."

Cricket—that sport with wickets. I lean back against the seat. I gaze out the window. We pass a field. They're not playing soccer. They're playing cricket. I wrap my arms tightly around the camera bag in my lap and try not to remember: "Gwenny," Coach had said on the phone. "We are cricket players first." But it was impossible to feel threatened by a sport I associated with the 1920s. I barely heard him. I could feel the rightness of Trinidad in my bones.

We arrive in the industrial suburb of Chaguanas. Ian introduces us to his family. We crash through the doorway, dropping our bags and waving shyly at two teenage daughters with braided hair and a three-year-old son who cries when he looks at Luke.

A giant pot of rice and beans steams from the burner. After an eight-hour delay, an eight-hour flight, and a two-hour wait standing in what we thought was the baggage-claim and customs line (it wasn't), we hadn't eaten in around eighteen hours. Ian serves us heaping plates. "Careful," he says, passing us a small bowl. "Pepper sauce—hot."

"We love hot," Ryan, Ferg, and Luke say in slightly staggered intervals, putting spoonfuls onto their plates. All three pride themselves on their ability to eat hot things. Once Luke special-ordered the plant of a pepper he read was the hottest in the world, currently used by the Indian army inside smoke grenades. He got on a wait-list at the local arboretum, tended it carefully for a year, and then cut tiny slivers and stuck them in his hummus, his salsa, his hamburgers.

I don't feel the same need for heat. I spoon on just enough to be polite.

When I feel the explosion in my mouth, I look over at the other three. They look like they've just been poisoned—faces flaming red, tears spilling out of eyes, hands reaching for throats—only they are trying not to show it, putting their hands back in their laps, murmuring *mmm* sounds.

Ian leans back in his recliner, chuckling as he bounces his son on his lap, who is still staring and wailing at Luke.

As Luke and I lie in bed later that night, he says to me, as though I wasn't there, "There was a delicious plate of food in front of me. I was starving. I wanted to eat it. I kept trying to eat it. Again and again, it burned. My lips, my stomach.

"I searched for a pocket of rice that wasn't contaminated. But I'd mixed it all around. Every bite—contaminated. I felt like a cartoon character with steam coming out of my ears," he mumbles as he nuzzles his face against the back of my neck. "A humbling introduction to the world."

I WAKE UP our first morning in Trinidad and feel panic. Before the trip started, there was the romance of abandoning job and home. But now that we're here, it doesn't feel like romance. It feels like idiocy; it feels like a mistake. I'm struck by the immensity of it: had I really thought it was a good idea to give up the place I lived in and liked in order to search for games that may or may not exist? And shoot a movie about it? Even though none of us had ever made a movie? In our grant proposals, we had pretended like we were seasoned experts, playing up those twenty-minute documentaries we'd made for college credit, making them sound like they were real films until we almost believed it ourselves. But now that we're here, I realize the truth: we don't know what we're doing.

I lie there in the very warm room, feeling jealous of Luke as I watch him sleeping soundly, sheets stuck to his sweaty legs. I crawl down to the end of the bed and put my face in front of the fan and try to calm myself down. It feels like pregame nerves, only bigger. Before track meets, I'd fall asleep on the blocks, head bobbing, my body shutting down in response to the hellfire of nerves. And it wasn't just sports; it was the beginning of anything. I can remember every first day—from kindergarten to college—along with the overwhelming desire to turn back.

Like when I was six years old and my dad forced me to be on the swim team. I sat in the backseat on the drive to the pool, crying and pleading. I did not want to do it. He kept driving toward the swimming complex, and my mom sat upright in the passenger seat, angry at him for making me. But after the initial minutes hanging on to the side of the pool, conscious of my chattering teeth and the white cap suctioning the top of my head, I started racing, and I liked it. Now I try to think of this trip like that. I just have to make it through the beginning.

I can smell food outside our door. I rustle Luke and get out of bed.

"They're up, they're cooking," I whisper-shout across the bed, poking at his calf. "Time to go."

WE EAT PIG'S tail and okra for breakfast and we do not use pepper sauce. At the table, I pull out the piece of paper where I had scribbled down multidirectional notes. "Ron LaForest" is written in a diagonal across the margin. He's a former forward for the Trinidadian national team who once scored a hat trick against Arsenal, and my first phone call.

"Hello!" I say, when Ron LaForest, national hero, picks up. I wind the cord of the rotary phone around my finger and announce with false bravado, "My coach said you're the man to call!" Then I explain that we're looking for pickup games. I don't realize that "pickup" doesn't translate.

At 11 A.M., we arrive at Queen's Park Savannah, the largest roundabout in the world. Trees line the two-mile perimeter, but the inside is pretty much just grass. Ian drives us around the outside, past the Royal Botanic Gardens and a stretch of huge eccentric houses built in 1904: a black-and-white castle built by a Scot; the Archbishop's Palace, a red-trimmed mansion with a chapel rising out of the center; the Mille Fleurs, a now-abandoned French provincial home complete with fretwork and balusters. They're so different than the gray, to-the-point buildings we've seen in the rest of the city, as if the settlers had put all their imagination into a circle.

As we pass the old, slightly crumbling palatial mansions, I repeat Ron LaForest's full name in my head. At first I thought it was "forest," as in the thing with trees, but now I decide that Trinidad's French influence means "forest" is pronounced for-ay. We're meeting him, with no idea what for, at the chunk of Savannah closest to the Royal Bank.

When Ian drops us off, we see twenty strong guys sitting in the grass, muscled legs extending in front of them as they lace up cleats. No one is smiling; no one is talking. As we walk toward them and into the silence, I know right away this is no pickup game. This is the anxiety that is a prelude to a practice. Something's riding on this, somebody's watching, and until you get the playing under way, and play well, there isn't a lot of fun to be had.

"Welcome," a voice booms out. To our left, we see Ron LaForest striding across the open field, dropping a cone every five yards. He has a musical
way of moving, like he walks to some aggressive beat he hears in his head.

He arrives in front of us and firmly shakes our hands, smiling a large,
gold-front-teeth smile. "I am Ron." He waves at the guys around him.
"This is my team. We are semipro . . . trying to climb to the next division. You are welcome to join our practice."

Practices are exactly what we aren't looking for, but we don't have the
heart to tell Ron. Luke and I join in. They've lost their last two games, so
Ron makes them run punishment fitness. (This helps explain the dark
mood we walked into.) Because Luke and I don't want to be the Americans who are too good for sprints, we run them.

Sometimes when you play against people who are better than you,
you're able to steal part of their gift—you play better than you are—and
I hope sprinting could work out like this. Maybe I can hijack their speed.

I'm so conscious of how fast everyone else is going that what I'm doing doesn't even seem like running. I feel like a marionette led by strings
in a play that someone fast-forwarded, my legs and arms rising at impossible speeds. I feel nothing. And I keep getting left behind, tall Trinidadians blurring by me. When Luke and I run sprints at home, I get a
five-second head start and then run like hell so he doesn't catch me. I
start trying to cheat a little now, taking off a half second before Ron says
go. It doesn't help.

Ryan and Ferg film the sprints for ten minutes, more for their personal amusement than for the movie. They sprawl out in the shade of the
giant oaks lining the field. When Luke and I come over during a water
break, they introduce us to a guy straddling a bicycle. "This is Carlan,"
Rebekah says, pointing up to him from her resting spot on the grass.
"He's a steel-drum player for the government."

"On slow days, when there's nobody to play music for, I ride my bike out
to the field," he explains. "I get a snow cone and watch whatever's going on."

"Good to meet you," Luke says. I am too tired to speak; I nod in agree-
ment. I put my hands on my waist and try to get my breathing back.

"I'll take you guys to a concert if you'd like," Carlan offers as he leans on the handles of his bicycle.

"Great," I say, still gasping.

Then Luke and I jog back to the field and the fitness.

WHEN THE PRACTICE ends, we try again to explain what we are looking for—informal games, games that don't count, games played just because.

"Ahh," Ron says, smiling hugely, his gold front teeth shining in the sunlight. "You want to take a sweat." We stare at him blankly. " 'Taking a sweat,' that is what we call it. You know, like 'work up a sweat.' " He jiggles his arm and starts dancing in place in order to demonstrate. "You must go to the fields at five P.M. You will see."

So at 4:35 P.M., we arrive at the fields. They are completely empty.

This is when we begin to deflate: we thought people play all around the world, but maybe we were wrong. Maybe this isn't going to work.

The four of us form a depressing little circle and begin to juggle.

Ten minutes later, over Luke's left shoulder, I see a man with a gym bag walking out to the field. Then I see another, and another, like the scene from *Field of Dreams* when the ballplayers materialize in the outfield.

And then we see the cricket bats. The bats, which look to me like kitchen rolling pins only flattened, are clutched in each of their hands. The players spread out in the grass and begin to hit tiny balls at wooden wickets.

We return to juggling. It starts to rain. I watch Ryan's face, his finely formed lips held tightly together, his chin pushed out. I feel the worst for him. He's not even a soccer player. (His juggling ability came from playing Hacky Sack as a fourteen-year-old.)

He'd trusted me; I'd convinced him of a great worldwide phenomenon. He dropped everything and came with us, even though he didn't know Rebekah and Luke at all, and in retrospect, barely knew me. He and I spent late nights in a ten-by-ten-foot editing room working on our

college docs together, but that was three years ago, and even then he was
private. Our social circles were separate: I fit the stereotype of the athlete
who spent all her time with other athletes, and he was the stocky frater-
nity boy who covered his greasy hair with a faded, sweat-stained baseball
cap. I'd pick up the camera bag from his Pi Psi house off East Campus
and wave uncomfortably at the guys half passed out on the five couches
in the giant living room. In the CDS basement, we'd commiserate about
how miserable it was to be in a windowless room at 3 A.M., but we never
really talked about each other's lives.

Now Ryan isn't stocky and Ryan doesn't wear baseball caps. His face
used to be handsome in a round, beer-thickened way, but now he looks
like a lanky male model—almond eyes, defined facial features. And he
had come out of the closet. "Uh, you know I'm gay, right?" he said with
a shy smile, hands tucked into his pockets, when we reunited in Durham.

"Yeah, kind of," I said. Not because he had any telltale gestures or
behavior, but because we'd sit alone together for hours without one hint
of chemistry or tension between us.

Ferg is also gay, which makes things easy and drama-free: we are one
straight guy, one straight girl, one gay guy, and one gay girl—a four-person
team. Standing in a roundabout in the rain in Trinidad.

To the left, another handful of men emerges from behind the trees. This
time, we're not suckered in. We continue juggling. We don't react. Until
they're close enough to make out an unmistakable Manchester United
jersey. And arms carrying unlaced soccer cleats.

I catch the ball in my hands. "It's real," I say.

Luke and I head over to the group of men, Ryan and Rebekah linger-
ing behind us, not wanting to alter the dynamics of our first encounter.

The guy closest has long dreadlocks and the stern facial expression I
always associated with my coach but am now starting to associate with
all Trinidadians.

I walk toward him, in his direct line of vision, but his eyes somehow
manage to skirt my gaze.

I stand next to him. He doesn't acknowledge me. I say, "Do you think we could play with you guys?"

He still doesn't look at me. He nods, almost imperceptibly.

Then Luke and I just stand there.

I can think of nothing to say.

I ask, "So are you from Trinidad?"

He nods.

I know Luke isn't going to help me, even though I have always been shy and awkward and he's always been easy and social. He doesn't force things, and I can feel him standing there, recoiling against the unnaturalness of this exchange.

I'm continually astonished by the gap between the way things play out in my mind and the way they play out in real life.

Before we'd left, I'd read the Lonely Planet guide, followed leads, and booked plane tickets, but I tried not to make a picture of anything in my head, stopping them as soon as they started, in the same way you hush someone who's about to tell you the end of a book or the final score of a game. But I had imagined things—and this awkwardness wasn't it.

By 5:15 P.M., dozens of games are happening across the grass—some of them cricket but most of them football, soccer, whatever you want to call it. And once Luke and I are playing, sending in passes that show the guy with the dreadlocks and everyone else that we know the same game they do, the awkwardness goes away: we are players, playing with everyone else.

Thirty- , forty- , and fifty-year-olds make up our game. Before long, there are too many people, twenty of us playing in a space the size of a penalty box.

We hear a finger-to-teeth whistle and see Ron shouting, "Come! Join my sweat!" He does his musical stride over to us and waves at everyone else, because everyone knows Ron, national hero. Luke and I wave goodbyes and follow him across the field.

WE PLAY UNTIL we can't see. It gets darker and darker, our feet finding the ball before our eyes do, but none of the games end, as though no one wants to be the guy who quits first. "The candle went out," someone finally yells once it's full-night dark.

Standing beneath a blinking street lamp, we listen to Ron. "Every day you will find Trinidadians scattered across the grass, hundreds of sweats going on in the roundabout until dark," he says in a booming, expressive voice. He again elaborates on the loose etymology behind their word for pickup games. "After work, you've got to get it all out, sweat it all out—take a sweat." This feels like a discovery: maybe every country will use a different expression. Maybe we can collect explanations all around the world.

But accompanying that discovery is another—the race against the sun. If 5 P.M., the hour when the sun is soft and the workday is over, is the international pickup time, it means we'll always finish in the unfilmable dark. The camera can't see anything but Ron's teeth.

"Anytime you want to come to this country, you call me," Ron says. He reaches his leg out and taps his cleat against Luke's and then mine. "This is what we do—if I think you are a good player, we tap. A player's handshake."

We try to watch the cleat handshake on film the next morning as we sit on the bed in Ryan and Ferg's room and log footage. Ryan had pumped the gain, but you still can't see anything; you can only hear it, a leather-cloaked *tap*. We log all four tapes, watching and time-coding: good move at 16:05, pretty wide shot at 21:14, interesting comment at 31:09. We have something on camera, we've started, and there's the relief of that. But Ron's comments in the dark are unusable, and it was hard to capture how many games were happening on the grass. Essentially we have footage of five or six scrimmages—no story.

CARLAN, THE STEEL-drum player, and his friend Andre pick us up at eight o'clock that night to take us to a concert. We pile into the '86 Accord, sitting four across the back, camera bags piled on top of us. A large rainbow-shaped SOCA WARRIORS decal arches across the windshield. We drive past packs of stray dogs and a goat tied to a telephone pole. Cars jam the street. Trinidad has more cars per capita than any country except the United States. The Trinidadians drive fast and without fear, aggressively nudging their way into intersections. The previous day we'd taken a walk with Ian's cousin Louis, and he had the same approach to traffic while on foot: he slung his arm out to the side so the four of us could follow him into the middle of an intersection. Louis, who was about our age and dressed in a beanie with a brim, sweatpants, and Lugz boots, said to us once it turned dark, "Without me, someone put you in a car and steal you. I'll protect your life." Things did look different at night.

The small Honda rides like a go-cart as we drive up and down the hilly back streets to avoid the traffic-stalled highway. We're listening to Andre—his English is easy to understand because he's spent a year working on cruise ships—tell us about the calypso concert, but we're also looking out the window at the dark, dark neighborhood we're driving through. "Malick is a rough area, one of the worst," Carlan says. A man walks in a slow diagonal across the street, headed nowhere clear. My eyes are following him, our car hurtling forward, when I see lights through the window—playground lights.

I turn around backward in my seat and try to make out what I'm seeing. There's a fenced-in court, and through the chain-link, I can see bodies moving. I hear shouts, game-sounding shouts.

"You want to stop," Carlan says as he watches the four of us crane our necks back toward the court.

"Could we?" Luke asks.

"I don't see why not."

The six of us walk up to the fence. Ryan, Rebekah, Luke, and I are quiet. We know what we're seeing: the game inside our heads.

Fluorescent lights make everything neon, pinging off gold necklaces, flecks in the asphalt, and the white sidelines of the basketball court. Small goals made out of steel bookend the game. It's three against three, and the players are loud: "You gotta mark the man, boy." "You taking too long, boy." And following the clanging of a goal: "All night baby, all night."

As we walk onto the court, two girls in short-shorts pass by us on their way out. One walks into Carlan, her shoulder nudging his chest. "What up, girl?" Carlan says, his accent thicker than when he talks to us.

A dozen teenagers are spread out along old bleachers. Off to the side, three older-looking guys lean against a defunct snack shop. A guy in a camo-print New York Yankees hat and an XL white T-shirt smokes a joint and looks out at the game. "They're older brothers of the guys playing now," Carlan says, his eyes following mine. "Two of them play in the Trinidad professional league." Watching every play, their faces giving up nothing, they feel like the godfathers overseeing the court.

I mess with the sides of the knee-length cotton stretch skirt I'd worn for the concert and move closer to the sideline.

In every pack of players, there are one or two ringleaders; you can pick them out by their ease, their confidence. My eyes land on a guy wearing red-and-blue swim trunks, nylon torn across the crotch. He's rubbing his buzzed head, his chin moving side to side as he bounces in place, all movement. He's maybe seventeen. His bare chest is still scrawny like a boy's, but he walks with the I-dare-you swagger of someone who feels older.

The ball skips across the asphalt toward me, and the ringleader is following it.

When he's bending down to grab it, a foot away, I ask, "Can we play?"

He frowns, points at my flip-flops. "You don't have shoes," he says, ball in his hands.

I glance down at his bare feet.

"But your feet aren't used to it," he says.

"They are," I say, feeling like I'm lying even though I'm not. I spent the last two months playing barefoot so I wouldn't be the American with soft feet. And Luke, who's part hippie, has always preferred playing barefoot.

"You play winner," he says, turning away from me, his face grim, like he thinks we're going to bring the game down.

I walk back to the bleachers. I like it when there is something to prove.

A younger kid, maybe eight, who's slouched against the stands, leaps up and runs to me. "What are you doing here? Where are you from?" he asks as he takes Michael Jackson slides backward, not letting the conversation slow him down. The kid acts as a foil—in his enthusiasm toward us, you can feel the lack of everyone else's.

"Lady, you ready to play?" the swim-trunk guy calls out as one group of players walks off the court.

A guy in a baby blue polo gets put with Luke and me. He isn't as good as the other guys. You can see it in the way he walks, guiltily, like he knows he doesn't care as much as everyone else.

On our side of the court, I stand barefoot on the asphalt. Adrenaline—there it is, taut in me, like it was never gone.

Then he's coming. A guy with a gold chain bouncing off his wet, bare chest, bright white high-tops looping around the ball. He touches it from his heel to his toe in one quick jerk—Harlem Globetrotter–style tricks, just for looks. He prances and I wait. Sometimes, although no one admits it, you know before a game starts whether you'll win or lose. When the premonition says loss, you ignore it; when it says win, you feel calm. There are smaller moments throughout the game with this same feeling, when you know what will happen.

As the guy with the high-tops dribbles toward me, I watch only the ball and then I take it. After I win it, when I can feel the stone-faced expressions break and hear the guys jumping on the bleachers and scream-laughing, I feed off it, dribbling down court with the confidence of someone who's just stolen it away. I scissor over the ball, get endline, and square the ball back to Luke.

At the beginning of a game, it's kind of cheating. Nobody thinks the girl will be good. When they come at you, they take you too lightly. Almost like they're flirting, putting on a show instead of playing. It's only after you strip it off them that the real game starts. Then they're serious, going at you as hard as they go at everyone else.

Luke taps the ball from side to side, a little showy, a little like an *AND1* video. Which is a surprise. In college, even though he was probably the most inventive player on his team, he didn't dribble in a game. A center midfielder found seams, opened the field, took touches that eliminated the need to dribble. He was a connector, good at making the game simple. But here he is, ball-dancing. It's that type of game, everyone offering up tricks. Luke stalls the ball on top of his foot. A guy in long plaid shorts reaches for it; Luke scoops it in a high arch over him. It's good; it's startling.

Now the kid in the swim trunks is grinning, looking excited, like we might be players after all. He claps his hands and then he goes at Luke.

He casually pushes the ball forward, waiting to see what Luke will do. When Luke moves in to defend him, he springs forward, using the sole of his foot to push the ball through Luke's open legs—a nutmeg. It's a *whoosh* feeling when it happens.

"I get me some white meat!" the guy yells.

The next five minutes are all-out. Then the guy with the white hightops hits a shot. It bangs the back of the steel goal, and we lose. I walk off the court and stand next to the bleachers, my whole body buzzing. I wanted to win, to stay on the court, but I played well and there's still the satisfaction of that.

I lean against the bleachers, half watching the game in front of me, half soaking in how good I feel. This game in Malick isn't the same as the one in Queen's Park Savannah. Those guys were older, people on the downward slope of their playing careers. There's still an honor to it: you're trying to play well enough to remember how good you used to be. There's a touch of dismay, flagged by the frustration of unclean passes and clumsy runs up field that are only a shadow of what you could've done ten years ago. But these guys in Malick are young enough to still want everything.

Before we leave for the concert, we get one more chance on the court. We play against the same set of guys, who still haven't lost. They ping it between one another, covering the court—left, center, right, up. And then they shoot, and then they score.

"Less than ten seconds!"

"You got cobo-ed, you got cobo-ed," the ringleader yells, coming toward us.

"What's 'cobo'?" Luke asks.

"It's when you don't get no sweat," he says, laughing. He rubs his head, shakes our hands, and heads back to the court.

"A cobo," Carlan tells us, "is a black bird that flies in . . . and then flies out."

We get back in our car and go listen to the steel drums. We pat our feet, bob our heads, try to show we can feel it, too. During the rest of the week, we juggle the ball with the men pushing ice cream carts in Maracas Bay and eat at Natalie's Bake 'N' Shark. We film scenics, anything we think might help us: machetes cutting into pineapples, chickens clucking around a coop, the mountains rising over Port of Spain. We "lime"— the Trinidadian word for relaxing, chilling out—with Ian and his family, Louis banging his knife on his beer bottle, making a beat. And at the end of the week, we take the ferry to Tobago, where we rent a car and drive on the left side of the street. We play with Guinean tourists on the beach in Store Bay. The playing fends off the island mosquitoes that come out at night, but Ryan, who stays still, trying to capture the sunset and our silhouettes, is eaten, bug bites in the shape of stars blooming across his face.

We end the week with eight hours of footage from T&T. But for all of us, Trinidad is that glimpse of the game in Malick. As we'd walked out of the court, I'd watched the kid, who was still bouncing up and down, begging the older guys to let him play. He held his hands together, like he was praying fiercely, and said, "Please, please." The skinny ringleader put his hands on the kid's shoulders, looked him very seriously in the face, and then smiled: "All right."

PELADA

1.

WHEN I SPENT the summer between my two years of grad school playing professionally in Brazil, I didn't call Luke. I told him it was because the pay phone was a two-mile walk and didn't always work when you got there, which was true, but really I didn't call because I was afraid to call. Luke and I met at a pickup game in South Bend. He'd been late, running from somewhere else, his face red and sweaty as he hurdled the wall around the court and shook my hand. He raked his fingers through blond curls, making his wild hair stick straight up, and when he smiled at me, dark blue eyes looking into mine, I felt shaken. We only had one month together. We drank wine out of the bottle and ate Taco Bell on the bench by the river when it was thirty degrees outside. We went late-night swimming in the empty pool of the old gym, kissed in the dark against the wall of the racquetball room. We got lost driving along rural Indiana roads, listening to Zero 7. He took pictures of old churches and dragged me to art exhibits and symphony concerts of people I'd never heard of. He told me he loved me by a street lamp. It felt hard to think, hard to breathe.

And then when he was gone, it felt harder to think and harder to breathe. Five weeks into the summer in Brazil, I'd been away from him for longer than I'd been with him. As I walked to and from practice, as I lay down on the top bunk and tried to sleep, I couldn't escape the fear that it would be gone when I got back, that I'd get off the plane and look out at a guy who was different from the one I remembered.

In college, I read John Updike's *Brazil,* a love story streaked with magical realism and sorcery, reality shifting beneath the lovers' feet as they combed the beaches, jungles, and deserts in search of the drug of each other. The fantasy from the novel seeped into my sense of the country. That summer, the feeling of unreality was reinforced by my hunger, fatigue, lovesickness, and soundlessness. No one spoke English; I spoke no Portuguese. We played seven to eight hours a day. We ate hot-dog buns for breakfast, rice and beans for lunch and dinner. As I walked the forty-five minutes to practice, I felt hollow inside, light, able to lift up and float down the street like a stray balloon. Sometimes we hitchhiked to practice, standing in the sun, holding out our thumbs, calling out to cars. Nice cars never stopped, but the ones with missing hubcaps slowed down, and we raced to catch up. Karen, my roommate, spoke to the driver in breathless rushes, and I sat in the backseat, listening to their voices. "Americano," Karen would say, slinging her thumb back at me. My team tried to teach me Portuguese on the walks home, drawing words with a stick in the sand, pointing at the sky or the rain, but as soon as I learned "sky," I forgot "rain." "It's OK, it's OK," Karen said to me as she patted my shoulder, her English growing faster than my Portuguese. At night, Karen spoke to me in Portuguese and I spoke to her in English, and some nights we feigned understanding, nodding, smiling, pretending. Other nights, we cut off each other's monologues: "Nâo fala português," I told her; "No speak English, no speak English, no speak English," she whispered as she fell asleep.

The whole summer there was a haze in my head, like the kind when you haven't slept, where parts blur and parts throb: ants crawling up my legs as we leaned against the wheel-less VW Beetle and put on our cleats.

Wading home through streets knee-high with rainwater. Paper plates stacked with marble-size balls of rolled dough, offerings for the Gods. Semipro basketball players who shared our dorms, their boom box blaring LL Cool J, their mouths singing sounds they did not understand: "Pride is what you had, baby girl, I'm what you have." Flavia, owner of a silver probe, going from room to room, stabbing lips, noses, and belly buttons. Karen discovering my Radiohead CD, lying every night with her face flat on the sheets, saying, "Love musica, love, my room sister."

I got on buses having no idea where we were headed; I followed girls to town, no idea why we were going to town; I put on whatever kind of clothes Karen put on. At practice, they put their hands on my shoulders and pushed me in whatever direction they wanted me to move. When the Brazilian winter dumped too much rain on the field, we trained on the beach, running suicides in the sand. Ice cream pushcarts wheeled by us as we did high-knees over hurdles made of cardboard folds, periodically grabbing them when the waves came too far up. On days when there were sitting puddles on the fields and high tides at the beach, we did agility work on the pavement of the main highway, our bodies taking up a lane, passing cars dousing us with sheets of water. On our off days, we cast fishing nets into the waves, floated down the river, washed our laundry in the stone washbasins in the back alley. As I scrubbed my jersey against the ribbed sink, they put their hands on my hips and tried to move me to the one-two-three rhythm of a samba.

When the summer ended and I flew back to Luke, I missed my connecting flight, arriving hours late. I had no way to call him, no way to let him know. I rode down the escalator and found him sleeping on top of the bag that arrived before me. He was asleep-asleep. I felt the shock of his realness as I stared down at him—brow furrowed, mouth open, hands curled against his chest—like he tumbled out of my imagination and landed at my feet. "Luke," I said, his name odd in my mouth, my voice odd to my ears. I crouched beside him and squeezed his shoulder. His eyes opened and I watched his return to consciousness, that second of confusion, then the knowing, the remembering. He swept himself up and then swept me up.

"You're here," he said, as he pressed me against him.

"You look different," I said, looking into the tan face that used to be pale, running my hands along the buzz that used to be curls.

"So do you," he said, his thumbs against my hip bones.

But we weren't different, it wasn't fake, and I felt the relief right way. We weren't in South Bend, where my tunnel-shaped apartment, his torn black futon, the winding river, the snow, and Notre Dame's gold dome served as the familiar backdrop to our relationship. We were in Los Angeles, California, place of sunshine, movie stars, and Joan Didion's Santa Ana winds. The setting had changed but he was still the guy who made me feel disbelief.

"You can understand what I'm saying," I said.

"Yes," he said.

"I can understand what you're saying," I said.

"Yes," he said.

"I haven't been able to understand," I said. I meant the language, I meant the country, I meant being without him.

HE TOO HAD been to Brazil, knew the country even better than I did. In the spring of his junior year, he lived in Rio de Janeiro for seven months. He learned his Portuguese playing in pickup games and talking to girls in bars. (He failed his end-of-semester paper because he tried to impress the professor with his arsenal of acquired slang.) On the beaches, he did like the Brazilians and donned a Speedo. (I found it in a box in his room and couldn't quite believe it.) Once, when he was taking pictures of tombstones in Cemitério São João Batista, accidental witness to a drug deal, he got held up at gunpoint; he used his Portuguese to talk the guy into letting him keep his camera. Before my turn in Brazil, he'd taken me through his Portuguese book, marking sentences for me to use, sounding it all out for me. But I'd never heard him in action, never seen him in Brazil talking with Brazilians.

Now, on the plane rides from Trinidad to Miami and Miami to Rio de Janeiro, Luke is studying his fat book, *501 Portuguese Verbs,* while I drink wine, watch bad movies, and try not to feel anxious.

Everything rides on Brazil. In the other countries, our movie idea is only a hypothesis: we think people play in pickup games. In Brazil, we know it; we've seen the games, we've played in the games. If we can't make it work here, it won't work anywhere.

By this point, we're starting to admit to ourselves that nowhere in our eight hours of Trinidadian footage is there a story. The Malick game is still running in my head—the lights, the guys, the steel goals, the asphalt, and the adrenaline—but we hadn't really gotten it. We'd played for only thirty minutes. We had no interviews. It wasn't enough. In Brazil, we're giving ourselves one month, twice as long as anywhere else. We need a story.

LUIS OLIVEIRA, A Brazilian living in California, saw an article in Luke's hometown paper about our project. He sent us an e-mail with the subject line "I will help you," and a week later we sat in his living room, eating Brazilian cheese bread. "My whole família lives outside of Rio," Luis said, rubbing his thighs excitedly. "Every day we play in the street! You will stay with them. Arnaldo, my brother, he'll help you find games!"

One month later we stand with Arnaldo around sunset, our bags still by our sides, looking out at the scene on the Oliveiras' street. Kids—sitting on the curb, leaning back on the palms of their hands, tapping their feet to Brazilian funk music. The smell of *feijoada,* a bean-and-pork stew, wafts out an open door. Older kids ride bikes, one on the seat, one on the handlebars. A six-year-old with an afro and pale blue eyes cartwheels by, pink tank top pooling against her chin. A ball pings around the street. A kid on roller skates nudges it forward; a trio of girls bumps it around like a volleyball; a teenager on a bicycle lowers one leg, drags his foot, and pushes the ball along as he rides. All at once a real game breaks out, three kids against three other kids, shooting on goals made out of flip-flops, until everyone is hot and tired and then it's back to the curb, where they drink guarana and catch their breath.

"Crazy alive"—that's Luke's description of Brazilians. (He has an unscientific theory that this irrepressibility is somehow related to the guarana, a Mountain Dew–colored soda they constantly drink.) Arnaldo— same curly hair and green eyes as his brother, plus the addition of a large gut—is as awed by this quality as we are and is determined to show it to us. He tells us he's too middle-aged and un-suave to know the scoop, so he's going to take us to somebody who will.

The following morning we drive to the office of an upstart newspaper run by twenty-year-olds. "Nova Iguaçu is a city of a million people, and we had no newspaper," Nike, a stylish guy with a head of dreadlocks, explains as he gestures around the wide room filled with computers and people in motion. "So we made one."

Gathered around a table, we explain our film. Making steeples with our fingers, it seems very official and important—and also silly. I wonder if all adults who sit at conference tables feel like that, like they're putting on an act. Plus we want pickup, something natural and spontaneous, so it feels ironic to sit in a boardroom and plan.

"We'll take you to where we grew up," Nike says. "It's a very small favela. Always there are games." Like Arnaldo, Nike's proud of his street.

A pack of kids shout Nike's name as we walk over what looks like an old-fashioned drawbridge, spanning a sewer instead of a moat. Ducking beneath an arch, we enter a labyrinth of very narrow alleys painted shades of purple, yellow, and green. Many walls are covered with someone's imagination—butterfly wings with perforated edges, a round-nosed shark, wandering, intersecting vines. It's not at all what I imagine when I think of a *favela*, the Brazilian word for "slum." Literally, *favela* means "wildflower": when people moved to the city looking for work, their improvised homes made out of scrap construction materials cropped up on the hillsides. Despite government removal campaigns in the 1970s to wipe them out, the communities grew as fast as their namesake. Governmentally shunned, the favelas didn't appear on maps and had no access to city services like water, power, and garbage removal. In the absence of the state, drug lords often took control, making some favelas more dangerous than others.

"Sandro," Nike says, pointing to the fifteen-year-old walking next to me, "is the graffiti artist. He paints the neighborhood." He's skinny, blue tank top exposing long, reedy arms. Holding a notebook in one hand, he shakes my hand with the other.

"A drunk truck driver ran over their goals last week," Nike says as teenagers drag construction cones into the center of the widest alley.

To the side, a ten-year-old with a pierced lip leans against the wall and watches. Behind the cone goal, three older teenagers listening to head-phones do a samba-infused break-dance. Several motorcycles, an electric blue car, and a grandmother weighed down with groceries pass through the center of the game, ball momentarily stilled.

As I take in the game, Sandro, the graffiti artist, rips out a page from his notebook and hands me a drawing of a girl with a long ponytail, big lips, a T-shirt with a United States flag, and very short shorts. She's swirl-ing, wavy lines shooting out from her hips, soccer ball at her feet.

I look down at cartoon me; it's strange to see yourself through some-one else's eyes. "Muito obrigado," I say, kissing his cheek, which is what I think a Brazilian would do. He walks away with his hands in his pockets, satisfied with his renderings of the world he sees, which strikes me as in-tensely familiar. At that age, like him, I'd try to get down my impressions, writing dangles of sentences; I threw pretty, dramatic words together— *"believing in the orchestra of passion," "racing against the rain of your love"*— things I was proud of until I read them again the next year and felt deflated and ashamed. (Word remorse hit a peak when three girls on my high school team found my journal and called out lines across the aisle on the bus ride to an away game; at first, as I leaned my forehead against the brown vinyl seat, insides rattling, I thought I was experiencing déjà vu. *Funny*, I thought, *I've heard those words before.* Then they called out the line that was unmistakable: "I WANT TO BE TOUCHED IN A WAY THAT MAKES ME TREMBLE." That ended journal writing.)

We play until the sun goes down. I had thought the dark might make the alleys look ominous and unfriendly, but it doesn't. Light spills out of doorways and TVs play *futebol* games that make people lift their feet and then drop them back down again.

"HERE, OUR KIDS are born with an understanding of futebol," a shirt-less man says to the camera. "Sometimes they can't say 'Dad' but they can say 'ball' or 'goal.'"

It's a Sunday, our last day with Arnaldo. He walked into the kitchen this morning as we drank coffee with his eighty-five-year-old father and announced he had something for us to see: on Sundays in small towns, they close side streets to traffic and reserve that space for games. We pack into Arnaldo's Fiat around noon and arrive in Mesquita ten minutes later. Arnaldo frowns as he glances down alleys that are not closed. He grasps the steering wheel tightly, neck craning, scared this great thing that once existed no longer does. We watch cars whistle over spots where games might have been. Right as I put my knees up against the seat and give up, Arnaldo taps the windshield: "Lá!"

Now we're standing on a roped-off street, cardboard sign attached to the twine: RUA DE LAZER, which Luke translates as "Street of Leisure." I associate leisure with luxury resorts and lounge chairs, not a ball scuffing along a street. But leisure, freedom from the demands of work and duty, looks like more than lounge chairs on the faces of the mothers who make up a small mob along the sidewalk. They wear tank tops that stop a half an inch above their belly buttons, and smoke cigarettes, expressions open but willful.

The shirtless man is combing his chest hair with his fingers and tell-ing us about his street's *peladas*. *Pelada,* the Brazilian word for "pickup," literally means "naked," maybe because it's the barest form of the game, stripped to the basics.

In front of us, kids play in a swarm. I sit down on the curb to watch. The ball is flat. Anytime a kid hits it too hard, it goes concave, shaped more like a crescent moon than a ball. While I'm counting how many passes they can go before someone takes too strong of a touch and kills it, a mother with a baby doll beneath her arm pulls me up by the wrists, tug-

Street of Leisure, Mesquita (Courtesy: Luke Boughen)

ging me through a dark doorway and into what appears to be a birthday party.

My eyes do the outside-light-to-inside-light flounder: I see cake candles and lots of small kid bodies packed into a kitchen. The mother is talking to me. The Brazilians look right in your face as they speak, extremely considerate, wanting you to be aware that they are speaking to you, for you . . . even though you can't understand anything they're saying. Still holding my wrists, the mom speaks intently, like maybe if she goes slower and I try harder, I'll be able to understand. She steers a spoon filled with what looks like chopped hot dog into my mouth, hands me a paper plate of chocolate cake, and pushes me back out the door. I stumble out of the room and into Ferg, who has a child hanging around her waist.

Ryan and Luke are surrounded by mothers. A tall woman in a floral skirt stands in the doorway and shakes a tambourine as the other mothers sit in 1970s-style patio chairs, drinking big bottled beers and dancing seated sambas. "We close the streets for the kids," a mom in blue says, exhaling on her cigarette. "We are old-school."

I wonder if this commitment to a fading ideal—streets set aside for play—is more central to the Brazilian madness than the guarana.

2.

When I went to stay with Luke in California, he was the guide and I was the visitor. When we go into the city of Rio, it's like California again, walking through spaces he already knows, while I try to keep up. He speaks the language, knows the streets, holds the maps. He leads us to the hut with the best-tasting coconut water and to the beach where he learned to play *futevolei* (volleyball with your feet). In the grocery stores, he knows how to weigh the fruit and where to find the hot bread. When we pass by a sandwich counter, the man in an apron calls out, "Ôpa! Lucas!" and rings up the same chicken *coxinha* Luke used to order. On Tuesday night, when we show up at the field beneath the apartment where he used to live, it's raining, and it's been three years since he's played here but nothing has changed: it's the same group of faces, the same tri-weekly *pelada*, the same slow walk out to the field. "Lukie!" they yell, smiling. One guy rubs Luke's buzzed head and says, "Onde que tá o cabelo?" *Where is your hair?*

Luke taps the guy's belly and says, "Cadê o gordão?" *Where is the fat man?*

Everyone laughs and I wait for Luke to explain that this guy, who gives no signs of being anything but too Brazilian-handsome to look at, used to be fat.

WE'RE STAYING IN Leblon because it's close to both Copacabana and Ipanema and because we've discovered that when you have four people, renting an apartment is cheaper than going to a hostel. Here there are tree-lined cobblestone streets. Doormen stand at the top of stairways, and old men with hands behind their backs walk beside small dogs. Women in designer heels swing shopping bags from boutiques, and men wearing sweater vests sit in cafés and sip cappuccinos. There's the sophistication of Manhattan and the breeze of a beach. Less than a mile away, thousands of shacks hang in the hills.

Rio de Janeiro has a murder rate comparable to war zones; most of those deaths happen in the favelas facing the city. During Luke's summer in Rio, he played in a Friday *pelada* between two warring favelas that neighbored his apartment. (They stuck the blond guy in goal until he proved his way out of it.) On the court, there were no problems.

According to legend, the Rio favelas may be where *futebol arte* was born. "After the British brought what is now the most popular sport on the planet to South America about 115 years ago, it was initially adopted by the elite," writes Brazilian architect Fernando Luiz Lara. "Around the same time, the occupation of a hill in downtown Rio created its first favela. Once the game reached the Brazilian peripheries, it broke away with the European formalism and transformed itself into the exuberant game now well known." Many of the one-name Brazilian stars—Adriano, Ronaldo, Ronaldinho—grew up in the favelas. On Thursday, a friend of Luke's friend will take us into Rocinha to see *peladas* in the largest favela in South America.

The rest of the week, Luke navigates us through the city. We go up Corcovado, the mountain named after its hunchback shape. Christ the Redeemer, a hundred-foot statue of Jesus Christ with his arms flung wide, stands at the top. We sneak out our camera, hiding behind Asian tourists, and film when the security guard isn't looking, unsure whether we're supposed to have a permit. Then we trek to the top of the neighboring mountain so that we can shoot the statue with the city spread out beneath it.

I lay on my stomach in the grass next to Luke and watch gray wisps of clouds pass fast in front of Christ, as Ryan and Rebekah take shot after shot, trying snap zooms, pans, and time-lapses. On scenic shooting days, we're at our most relaxed. If you miss a shot or an opportunity in a game, there's no getting it back. But scenics you can film again and again until you get it right.

Luke's into statues. I am not. But this is a statue that reshapes my thinking. Up there, twenty-three hundred feet in the air, at the tip-top of Corcovado, soaring over the beach, the favelas, Maracanã Stadium, and the Rio-Niterói Bridge, he looks like he's opening his arms to all of Rio de Janeiro . . . and he looks seconds away from a swan dive, unafraid of it.

We see a man in a Speedo holding out his arms in the exact same shape—as if to say, *World, I am ready for you*—as we wander around Copacabana the next day. A dozen or so people like him—meditating, God-calling figures—dot the beach, oblivious to the stares of the sunbathers who surround them. Vendors zigzag across the sand, strapped down with ice chests full of beer and poles blooming with multicolor sarongs. Circles of people stand at the water's edge and keep the *futebol* up. While in the U.S. we play paddleball and throw Frisbees, the Brazilians juggle, daisy-chaining down the beach. Their bodies are superhero hard, wet chest muscles glistening in the sun. Their tiny bikini bottoms, *sungas,* make for a whole lot of thigh. They kick the ball higher and higher, doing kick-boxing-style pirouettes, timing the swing so that the heel of the foot connects with the ball and sends it straight up. One girl plays; she's got Gisele Bündchen hair, deep tan skin, and tiny white bikini bottoms that creep up the kind of butt I didn't think was real. And she's good, her leg pirouettes prettier than the men's.

Higher up the beach, by the boardwalk, we see a game. I've played on the beach before but always in the packed-down sand by the water, not up here, in flour-sand that betrays you, giving way beneath you as you try to move.

You can't dribble: the ball gets stuck, you get stuck. The other players understand that you don't move it on the sand; you move it in the air. It levitates from foot to foot. I can't do that. I never learned how to lift the ball over someone, because it didn't look like something that could be learned. The scissors, the stepover, the Cruyff, all the earthbound moves—those I could memorize. But that little, unexpected poof—that was nothing that could belong to me.

When I pass the ball across the sand, it looks like a rock skipping across a lake. It never goes where I try to send it. So I try dribbling again, but the ball doesn't roll, it dies, my scissors doing nothing but making a tangle. (Even when I'm not on a beach, a scissors move makes me feel sheepish; it's like the conversational "um"—what I do while I try to think of what I really mean to say.) The men volley it forward, the ball sailing over me, to the left of me, to the right of me.

Updike isn't the only one to paint the country as enchanted; the whole footballing world thinks it. Brazilian players—they are magic wielders. One guy with power quads keeps holding the ball up, baiting me, but when I reach for it, the ball vanishes. I'm looking up into the sun, trying to find it. It's nowhere. And while I'm disoriented, spinning, he reappears it, flourishing the ball in front of me.

Another man—gray chest hair, wrinkled black skin, shriveled muscles—is wearing napkin-size trunks and a bandage around his knee. His feet can catch anything. He loops the ball back and forth with the man with the quads.

There's also an angry teenager playing. Standing in the corner of the field, he's bitching, he's moaning, and then, out of nowhere, he's doing a bicycle kick, a spectacular one, wrenching his rage-filled body up like an acrobat. (We grew up trying bikes—usually forgetting the jump part, just kind of crumpling to the ground and hoping our foot connected—but nobody ever pulled one off in a game.) Here, no one reacts, as though a bicycle kick is passé, like he should come up with something more original next time.

After the game's over, we sit along a short concrete wall. With my finger, I push sweat off my shins. I'm thinking about the first time I got beat in the hundred, running as fast as I could and watching myself get left behind. I felt surprised, helpless. That's how I feel now. The old man and the strong man stand in front of us, squeezing a water bottle over their faces.

The man with the thighs passes the bottle to me. "Muito diferente, eh?" he says, smiling at me. The Portuguese "t" turns into a "ch," but "dife-renche" is close enough to "different" for me to understand.

"Muito," I say.

He says something else and I look dependently at Luke, who's bent over, pouring water over his neck. "He can tell you'd be a good player on the field."

I stare into the man's kind, generous face. Why is this so important to me? Why do I need people to believe that I'm good?

In graduate school, I tried not to tell anyone I was a soccer player. I wanted to see what it would be like. I didn't make it past the first week. It was a Saturday night at the Oyster Bar, and they were talking about *Moby-Dick,* a book I hadn't read. I drank down a gin and tonic and announced, "I played soccer. I'm a soccer player." I needed them to understand that there was at least something I knew about.

WE WALK BACK to Leblon along the boardwalk.

"Did you get the bicycle kick on camera?" I ask Ryan. I'm conscious of my tone. I try to make it airy.

"I think so," he says, a little badgered by the high hopes I'd failed to muffle. "But it wasn't a perfect angle or framed well," he warns, adjusting the straps of the backpack.

As we walk, I notice for the first time how hot it is. When you're playing, the beach breeze against your wet skin keeps you cool. But when you're sitting there, too much equipment strapped to your body, you are not feeling cool. Ryan's hair is a sheet of grease, and his T-shirt, once navy, now looks black. Ferg's shoulders are bright red.

I wonder if Ferg wanted to play. I asked her midgame if she wanted on, and she waved me away. But that didn't necessarily mean anything.

"Was it hard to watch?" I ask.

"A little. But that soft sand looked like it sucked. And I was hot . . . so . . . nah."

"Gwendolyn," Ferg says now. It's strange, ominous, to hear her say my full name. In college, I was G, much easier to say during a game. "When you're playing, you just need to play."

Occasionally, in the middle of a game, I see details I feel passionate about. The kid wearing one shoe. The word CARIOCA (the term for a Rio native) splashed across the butt of someone's Speedo. It's annoying when someone tells you what to film, so I try to shut myself up. Sometimes though, I still jog to the side and say, "The shoe!" Those shouts, understandably, aren't always well received.

I continue walking, my head processing the rightness of her statement.

A man hawking fried cheese passes us, and Ferg and I both want it. We eat more than Ryan and Luke, who don't remember food until their stomachs growl. We sit down in the white patio chairs on the boardwalk, sucking on cheese sticks, staring at striking faces. Whenever I get caught, a pair of eyes looking back into mine, the Brazilians smile, accustomed to admiring gazes.

MY WHOLE LIFE, anytime I see a goal, I point out the car window and cite my finding: "Field." In Brazil, this habit doesn't go away, but now there are goals everywhere so it sounds like a tic. "Field, field, field," I say as we walk from lifeguard post 1 to 9. Every block has a court, every court has a game. It's hard to choose a place, hard to walk by, hard to come up with any one plan. Luke keeps talking about Aterro do Flamengo, quoting facts from his architecture class: "It's the biggest urban park in Brazil." He studies the map and the street name and the best way for us to get there, as though we've already agreed that that's where we should go. "It's a cool place," he says.

He doesn't say anything else. Luke always leaves you a little in the dark, as though being too informed will kill the mystery of what you find.

While we'd planned the trip from our kitchen table in Asheville, he told us about courts that stay lit all night long, about games among doormen and waiters, who, after late-night shifts, play until three and four in the morning . . . but he in no way makes it clear now that Aterro do Flamengo is where these games happen.

"Why should we go there?" I say.

"It's a good night to try to catch the waiters," Luke says, as though we all knew that's why we were going there.

It's raining when we arrive in Flamengo, lightly at first but then flee-beneath-the-bank-building hard. We cower next to marble pillars and people in parkas and hope it will pass. The storm comes in and goes out. We take our time getting to the park, walking slowly. It's still drizzling and I wonder if these fields that Luke says are always full will be empty, but as soon as we walk in we can hear the squeak of shoes on wet turf and the skip of balls on water.

Wandering through the park is like being inside one of the Choose Your Own Adventure novels I read as a kid. Every time we reach a new corner we wonder which direction to go. There are small fields, big fields, turf fields, grass fields, concrete fields. There are dark guys, light guys, old guys, out-of-shape guys, bodybuilders, teenagers with faux hawks. Then we see a girl field; it looks like a practice, not like pickup, but still we go watch.

We all see the kid at the same time and go silent. We stare at the tiny blur who's toying with the ball, laughing every time she dribbles by someone as though she's just pulled off a fantastic joke.

"Um, she's really good right?" Ryan asks as we all put our fingers up on the chain-link fence and try to get closer.

"How old can she be?" I ask.

"She doesn't look more than eight," Ferg says.

Our movie's going to be about pickup games, not eight-year-old superstars, but we keep watching anyway.

"We might as well see about her," Luke says.

When the practice is over, Luke lingers weirdly next to the coaches and waits for someone to notice him. The coach, a gray-haired thin guy, is stuffing cones and pinnies into his bag when he looks up at Luke, who clears his throat and points at me. I hear him say "futebol feminino" and "Santos," and I assume he's saying, "My girlfriend's a soccer player, too," hoping this will somehow help us.

Then Luke points at the tiny kid.

The coach startles us by responding in English: "They call her Ronaldinha." He throws the bag of pinnies over his shoulder and says, "Have you eaten? Let's go to dinner."

We follow him around the corner to a Chinese restaurant (just like that, going to dinner with us, people he's never met).

Over sweet-and-sour chicken we never would have eaten on our own (because who goes to Brazil to eat food from China?), we tell him we're looking for stories of *peladas*. Sometimes it's hard to explain; people want to take us to stadiums, to real games, not games that no one pays attention to. *Peladas* are natural, part of the daily routine. To a Brazilian, making a film about them seems about the same as making a film about after-dinner walks. But Alejandro, the coach, gets it right away.

"Ronaldinha grew up playing *peladas* with the neighborhood boys—they're the ones who nicknamed her," Alejandro says. "There's a dirt field right beneath her house. You should go there."

On his napkin, he draws Luke a map out to Niterói, a suburb on the outskirts of the city. He sketches out a bridge and writes down the bus number. "Ronaldinha's special," he says. I think about the hope inside her nickname.

As we walk out the door, Luke asks as an afterthought, "Know any waiters who are playing tonight?"

Five minutes later, Alejandro drops us off in front of a yellow awning that says PIZZA GAMBINO. "This is the place. Good luck," he says. We shake his hand and thank him, a guy who will probably never see us again but who had no problem helping us anyway.

So Luke stands behind the families waiting for a table, and when it is his turn in front of the host stand, he says, "Desculpe," which means "excuse me," the phrase that almost always starts our *futebol*-based propositions. I wait to hear the throat-clearing sound that will come next as Luke tries to sort out his rough voice, garbled with nerves. "Cê joga futebol?" he coughs.

The guy, who'd been shuffling through menus, looks up. He has the shape and coloring of a leprechaun. "Claro," he says, nearly defensive, as though insulted by the possibility he might not play.

"Cê vai a jogar esta noite?" Luke asks. *Will you play tonight?*

"Sim," he says, nodding his head and tapping menus against the stand.

BY MIDNIGHT THE restaurant has emptied out. While there was the sound of families, crying babies, and gesticulating men cursing at the Flamengo game, now it's quiet. The waiters sit down at the table around the television, undoing bow ties, silently watching the end of the game . . . until the goal, and then there's a great leap up, chairs crashing. The lone waiter still washing the floor pumps the mop in his hand, water dribbling on tile.

At midnight, we walk out of the restaurant with Etevaldo and Reinaldo, two of the waiters playing tonight. Etevaldo has changed into a wife beater and yellow-and-blue floral board shorts. As we pass another restaurant, Reinaldo knocks on the window. A waiter slides it open and leans out of it as Reinaldo says, "Nós estamos indo pra quadra."

Nos means "we." *Indo* means "going." *Quadra* means "court." I add it up and feel proud that for one second I know what's happening.

We walk in a cluster down to the field. Before you've played, things are still polite, silences vaguely uncomfortable. During my summer playing in Santos, I'd learned how to ask basic facts, weirdly personal questions you'd never lead with in English, like, *Do you have brothers and sisters?* So I try it now.

"Brothers?" I say. "Sisters?"

"Sim," he says. "Uma irmã, um irmão."

"Older?" I ask. "Younger?" These are words I think I remember. I raise my voice, like volume will help me be understood: "Mais vieux? Mais jeune?" Really, *vieux* and *jeune* are French, a language I don't really speak (worst grades in college) but that keeps coming out of me when I try to speak Portuguese. I should be saying "mais velho, mais jovem."

They stare at me blankly. Luke makes no move to help me out. He gives me a look that says *You're being unintelligible.*

Next I try gestures—when I say "vieux," I throw my arm over my head, as if to say "big brother," and when I say "jeune," I throw my arm low, as if to say "little brother."

Everyone—Ryan, Rebekah, Luke, and the Brazilians—laugh. I don't get it, don't understand why they're laughing. "What?" I ask, smiling.

"Your hand gestures," Ryan says. "It just kind of looked like you were asking, 'Giant? Or midget?' "

Etevaldo puts his hand up by his ear, as if to say "regular-size, regular-size."

I laugh, defeated.

We come to a *passarela,* a footbridge that reminds me of a Paris postcard, except instead of the Seine below us, there are fields, rolling out in all directions. It's midnight by now and many of the *quadras* are empty, wide open, each one calling out to us.

As we sit down on the benches at the court closest to the beach, Reinaldo passes me one of his earbuds. We're listening to the *Rocky* theme song when a group of waiters walk over the *passarela,* waving their arms at us and whistling.

A big guy tosses an armful of pinnies onto the ground and shakes my hand with both of his hands, really jiggling my arm, like he's miming an introduction rather than making one. "Olá, Olá," he says. "Caipirinha?" He holds up a jug of yellow liquid, ice, and lime slices. "Sim, caipirinha," he says, answering for me. "Hora de beber!" *Time to drink.* He lines up a dozen plastic cups across the bench.

Reinaldo pulls a bib over his head, clearing the cigarette in his lips so fluidly it looks like this is how he always puts it on.

On an asphalt court, beneath the lights, we play for hours. It's 1 A.M., 2 A.M., 3 A.M., and then 4. I'm yawning, I'm floating, I'm clapping my hands against Etevaldo's after we combine around the waiter from Beer Haven. I watch the big guy in goal blowing his nose into a crumpled tissue, and Reinaldo as he sits down in the middle of the court, mock-screaming as someone hurdles over him.

Around daybreak, the game dies out. Etevaldo sits on the bench with his hands resting against his muscled arms. Luke asks him questions and I listen to the steadiness of Etevaldo's tired voice. "I wash the dishes, I sweep the floors, I put the chairs up on the table," he says, "and then I come to play, to live."

3.

A CAB DROPS us off at the base of Rocinha at 6:45 the next morning. This favela's not quiet like the one we went to with Nike. The Internet told us it's home to somewhere in the narrow range of fifty thousand to five hundred thousand people.

We didn't want to be late so now we are early. This is the city where you don't stop at red lights at night unless you want to get robbed, the city where people get sandals stolen while napping on the beach, the city where Luke got held up at gunpoint. And we are four tourists hanging out in front of a favela run by drug lords.

I've got *Tropa de elite* on my mind, the Brazilian movie about heavily armed police squads trained in urban warfare who come into the favelas to clear out drug traffickers. Even though the film hasn't been released yet, most of Brazil has already seen it; bootleg copies of a leaked cut were sold all over the street. The four of us watched it, no one but Luke understanding anything, but I think all you really had to hear was the gunfire.

City of God, the other famous favela movie, put all of the action—the shoot-outs, the drug wars—to the sound of a *cuica,* a samba instrument made to imitate a monkey's screech, a sound that makes it feel like something is going to happen. That's the sound I'm hearing in my head as we stand and wait.

The drug lords is the part that scares me, even though Luke explained that, weirdly, the drug dealers make the favela safe: everybody follows their law. Even to enter the favela, we need approval from the gunmen. We're waiting on Washington and Emerson, Brazilians with names that sound more American than our own. They run an after-school program in Rocinha and are willing to get us the drug lords' permission.

In front of us, commuter vans empty out and then fill up again, women off to work, boys on their way to sell soft drinks or sunglasses on the beach in Ipanema.

"Lucas?" we hear as two guys approach. We shake hands, and then Emerson says, "Shall we go?"

We weave between men selling acai, tank tops, and cell phones. Washington walks with his hands behind his back and whistles something eerie, something that sounds startlingly familiar.

"Is that what I think . . ." I whisper to Ryan.

"Yes," Ryan says.

To the soundtrack of the *Kill Bill* whistle, we enter Rocinha. Guys on both sides of the road carry guns so big they look like toys. Right in front of us, a teenager props himself up on an AK-47 the way someone in an old-fashioned photo might lean against an umbrella. He's smiling and it seems like he's smiling at us, but I'm also trying not to look directly in his face, so I'm not really sure until he says in perfect English, "Hello, my friends. Welcome to Rocinha, the most beautiful place on earth."

I keep my hands on the straps of the camera backpack and stare ahead of me as we head into the favela. It's like walking into a cross between *Alice in Wonderland* and an M. C. Escher. Homes web up the steep hillside and into the horizon—homes made out of exposed terra-cotta, concrete oozing out from between the blocks; homes made out of cement, blotches of mildew staining their sides; homes coated in brightly painted stucco. Most are three or four stories, stacked topsy-turvy on top of one another, the floors on the bottom often smaller than the ones on the top.

The base of Rocinha bustles with business: Internet cafés, local bars, and stands with blue-tarp roofs selling candy, jewelry, and electronics. I stare at a telephone pole with hundreds of cables shooting out from it, crosshatched like an Etch A Sketch drawing. A dozen motorcycles wait at the bottom, ready to taxi people up to the top.

All the sound is morphing together. Cars with giant speakers bungee-corded to their roofs blare advertisements. A man hawks pirated movies, chanting, "DVD, DVD, DVD." A chicken roasts on a spit on the sidewalk. A television blares a rerun of the Flamengo match, an announcer shouting, "Bellllllleza." Washington's whistling, the *cuica* noise is playing in my head, and I can still hear the gunman saying *The most beautiful place on earth.*

The road, while wide at the bottom of the hill, contracts as we climb higher, too narrow for cars. We walk along winding mazes that shrink smaller and smaller before opening up again. Sound softens as we turn down side streets; noises are delicate—the echo of kids laughing, the voices of a *telenovela* escaping through an open window, the distant rumble of a scooter funneling down the alley. A boy on a tricycle streaks by us, heading straight down the hill. We walk through a doorway, down a teal blue hallway, and up a winding staircase that leads to the roof.

Up top, we look down at the favela. Washington's next to me. He seems like a guy we'll never know. No telling what his mind's doing while he's whistling, hands in his pockets. I lean over the side and look out at his neighborhood, the Jenga-like towers of homes, rooftops dotted with blue water bins, and mothers pinning T-shirts onto clotheslines.

"Do you play?" I ask Washington, my foot nudging the ball toward him.

"No . . ." he says. His pause stretches out. "But later, I'll take you to people who do."

AROUND 8 P.M., Emerson drops us off at the big field on the outer lip of the favela. Men linger in pockets around the dusty sidelines. The sun has just gone down. The lights around the field are not bright. Each gives off a six-inch glow, making it feel like we'll be playing in candlelight. It's too dark to film.

One guy wears a shirt with green and white stripes that make his belly look even bigger than it is. A gold chain and a bright pink stopwatch hang around his neck. Everyone comes up to him, giving him a hand-over-fist shake. I get the sense that he's the center, the one who runs it.

The guys put Luke on one team and me on another. My team is off first, so we sit on a bench off to the side and watch. I don't try to talk to anyone. I wouldn't even if I spoke Portuguese. You don't talk if no one's seen you play.

Watching the game, I realize there's a good chance I'm not going to be good enough. The *futebol* in front of me is everything Brazilian soccer is supposed to be. Players invent in the dust. I'm jealous Luke gets to play right away, while I sit here and psych myself out. I've never been good at watching. I get sucked in, transfixed by everyone else, less sure of myself.

I don't understand what makes the game end, but it does, and my team starts walking out onto the field. Someone tosses me a red bib that says FAMÍLIA VALÃO in a font made to imitate dripping blood. *Valão,* Luke tells me, is the name of the street they all live on in Rocinha. The word means both "sewer" and "open grave." A big sewer runs under their street; the blood-dripping font presumably takes advantage of the word's other, more-intimidating meaning.

"Que posição você joga?" one guy calls out to me.

"Meio-campo," I say, hoping I'm saying "midfield." He points to the center of the field. By midfield, I'd meant outside, on the wing, where you can turn it into a one-on-one battle. I had not meant to ask for the all-the-best-players-play-here center.

I jog to the middle, my heartbeat scattered and out of control. The whistle blows, the game begins. A center mid has to check to the ball, which means you've got to think you deserve it. I know if I can win a tackle, my confidence will shoot up enough for me to go ask for the ball.

A player on the other team is close to me, and his touch, while not sloppy, isn't perfect either. I lunge hard for the ball and knick it, slipping in the dust but catching my balance enough to break for it, getting my body between the guy and the ball. I take one touch and send it to the forward. I overlap up the field, and the guy lays it back to me. I one-time it, taking a left-footed shot that has decent pace. The keeper catches it easily enough, and I start jogging back the other direction, keeping my face blank, even though what I feel is unbelievably lucky.

Now I have to maintain it. My mom always told me, "Fake it 'til you make it," and I never liked the expression—I thought it was too cutesy—but that's often what I end up doing. I pretend like I belong until I believe it.

Center midfielder—the person who's everywhere, all the time. On the wing, you can go long stretches without seeing the ball. It's easy to fall into a trance, to watch. There's no risk of that in the center: all points connect through you.

I get megged once—the ball whooshing between my legs before I know what's happening. The move's so fantastic I don't even feel bad about it.

And otherwise, I'm playing well. I check to my forwards and my defenders and then I lay it off, my passes clean. I'm not stupid enough to try to dribble. It's cluttered and cramped in the center; taking more than two touches is asking for it. Someone will appear out of nowhere, materializing right in front of you, usurping the ball. On the field, there's very little worse than that.

Of course, I want to dribble, I want it badly. Dribbling is what I'm good at, even though it feels stupid to say that in Brazil. I'm good but they're better. Still, I want to impress them. But I've got to wait. You have to fan the field with passes so consistently that no one will expect you to dribble—and that's when you go for it.

The big guy wearing the bright pink stopwatch blows a whistle. Our game is up. No one scored. I head back to the bench, Luke touching my hand as he walks by me.

Now that I've played, it doesn't feel bad to watch; I can sit back and appreciate. I see the meg again, the one that got me. A man charging forward suddenly changes directions, turning right into the person chasing him. Using the sole of his foot, he pulls the ball through the outspread legs, going through the defender so completely it's as if the guy was never there.

When I go on again, it no longer feels like there's an earthquake in my heart. This time my team puts me on the wing, space I know how to navigate. I hit in passes, one and then two and then three—and then I try something. I don't know what, I'm just moving, sprinting down the line, feigning a cut right but continuing left, my legs making a bow around the ball until I've stolen a couple inches of space. I shoot the hell out of it, as quickly as I can, scared I've taken one touch too many and that I'm about to get caught. I hit it cleanly. I hear the bang of the crossbar and the ripple of surprise.

For the rest of the game, the guy running the wing with me lays down move after move. I grab his shorts and try not to lose him. He beats me a lot. But I feel sort of proud about it, like I've proved I'm good enough to be worth beating. I'm playing as hard as I can, the kind of hard playing you don't even feel.

At midnight, Anderson, the man in the green and white stripes with the pink stopwatch, whose name we know from hearing everyone call it on the field, blows the whistle again, and this time it means the end.

Everyone stands clustered together, pushing down socks and taking off bibs, running fingers through sweaty hair. One guy brushes my shoulder and says, "Joga bem." *You play well.* He's the one who kept beating me up the line. My hands are on my waist, and my breathing hasn't quite evened out. For as long as I can remember, *futebol* has been how I come all the way alive.

ON VALÃO STREET the next morning, we walk toward Anderson's house. Peeking into doorways I see a doily-style tablecloth and a flat-screen television. My thoughts get stuck on the TV. I thought favelas were poor, and they are, one room topped upon another room . . . but there are also flat-screen televisions.

Anderson's home is three-storied, a different generation on each level—his grandparents on the top, his parents in the middle, Anderson on the bottom. *Futebol* trophies fill one corner; colorful kites stacked on top of each other fill another. "The big man is a little boy," says Emerson. "Always flying his kites."

I'm guilty of projecting personalities upon people. The other night it was dusky. Anderson wore a thick gold chain. He had meaty forearms. People kept coming up to him, doing covert handshakes. His whistles signaled both the beginnings of the games and the ends. Which all felt Mafia-like to me. I thought he was a hidden-thunder type of man. But as I lean against the doorway, listening to his soft-spoken voice as he talks about his passion for *futebol* and kites, it's clear that I'd gotten him wrong.

Anderson slings his knapsack across his chest and winds through the narrow passageways. The morning papers are clothespinned onto a laundry line. He shuffles behind a group of men reading the headlines until he can see: MARTA, MARTA, MARTA / BRAZIL 4, ESTADOS UNIDOS 0. Motorcycles honk as they weave through the crowd of people striding toward their mornings. Anderson stops into his grandfather's bar; his grandmother is behind the counter, shaking coffee through a water filter. He chugs down a cup of coffee, watches the Flamengo highlights, and kisses his grandma on the cheek on his way out of the bar. As we leave the Valão alley, he points out words that have been painted over but that you can still see: FAMÍLIA VALÃO, GOOD AT FUNK, JUJITSU, WOMEN, and FUTEBOL.

THE RIO WHIRLWIND—people with unbelievable wattage appear in your life and then move out, waving as they walk away down the sloping alley, sidewalk, or beach. Experiences overlap: Etevaldo bouncing the ball against concrete and yawn-smiling; the casual magician on the beach who looked at me like he knew what I loved—and he did, because here, *futebol* is what most people love; the graffiti artist sketching visions on a notepad. (Luke pointed out what I'd missed—how in the drawing Sandro gave me, the stars and stripes of the United States flag melted into the disc and diamond of the Brazilian, as though I was becoming *brasileira*.) And now we are leaving, headed to the other side of the bay to see the tiny phenom.

FUTURE, PRESENT, AND PAST

1.

WE STAND IN front of three terra-cotta-block houses. Ronaldinha says, "Adivinhe qual é o meu," and Luke says, "She wants us to guess which one is hers."

We choose the one to the right and then the one to the left and finally the smallest one in the center, the address 811 spray-painted on a house the size of a garden shed. "Sim," she says, clapping her hands and smiling.

The dirt field her coach had told us about sits directly beneath the neighborhood bar, the smell of barbecued liver wafting down from the grill. Since it's Saturday, a dozen adults stand beneath the overhang, eyes on the field.

"She plays like Ronaldinho and she looks like him," three boys sitting behind the goal tell Luke. "She's only missing the big teeth." She has his eyes, his cheekbones, his grin, his *ginga*—a Brazilian term that refers to a kind of sublime deftness, something to do with the sway of hips and imagination.

We thought Ronaldinha was eight but she's really thirteen and small for her age. Playing against her in the dirt, I have her in size and speed, but already she can do things with the ball that I've never thought about doing. Ryan keeps scampering into new positions, wiping his sweaty bangs off his forehead and cursing from behind the camera. "I can't get her," he says. "She keeps faking me out. I've missed all of her best moves, all of them." He takes off jogging again, holding on to his pants because he's forgotten his belt, hustling to catch Ronaldinha as she attempts to juggle the ball over Luke's head. She nearly pulls it off, her touch so good that for a second I think Luke will let her have it—but he boxes her out with his adult body at the last second, not quite ready to be served by a thirteen-year-old girl.

We're trying to figure out how we'll make Ronaldinha's story fit in the film, and one idea is to compare her to me: she's a girl, I'm a girl; we must have a lot in common. Luke asks me if she reminds me of myself. She told us, "When I was little, I started playing because I thought the ball was beautiful. I asked my brother to teach me how to play." That story sounded like mine. But the look in her eyes is different than the one you would've found in mine. My look was beseeching; her look is fearless.

Ferg is up top, filming the adults who huddle together and stare down at the neighborhood star. Ronaldinha knows what they're saying—that she's going to be the one who makes it. It doesn't faze her. She moves like she's ready for the pressure. If she's like me, the expectation the adults put on her is nothing compared to what she puts on herself. "Futebol vai me dar um futuro," she tells Luke later, smiling and mumbling into her Mickey Mouse sweatshirt. *Football will give me a future.*

The barbecued liver is ready around sunset. Ronaldinha slings her arm around her mom's neck. Everyone sings a Vila do Ouro samba, and Luke translates the lyrics for me: "This game will have love/I want to win/This game will change."

The kids run down to the field, where they find a wounded bird. Ronaldinha scoops it up and talks to it.

Her mother looks over the edge of the bar at the field. "My daughter is poor," she says. "If she rises, it is out of nothing."

"Thank God she has football. I've saved money for clothes, sandals, and food, for her travel with her team, so that no one will think she is inferior. She wants this and I want it for her. I'll be behind her no matter what."

BECAUSE THE 2007 Women's World Cup final comes on at six the following morning, we spend the night at Ronaldinha's house. Luke and I sleep in the foot-and-a-half strip of floor between the bed and the chair. Ferg sleeps with her legs hanging over the chair. Ryan's sent to the neighbor's house, where there's more space, but around 1 A.M., he knocks on the cardboard door. He's got bed hair and he's holding a blanket in his hand, looking like someone fleeing a fire.

"Uh, the lady's husband came home. There was a lot of shouting, wild gesturing. He came into the room and yanked me out of the bed. I couldn't understand what was going on. But my guess is that he didn't like a strange man inside his home."

Ryan lays down next to me, which is pushing spatial limits, but if we all spoon and no one tries to flip over, we're fine through the night.

RONALDINHA COMES IN at five and crawls in bed between her mom and brother. She's been out all night. When we left her, she was samba-ing with a dozen other kids. The samba may be Ronaldinho's trademark: when he finds the back of the net, his toothy smile and celebratory samba by the corner flag light up the stadium, the crowd, the country, the world. It is also what gets him in trouble, tabloids running pictures of Ronaldinho shaking tambourines and dancing into the early hours of the morning, earning him a reputation as a man whose partying gets in the way of his performance.

At 6 A.M., Ronaldinha's mother shakes her awake and turns on the small television. Ronaldinha rubs her eyes, pulls the covers up beneath her chin, and watches her country's chance to be World Champions.

The Germans are strong, their passes precise, but the Brazilians are the ones who thrill enough to keep us awake. Marta, Cristiane, Daniela— they invent. The first time I watched Marta play she was sixteen and uncontainable. I moved off the couch and onto the coffee table and couldn't believe what she could do.

Brazilian imagination dominates the game. The Germans flail to defend.

When the Germans score an ugly, skipping goal, Ronaldinha throws her arm down against the bed.

We all slump, resigned to witness the game's oceanlike power, the way it sometimes gives and sometimes takes away.

But then Marta's brought down in the box. We watch for the downward point of the referee's arm, a gesture that always feels like it happens in slow motion: penalty kick.

Ronaldinha's arms fly out of the covers. She taps the ten-by-ten-inch TV and yelps.

I study Marta's face as she walks into the box, looking for signs of penalty-kick inner turmoil, that talk you have with yourself where you try to command your thoughts into sureness.

"Eu nem olhar!" Ronaldinha cries, and because her hands are covering her eyes, I guess this means "I can't watch."

She keeps her eyes shielded until after it's over, only looking after she hears her mother yell, "Puta" and the rest of us moan. Then her eyes search the screen, stunned.

WHEN THE REFEREE blows the final whistle, we watch the alternating shots, first the Germans, arms around one another's shoulders as they jump in a circle, and then Marta as she walks the field alone, face vacant and unreadable.

When the reporter holds up his mic in front of Marta, she looks wiped out and miserable, but she puts her hands on her hips and says to anyone watching, "Now you have to lift your chin and keep working."

Ronaldinha lays there for a few minutes, grabs her shoes and a pack of crackers, and slams out the door, headed to the field.

She shoots on one goal, retrieves it, and shoots on the other until her brother joins her. More kids hear the sounds and come down to the field, the *pelada* swelling larger and larger, adults again leaning over the side of the bar.

IN THE NEIGHBORING town, we walk with Ronaldinha. The image of Ronaldinho, her namesake, is spray-painted onto every third wall, bigger than life. Some look officially sanctioned; some do not. Luke nudges me and points out graffiti of a blue wizard's cap resting on a ball. Four words are scrawled beneath it: A COPA É NOSSA. *The World Cup is ours.* It, unfortunately, had not been theirs. In 2006, they lost in the quarterfinals. Ronaldinho scored zero goals. Even though fans destroyed his twenty-three-foot statue in Chapecó, nobody's painted over him here.

Standing in front of a washed-out image of Ronaldinho, Ronaldinha performs a little samba, arms swinging, feet shuffling. She puts her face next to his; holds up both her thumbs, pinkie fingers slightly extended, a signature Ronaldinho gesture; and smiles at the camera.

2.

Ronaldinho's real name is Ronaldo. Since that one-word name was already taken, the Brazilians added *inho,* an affectionate tweak for their new hero. Not unlike the neighborhood boys' adaptation for their local star— Ronaldinha. One career fades out while another one begins.

And now we're headed to Santos, where I used to play, to meet the women who play there now. They're the best team in Brazil, the team someone like Ronaldinha is aiming for. Marta herself will star on their front line in 2009. Everything in Brazil feels interconnected and fated.

Ryan's sister, incredibly, married a Brazilian a month before we arrived in Brazil, and his entire extended family offered to take us in. Dani and Suzel, Ryan's new aunt and uncle-in-law, have an apartment in downtown Santos. We calculate the cost of four bus tickets and try to find a taxi driver who will take us the scenic route up the coast for the same price. We listen to Seu Jorge remixes, windows down, air blowing against our sunburned faces as we stare out at empty beaches and move away from the clasp of Rio.

If Rio is Luke's city, then Santos feels like mine, even though I actually lived in Itanhaém, the rural beach town two hours south. The only time I went to the city was to watch the men's team. I don't remember what Santos even looks like, only Robinho—the best player I've seen in person—and the ring of chaos around the stadium, blue smoke bombs zinging down the alleys.

When I e-mailed Kleiton, my Santos coach, and told him we were coming to the city, he wrote back, "Gwendolyn!" (I could hear him saying it: "Gend-o-lene," the *Gw* sound as hard for the Brazilians as the rolling of the *r* was for me.) "Your timing is luck. No game this weekend. We will do a brincadeira on the beach."

OFF THE FIELD, *brincadeira* means "joke, prank." On the field, it means the same thing. There's no American equivalent. A *brincadeira* is half game, half performance. The whole point is to surprise. Feet hovering over the ball, you wait to see what you will make. Defense is light; tricks are prized.

I get philosophical about *brincadeiras*. My summer in Santos, we played them the day before every game. In college, the day before games, Americans do walk-throughs, shadow play where you go over all the runs you're supposed to make. What you're told to do versus what you're inspired to do. Maybe this is why Brazilian soccer looks more magical than anyone else's.

Early Sunday morning Ryan, Ferg, Luke, and I head to the beach in front of Canal 2. Old couples in visors are taking walks along the water. It's quiet, nothing but waves, and the sun hasn't spread out yet. The Santos girls arrive on bicycles, whizzing along the sandy sidewalk. They jump off the bikes smoothly, flip-flops making popping sounds as they land on concrete.

I brush a ladybug off my arm and feel shy. I keep waiting for the girls I know to arrive, but they don't. They're gone, off to new teams or back to the cities they came from. I guess I thought they'd still be here. I expected Nenê to flick my earlobe. I imagined Karen putting her arm around my neck and saying, "Hello, my room sister."

The Santos girls rub goose-bumped arms as we tiptoe-hop across cold sand, scattered orange peels, and beach hay.

Sometimes games take forever to get started—you stand there and juggle and juggle until someone finally realizes he's going to have to be the one to push everyone into action—but this game starts right away. Four girls roll out bikes, flipping them over—makeshift goalposts. As half of us peel off T-shirts, someone's already running toward the goal.

The old couples walking stop to watch, squinting into the sun, staring at us. The players are a lot to look at. Hoop earrings and glittery neck-laces, smeared mascara, low-cut sports bras, pierced belly buttons, painted toenails. Black skin, brown skin, white skin. Braided heads, short boy-cuts, ponytails shining in the sun. Faces that are cover-model pretty, faces that look worn and old. Waistbands of shorts rolled over three times, exposed long legs. Girls who walk like dancers, girls who walk like baseball catchers. Girls from small interior towns in the south, girls from northern jungles, girls from the beaches of Floripa. All of them dazzle, stealing the ball away from one another, dribbling down the sand side-line. A girl named Erica keeps doing rainbows, real ones, arching the ball right over a defender's head. Ball attached, her foot moves like a queen's hand waving to a crowd. They laugh the whole game. Goals mean shriek-ing and then sambas—saucy facial expressions, arched wrists, hula-ing hips.

The ball splats down in front of me. I try something fancy. When you're in Brazil, it kind of works, your feet under a spell, doing things they're not capable of, like you've siphoned some *ginga* for yourself. In bed at night, Luke and I talk about this phenomenon, wondering if there's any way these powers could last. Or if, like the game we will play in tomorrow, it is only possible in Brazil.

SOMEHOW WE'VE DIPPED into a time-lapse sequence—able to move rapidly through the stages of a player's life span, witnesses to the begin-ning, the middle, and, on our final day in Santos, the end.

"The old men play very early on Sunday mornings," Dani had said as we'd stood in the laundry room of his sixteenth-floor apartment, looking down on a full-size field. "A flock of birds—that is their sound."

Now we're posted in the laundry room, T-shirts brushing the back of our necks while we stand at the window and wait for players to arrive.

At 6:15, a man sits down on the ledge of the canal and opens up a newspaper, a *futebol* resting beneath his sandaled foot.

AN HOUR LATER, the sidewalk is crowded with old men, gym bags slung over shoulders, laces dangling down from unzipped pockets. They smell like aftershave, strong coffee, and Icy Hot. Some wear sweaters, some wear 1980s hip-hop-style windbreakers. There are trucker hats, board shorts, argyle sweaters, tweed golf hats, and thin T-shirts. The men boast, heckle, and pat shoulders. Luke is folded into their routine, a listener for jokes. They approve of him instantly. Maybe because of his interest in them, maybe because Luke makes a natural old man—he's got the calm it should take five decades to find. Or, most likely, it's his Portuguese. He's blond, he's American; no one expects him to be able to start rattling off *ch* sounds. They raise wild-haired eyebrows and look more closely at him.

I stand close to Luke, as though I can absorb his understanding. I look into their gray-lashed eyes. Luke, so taken by them he can't help but share with me, relays comments:

"The women kick them out on Sunday mornings."

"He says they don't know how to play, just how to talk smack."

"They're here under doctor's order—good for the heart."

"They call it *grama molhada*. The 'wet grass' game—the only thing they're good for is playing away the dew."

A man with a gray crew cut who introduced himself as Douglas is sitting on the ledge and flipping through a *Playboy*, whistling every few pages. He smacks it shut, pulls a crumpled roster from his pocket, and spreads it across the cover, divvying names onto teams.

At 7:30, Douglas unlocks the gate, rolled *Playboy* tucked beneath his arm. The players follow him along a dirt path, stopping off at a temple beside the field. They groan theatrically as they kneel down to pray.

We gather around tables in a courtyard beside the field. I wonder how many more stops we'll make. Since we arrived at the ledge of the canal a little over an hour ago, we walked to a café, where four men sipped espressos and told a story all at once (hands fluttered over coffee cups, rising higher and higher until they were making wide impassioned rainbows with their arms); came back to the canal ledge; stopped off at the temple; and now we're sitting in patio chairs, playing cards, stretching sore backs, and flipping through Douglas's *Playboy*.

The tall man on the other side of me, Lulu, runs his hands through his full head of hair, as white and bright as his leather penny loafers. In contrast to his hair, his face looks tanning-bed dark. The top two buttons of his collared shirt are undone, gold chain and chest hair on display. As I eye his huge calves—the white curly leg hair the only hint they do not belong to a young man—Luke tells me the guy played keeper for Santos while Pelé was there. This fits: he has the long-lasting swagger of a professional.

Douglas raps my arm and points at a man who's just walked up. "Marta," he says, moving his hand like a fish swimming through water, like a player weaving up the field. It takes me a second to register that he's making a comparison, Marta being his choice as the ultimate beacon of skill. I make an *Ah* sound that I hope will convey understanding and appreciation.

Most of the men disappear to the locker room (location change six), and I sit down on the bench with three guys who show no intention of playing.

The guy standing behind me already has a beer in his hands, even though it's not yet 8 A.M. He points at me and says, "Alema?" Which I know means "German." This is not the first time this has happened. "No," I say.

"I speak English, I speak English," he says, patting his chest. "You are from Germany?"

"No," I say. "United States."

"Ahhhh, Germany."

On the other side of me, a small man crosses his legs and unfolds a newspaper, not listening to us at all. His outfit looks like what hipsters try to clone—tortoiseshell eyeglasses, cardigan sweater, black loafers without socks. Once the men have taken their places on the field, swinging legs, jogging in place, he lowers his paper and stares out at the field, as though mystified by his friends' desire to run around.

Half of the men are barefoot, half wear flats. (Lulu, in the goal, is still wearing his white penny loafers.) In each touch, you can see the great familiarity with the game.

While gentle with the ball, they're not gentle with one another—no consideration for old hips. They tackle hard. Bodies fly. On the bench, Luke and I turn to each other, wincing, sure that we will hear the cracking of brittle bones.

A half century of experience makes for opinionated players. They gesture wildly and yell at one another:

"You always do this!"

"Oh yeah, and you never foul."

"Make a goal, asshole."

"This game needs a nurse."

"What, so I hit it with my hand—big deal."

"He's trash, he's trash—pass the ball to me!"

"You just passed it to my knees."

"All the world's going to see this, and you're playing like this!"

There are balls they don't get to. When someone sends it long, the man on the receiving end pumps old arms in vain. He tosses his hands and mutters, and I know what he's saying because I've heard younger men say the same thing: "Maybe a few years ago I would have had it."

Glancing at me, the guy in the cardigan folds his newspaper and stands up. He beckons me up from the bench and says what must be, "Go on, get in there." He pushes me into the game, vaguely annoyed, recognizing that we would sit there forever unless someone told us to go in.

"You too," he says, throwing his hand at Luke.

When we walk onto the field, I can feel the old men looking at me. They are seventy-year-olds playing barefoot, but in their eyes I am the spectacle. They chuckle with pleasure.

My teammates find me often. When they pass the ball to me, it feels like old-timer courtesy, like opening the car door for a date.

On the other side of the field, Luke's play is relaxed and unhurried, not wanting to be the twenty-four-year-old hotshot. He focuses on serving balls to his teammates. In any game, if someone goes through the trouble of making a run, you feel obligated to play them, to reward them; in this game, where you can feel the effort behind every run, this is especially true.

Douglas is running, going as fast as he can, and I'm watching his wrinkled elbows as he hauls his body up the sideline, and then, out of nowhere, he's down, sprawled out on the grass. He lays there for a second on his side, propped up on his right elbow like someone lounging in a park. He soaks in the tragedy of it, the unjustness of his fall. When someone on the other team comes over to help him up, he pats the ground in front of him, as if to say, "It was the grass, it was the grass."

I look up from Douglas to see the keeper hopping sideways, batting away a shot. Then he poses, leaning nonchalantly against the goalpost, one hand on his hip. (Luke thinks he leaned against the post in order to demonstrate how much saving that shot took out of him, while I read it as: *Oh that? That was nothing.*)

His teammate jumps on him in celebration. When the whistle blows, they walk together off the field, one man's arm hung round the other's neck.

The men disappear into a locker room and come back smelling like cologne, their gray hair wet and combed. A man behind the bar guns Brahma beer into big glasses. I don't like beer, but I'd rather drink it than admit that to grandfathers who are offering it to me. "Saúde," I say, clinking my glass against theirs.

"We call it the third half," Douglas tells Luke, tapping his beer and making a little party with his thumbs, tipping them toward his mouth. "The first two playing, the third one drinking."

When he stops laughing, Douglas swirls his beer and says, "All week we wait for Sunday."

WE DOUBLE-KISS THE old men good-bye (it's one kiss in Rio, two in Santos) and board the first of three buses that will eventually land us at the home of Nenê, my former teammate. On the ride, I replay our *pelada*, feeling like the old men had just taught us something important: we get old, the game does not.

The men in Santos keep coming to the field. From what I can tell, when someone's counting on you to play the ball well, the game offers as much meaning at the end as it does in the beginning.

3.

"If you're alive, you show up": that's the translation of the graffiti scrawled across the waist-high cement wall surrounding the *futebol* court at the base of a São Bernardo favela.

This is the court where Nenê grew up playing. It's also the court where her brother was stabbed to death. The summer I played for Santos, Nenê told me about her brother by miming it out for me, driving her fist into her neck.

Nenê, at twenty-seven, had been one of the oldest players on our team. She'd already quit soccer once, taking a job at a toy factory in order to make more money for her family. But she missed *futebol* too much and came back. Nenê's Happy Meal–like toys decorated our dorm rooms. Karen and I had a *Finding Nemo* fish sitting on our dresser.

I knew Nenê had eleven siblings—she sent most of her forty-dollar monthly paycheck home to her mom—but I was still stunned to see every-one packed into the kitchen when we arrived last night in São Bernardo.

Nenê's mother wore eyeglasses and a knee-length skirt and reminded me of a convent nun. She asked us questions in slow, considerate Portuguese that I could sort of make out.

"Onde você mora?"

"Nor-chae Caroleenah," I say, feeling pleased with myself for remembering to convert my *t* into *ch*, not realizing they only make that sound in the state of Rio. (I should also be saying "Carolina do Norte," not Norte Carolina.)

"E sua família?"

"Florida."

She frowned. "Por quê?" *Why do you live in North Carolina if your family lives in Florida?*

I thought about my family and I looked around the kitchen at Nenê's. "I don't know," I said, and for that second, I didn't. I had no idea why we spread out, scattering ourselves across distant places. I thought about it again as I went to sleep on the floor of her living room, sweatshirt balled beneath my head. Our great American mobility. We leave for schools, jobs, and chances that take us very far from home.

Through *futebol,* Nenê has also followed chances, playing for teams in Minas Gerais, Santos, and São Paulo. When her contract ran out, she came home. "The season would end and I wouldn't have any money. I'd rob people, fight. Like my brother, I was going in the wrong direction. I didn't know why . . . just that I was going. I wasn't part of a gang—I was my own gang. I passed through the favela entrance, the mouth of smoke, no problem," she told Luke as we sat in her bedroom. "I knew what people said about me—that I had the face of a thief. But I was also known for my futebol. That's what I had going for me. I never missed a day on the court. If I wasn't there by two P.M., people worried about me."

Many of the guys she grew up with went somewhere to play—some to São Paulo, one to Spain, one to Portugal. Nenê's career is over. "We can't all be Marta. I didn't move forward," she said. "So I went to work." She's back at the toy factory. In Santos, she was our goal-scorer. Having witnessed her gift, it's hard to wrap my mind around the idea that she's done, talent stilled. In the factory, she sat on a stool, spray gun doling brown paint onto a Shrek doll. She says she enjoys it. In her bedroom, dozens of small plastic dolls sit on her dresser. "I don't know why I like them so much. Maybe because I painted them. And we never had any dolls when we were kids. Now I want them all."

Her contract with the toy factory is up at the end of the month, and she's not sure what she'll do next. "I don't pick what I do—things show up," she said, rolling a Hello Kitty–looking doll in her hand. "I was always playing futebol, playing futebol. And then you look for a job? Futebol's not on your résumé. My résumé was blank. It's hard in Brazil. But I've always found something. Clean up trash, watch people's cars, help people build houses—anything, I don't care . . . it's honest, there is dignity." She leaned back against the bed, looking up at the underside of the top bunk, yellowed newspaper clippings of *futebol* stars stuffed beneath the wooden slats.

Nowadays, Nenê usually only plays on Sundays, after she's coached kids for two hours at the church. Almost all of the guys she grew up with are gone. But the players at the court now still know who she is. "Sometimes people will say, 'Who's that? What's she doing out here?' But someone else will say, 'That's Nenê' and they'll tell my story."

AT THE COURT, the tricks are jaw dropping. The nutmegs are a slightly different version of the ones we saw in Rocinha, which fascinates Luke. "It's like every Brazilian neighborhood comes up with their own tricks," he says.

"You Americans plan—mechanical," Nenê says. "Brazilians try new things, invent. We care about the moment."

A guy wearing a trucker hat, a hoodie, long shorts, and red-and-white high-tops splashed with cursive—a look that says *street*—steps on the ball and trips, his long body sprawling out across the court. You don't expect someone as tough looking as him to go down.

The guy everybody calls Negão, which means "big negro," is six-three, shirtless, and has a cast on his right arm. "He's the drug dealer, one of the guys who runs the area," Nenê says, her face somber. Drug dealers killed her brother; I wonder if he's on her mind when she's out here. "I wanted to find whoever did it and kill them," she'd said. "All of them."

Nenê's relationship with her brother was complicated; on our Santos team, many brother relationships were. Too often, our brothers, the ones who taught us how to play, had lives marked by violence and crime. Nenê said her brother sold her bike, her shoes, her cleats—enraged her—but you never stop caring about your brother.

It seems very hard that her tragedy happened on the court, the place where you're supposed to be able to forget.

At dusk, Nenê sits down with her back up against the wall, her knees tucked up to her chest. A kid about Ronaldinha's size sits down next to her. He messes with a ball, rolling it around, waiting for his turn. They lean against the graffitied wall, looking out at the game.

SAUDADES

THE LAST STORY from Brazil is hard to believe.

In Santos, after a day shooting scenics of ocean and white sand, we laid down on the beach in our sweatshirts, looking out at the waves. It was brisk outside, wind whipping. Down the beach, solitary figures walked by the water. One man came toward us, wind pushing him forward, his hoodie pulled over his head, shadowed face hard to make out. We watched him approach, waiting to see if he really was walking toward us.

Up close, his face was striking, beautiful. He had the chiseled bone structure and two-week beard of some movie star you can't quite place. His eyes, the same dark brown as his hair, were framed by long lashes and fine lines that made him look like a bearer of wisdom.

He held out his hand, a mystery fruit resting on his outstretched palm. "Gostaria de uma fruta?"

"What is it?" Ryan asked Luke, looking at the fruit as though it were the apple from *Snow White*.

"No idea," Luke said.

We accepted the fruit and thanked him.

The man who introduced himself as Ilson laid down on the patch of sand next to us, chatting with Luke, looking him very deeply in the eyes before standing up, brushing off sand, and walking away. We took turns biting into what might've been a kumquat while we watched him waft away with the wind.

A week later, we took an all-night bus ride to Curitiba, a four-hour bus ride to Floripa, and one more two-hour ride on a local bus down dirt roads, stopping ever so often to pick up schoolkids. Eight hundred kilometers later, when we pull into Guarda do Embaú, a fishing village of three hundred people, there he is—Ilson, the man with the eyes, standing in the center of a deserted town, sweeping dust on an empty street.

When he sees us, his face registers no surprise. He holds up his hand as though he's been waiting for us.

"Not possible," Ryan says as he stares out the windshield.

The eeriness is reinforced by our location.

Ilson walks alongside our car as we roll down a cobblestone street that ends at the beach. We stand on the shore. We stare out in front of us. Shafts of sunlight spill down through dark storm clouds, lighting up a cantaloupe slice of white sandbank, formed where the diverging river meets the ocean. A dozen brightly colored rowboats rock softly as the wind passes over water.

This sandbank is why we're here. Anderson, a local who grew up in Guarda, wrote to us about his town's river, the way it splits and then heads out to the ocean, forming the tiny island where the riverboat guides play in sunset pickup games. But all that was just a couple of typed sentences in an e-mail from a stranger; now it's a paradise we're standing in.

We'd been careful not to get our hopes up—a game with riverboat guides on a sandbank? It sounded like the most spectacular thing in the world, so we spent all five bus rides reminding ourselves it probably wouldn't be quite so spectacular. It is.

Ilson, who's wading in the water, pushes a rowboat toward us. "Entrem."

"I figured out who he looks like," Ryan says as he squints at Ilson's sunlit face. "Not a movie star . . . Jesus."

"Well," Luke says, "he did just tell me he's a shaman."

A shaman who looks like Jesus is leading us through parted waters. I stare at Ilson's bamboo stick as it rises up and then sinks down again as he pushes us forward, a ripple blooming across water.

We beach the boat on the other bank. Ilson disappears through a hole in the trees we wouldn't have seen. We hunch our heads down and follow him through a canopy of trees, toward the patch of light ahead of us, popping out on top of rocks that are clay-red. Howling wind whips at my hair and my skirt as we walk out on a cliff and scale its side. I look down at the straight drop into ocean slush, waves crashing into boulders a few hundred yards beneath me.

Once we make it around the other side, we look out at new scenery—sweeping sand dunes. Just beyond the dunes, it looks like we can see Ireland. I wonder if I'm in a science fiction film where one landscape can just melt into another—we float across a river, down empty white stretches of beach, through green rolling hills, weave between scattered cows, into a world made of rocks, through a tangle of jungle, and out to another shore that recedes into pool-colored waves.

Back in the boat, Ilson guides us through marsh canals that look like bayou, with horses standing on grassy banks.

There's no chatter, just the sound of the boat gliding through water. Ilson's voice lures us out of our daze. "Futebol?" he says. "Quer jogar futebol? Aqui."

(Even that sounds to me like something out of *The NeverEnding Story,* a mystical stranger guiding us along on our quest.)

On the shore in front of us, two Adonises in Speedos stand with feet planted wide, hulking arms folded in front of puffy chests.

WITH THEIR HEELS, the men draw sidelines in the sand, making not only the penalty box but also the half circle on top of it.

Their play is riverboat-guide relaxed, muscle-bound bodies fiddling with the ball, plodding down the beach. I get megged again: the man in the red Speedo stands with both feet on top of the ball, and when I go to kick it out from under him, he hops off and plays it through my legs, continuing down the beach, slotting the ball through the driftwood goalposts.

Dark storm clouds creep across the sky. Ilson stares into the blackness and announces, "We must leave."

The raindrops pelt us as our boat streaks across the water.

Under the cover of the beach-hut bar, two riverboat guides play guitar and sing a Portuguese version of "No Woman No Cry." People fleeing the rain arrive breathless, shivering, and wet. In it together, we watch our hut fight water. The sound becomes suddenly more violent. It takes a second to realize that one hour ago we were getting sunburned but now we are getting hailed on. The ice pellets bang louder and louder against the roof.

A woman weaves out from behind the bar and into the crowd of wet beachgoers, holding a frosted tin pail over her head. "Caipirinha!" she yells. "Gelo do céu!" A pail of caipirinha—made with hail—gets passed around the bar.

The riverboat guides sing with closed eyes. Couples dance, pulled into each other for warmth, women's faces against men's necks. Luke folds me into him, my back against his chest as we watch the waves crash against the shore and the hail crash against the roof.

I know hardly any Portuguese, but four expressions I do know I'm sort of obsessed with: *favela,* which also means "wildflower"; *pelada,* which also means "naked"; *brincadeira,* which also means "joke"; and *saudades,* the term my team taught me last time I was leaving this country, a one-word way to say "I miss you." It describes "the feeling of absence for someone or something you wish was still present." All month I've said it, *saudades,* to Arnaldo, Nike, Sandro, the waiters, the old men, Família Valão, Nenê, and Ronaldinha. *Saudades* slinks into me again now. I can imagine us combing streets in other countries, our minds always drifting back to Brazil.

PICADO

THIS IS WHY we love Buenos Aires: the men hum tunes to themselves as they whisk by us on the sidewalk, and the women wear leather heels in distinctive colors—magentas, mustards, and teals. Bookstores and trees line the sidewalks. There's the corner bakery where we buy baguettes for two pesos and the old café where Jorge Luis Borges came to write. When we wake up, we sit on our balcony and drink *café con leche* while watching boys hang out the windows of the school across from our apartment.

This is why we're frustrated with Buenos Aires: we get mugged on the Subte (Ryan's wallet deftly removed from his pocket); it's raining 90 percent of the time, and when it's not, the tipa trees spit sap onto our faces; the bookstores boast of novels in English but only carry the young adult series Sweet Valley High; and worst, we can't find *fútbol*.

Ferg and I eventually walk into a used bookstore with dark, secretive aisles lined with English finds: Charles Bukowski, Ken Kesey, a photo series of Hemingway in Africa, a collector's edition of Jack Kerouac's *On the Road*.

And finally, after three days of nothing—facing blank stares when we ask about *picados,* showing up during prime playing hours at deserted fields, taking the subway from one end of the city to the other, empty courts shuttling by our windows—we begin to notice the men. It doesn't happen right away. It's a city; floods of people come at you. There are sirens, honking horns, and taxicabs that pull up to the curb. So it takes a while before I glance down and see a pair of shin guards in the crowd. I spin around on the sidewalk, trying to follow the legs, but they're gone, swallowed by the crowd, my sighting so brief it's hard to know I really saw it.

Twenty minutes later I see Ferg turning against the flow of the crowd, standing up on her toes, reaching with her neck. "There was a man," she says as she jogs to catch up, "with a briefcase. And a suit jacket. But underneath . . . a jersey. Soccer shorts. Soccer socks. I know it."

Somewhere very near here, people are playing.

We walk up and down the streets, staring down alleys, into windows, up at roofs. Ferg and Luke pick off the straggler in each crowd, asking the Argentines what they know, like somewhere there's a secret door everyone but us knows how to push.

They come back without answers. "They say there's no field anywhere around here."

We walk slowly. I start forming opinions about Argentina, adding up three days' worth of observations, making sweeping judgments on a country. The Brazilians are open, embrace everything, while the Argentineans are aristocrats who tie sweaters around their necks and lean back in restaurants, legs crossed, watching the game instead of playing in it.

I feel hot, clammy. Just because our movie idea was possible in Brazil doesn't mean it is possible anywhere else. If we can't find soccer in Argentina, land of Maradona, Messi, Tévez, and Batistuta, how will we find it anywhere else?

Someone left-brained would have gone through appropriate avenues, contacted the clubs, the breeding ground of players, been directed toward men who wear polos embroidered with league insignias and who hold keys to every field. But we hadn't wanted to set up a game. We were pickup romantics. We wanted to just go to a place and find it.

We gave ourselves a month in Brazil, time to screw up, time to get lost. But we had only two weeks in Argentina, seven days in Buenos Aires, and three of them were gone.

Then, suddenly, they are right in front of us—the men—sitting down on the sidewalk, jerseys on and soccer bags out, passing crowds weaving around them, stepping over outstretched legs.

"Dónde está la cancha?" Ferg asks, leaning over them. *Where is the field?*

"No sé," they answer, shaking their heads, continuing to push down socks, remove shin guards.

She stands there, her eyes running over all the evidence of *fútbol*— the bags, the cleats, the knee braces, the sweaty faces.

Her hips twist, ready to walk away, but then it's like her mind says, *Hold it. This has to be it.* "Where are *you* playing?" she asks.

"Aquí," they say, tossing their thumbs behind them.

Rebekah stares through a window stenciled with pizza slices. She looks back at the man, and her facial expression says, *Please explain to me why you're pointing into a room full of pizza and telling me there is soccer.*

A tall man with shaggy black hair stuck to his wet forehead says something, but his words are too fast, Ferg still dizzied by the gap between classroom Spanish and Argentine Spanish, where *ll*'s transform into *juh*'s. He sees the blankness on her face and stands up, leading her through the door to the pizzeria, to the portal, the game waiting just beyond.

FROM THE STREET, you see only restaurants. But inside, tucked behind the tables and the diners, *fútbol* courts spread out before you. In the morning, we track through the city, scouting what feel like magic tricks: we walk into restaurants and out onto fields. (Club Eros is my favorite: green plaid tablecloths, Chianti wine bottles splattered with candlewax, men in suits cutting into *bife de chorizo* as they sit at tables overlooking a checkerboard court.)

At 4:30 P.M., when the Argentinean men wrap up workdays, we enter Club Arroyo. Two women sit behind a concession-stand-like window.

Above them, a black letter board, the kind you'd see at an old-fashioned bowling alley, advertises rates by the half hour.

As we stare at the unevenly hung white letters on the sign, trying to figure out if there's any way to play with other people, the two ladies behind the counter stare at us. Luke's blond hair is a torch of unbelong-ingness. And I'm a girl; based on the fifteen men standing with us in the lobby, that's not ordinary, either.

When Luke tries to ask them questions, the women's eyes grow larger and larger. (In Brazil, Luke was language king. He had the inflections, the rhythm, the ability to bounce his body around in the same way the Brazilians did. Here, when he opens his mouth, Portuguese is stuck on every syllable.)

They reiterate what it says on the sign—100 pesos to rent a field. We could rent one but we'd need ten friends. We don't have ten friends.

"But, they said we can play if anyone's short on players," Luke relates back to me as I follow him out the lobby door, holding our ball in my hands.

WE MOVE FROM field to field: a guy with a gelled haircut turns us down right away, with the guilty discomfort of someone turning away a panhandler. A group in their late twenties tries not to acknowledge us. (They're the type who made me nervous in high school and whom I guess still make me nervous now—nonchalantly arrogant facial expressions, athletic builds, clothes worn carelessly well, old sweatshirts, cutoff warm-up pants, pushed-down soccer socks.) As Luke says, "Mi amigo, puedomes jugar?" they keep their eyes on the court, shaking their heads without even looking at him.

It goes a little better when Luke approaches a skinny fiftyish-year-old with a balding head and bright eyes, a guy who looks like somebody always inclined to say yes. Ball under his arm, he looks at me with raised eyebrows. "Usted sabe cómo mover la pelota?" he says, which Luke explains to me means, *You know how to move the ball?*

I nod and smile. "Buuuuennno," he says, dragging it out.

He puts his arms around our shoulders and welcomes us to the court. We're passing the ball around the field with everyone else when two late-comers jog up, bent over and hopping, tightening laces on the go. Their arrival means our exit.

Everyone at a club has a stake in the game: we saw men thumbing through bills in the lobby. Someone who's paid money to be there isn't going to give up his spot for someone who hasn't. This makes complete sense to me. I just have no idea how we're going to get a game in Buenos Aires.

We wonder if we'll have better luck if I try. Sometimes guys have a harder time saying no to a girl. Luke goes over it with me: *Está completo. Está completo.* When I stand in front of strangers and try to say my line, the words disappear. I lose them completely. New words come out, "Ju-gador completo?" *Player full?* No one can make out what I'm saying.

We stand in the area between two courts, watching the games on both sides of us, silent.

"What are you doing?" a voice asks from behind us.

English—so far it's been rare in South America, which I admire: I like it when locals expect you to figure it out on your own. But that doesn't mean my hopes don't soar when I turn and see a guy who might be will-ing to tell me where the soccer is.

I tell him—a man with a dark ponytail and pale skin, who has wit-nessed our string of propositions and rejections—that we are looking to play. We think the word for "pickup" in Argentina is *picado* or *picadito*, but so far those terms have only led us to clubs.

"Are there any places beside clubs?" I ask. "Places where you don't need money or friends?"

"You know you are in a city?" he says. "There is no space. Buenos Aires is not the best place to look."

"Rio de Janeiro is a city. That doesn't stop the Brazilians," I say, my voice kind of haughty, as though I have a right to Brazilian pride.

He tucks a piece of hair behind his ear and frowns. "To find the real fútbol you'd have to go to the villas. But you cannot go to the villas."

I scrunch up a sleeve of my T-shirt and look closely at him.

"Places like Villa 31, Villa Lugano—the bad neighborhoods. For outsiders, it is too dangerous. It is impossible."

We try two more restaurant clubs, but now as we go from field to field, I've got the word *villa,* prounounced *vee-juh,* rattling around in my head.

I don't want to come to Buenos Aires and film club games—games we can't get into, games you have to pay for—while there is "real *fútbol*" happening somewhere else.

THE NEXT MORNING we leave the cameras at the apartment and take the blue Subte to the end of the line. We ask a man selling bread how to get to Villa 31. Turn left, then right, head out along the railroad tracks. "Es muy peligroso," he says, glancing up at us. "Usted no debe ir allí." *It's dangerous.* You should not *go there.*

With a dozen or so other people, we walk fast along the tracks, which makes it look like we're riding a conveyer belt forward. A train thunders by, depositing people on platforms that had been empty. We hear a scream, the sound of movement, a man running. The woman in front of us doesn't glance over, so we don't either. My heart pounds as the sound of footsteps gets closer, but he runs right by us, sweeps past us. And soon we are in, the neighborhood of cinderblock houses spread out around us.

We'd been told that Villa 31 is built under a highway overpass, but that hadn't really meant anything to me. Now as we walk, we can hear the zipping sound of cars and the longer, charging rumble of the semis as they pass over the top of us.

Soon we hear the yelling of a crowd and then, once the narrow dirt road opens up, we see it: a new world spread out beneath the interstate, hundreds of people crammed around nothing other than a *fútbol* game.

It's a Sunday tournament, and the villa's main road doubles as a field.

We drift into the crowd, good and dumbstruck. A boom box blares Latin music. Kids ride dads' shoulders, hang on moms' legs, play with piles of peanut-shaped Styrofoam. A man tries to sell the huge parrot riding on his shoulder; the bird plucks at his shirt buttons. Bicycle carts topped with umbrellas weave through the crowd, men offering colas and candies. Stray dogs pant their way past each set of legs, scanning the ground for food. A boy leans up against the interstate piling, holding a ball beneath his arms as his eyes track the movement of the game.

After a forward streaks up the part of field closest to him, pushing left and then cutting right, the kid jogs to the space shadowed by the highway above and mimics the movement of the forward, throwing his small shoulders left, lunging back to the right. Then he returns to his spot and continues to watch.

ON SUNDAY, SEEING the families, the men selling ice cream, the kids drawing pictures with chalk, they didn't look like people to be afraid of. People keep telling us Villa 31 is dangerous—*peligroso, muy peligroso*— one of the few Spanish expressions I've heard enough to remember, but I liked that game and the kid on the sideline.

When we come back the next day, three separate policemen try to stop us. The first one says, "Don't go there," shaping his arms into an X. The second tells Luke, "It's your life, not mine." And the third one says to Ferg, "Last week, Channel Two came. They stole their cameras and bashed in their heads." That last one carries the most weight, even though we tell ourselves he's just saying that to turn us around. It feels naive not to be scared. All the festivity of yesterday has gone silent—no music, no cheering, no laughter—just the whistle and thunder of the semis.

We attempt to turn down the same street as yesterday. I'm trying to recognize a laundry line, a graffitied post, something, when we come upon a field, a new field, one we never saw yesterday. Even though it's 2 P.M. and hot, people are playing.

We stand a few feet back from the endline and watch. A row of favela-like, unfinished cement buildings tilts sideways and backdrops the field. The ball shoots out of bounds—toward us—and my heart starts up with the pounding, because I know it's our chance and I know Luke will take it.

He chases the ball down, volleys it back, and calls after it, "Perdón . . . podemos jugar? Uno a cada lado?" *Can we play? One on each side?*

You don't spend three days getting rejection after rejection without expecting another one. I'm gnawing on my fingernail and looking at Luke, at this man I love (I don't know if I've ever thought of him in this sentimental way before, but that's what I'm thinking now as I watch him dangle himself out there and speak his Portuguese-tinged Spanish).

Like me, the guy stares at Luke. His tan, sweaty face is wadded into a grimace. "Huh?" he says, that international sound.

Luke repeats himself: "Podemos jugar? Uno a cada lado?" He says it louder, determinedly confident, like he knows he's saying all the words right. (This is a secret he learned in Brazil: even if your pronunciation is perfect, if you sound hesitant, they think they can't understand you. You've got to infuse each word with enough bravado to convince them.)

"Ahhh," the guy says, ball in one hand, beckoning us with the other. "Claro, claro." *Of course.*

We walk out onto the dirt field scattered with rocks, plastic bags, candy wrappers, shattered glass, a stray sneaker, and a discarded cabinet door. I shake hands with a guy who looks at me like I am a hallucination. I smile at him. He smiles back but still looks flooded with confusion, like my arrival wars with what his thirty years of playing *fútbol* at this field have taught him to expect.

A FIFTEEN-YEAR-old with a skinny chest hurdles a stray dog whose path intersects with his own. He plays the ball back in, sending it to a middle-aged guy who ends the game with a rocket into the upper V. Through the vibrating netless goalframe, the Buenos Aires skyline rises up behind the slum.

Out of breath, our wet shins caked with dust, we stand together along the endline. The *fútbol* was rough, intense, the kind I love. (When Luke got endline, he landed on a rock, a big one. His ankle rolled out, but he kept running, pretending like there was never a rock.)

A fortyish-year-old with tattoos on his forearms leaps up to grab the T-shirt draped over the rusted crossbar. He whips the teenager closest to

Villa 31, Buenos Aires (Courtesy: Ryan White)

him, slings the shirt over his shoulder, and gives us a low wave good-bye before walking back into the villa.

A credit-card-size bandage covers the right cheek of the guy closest to me, making me wonder what's under it. He smiles at me—he looks about nineteen—and while the other guy's smile was a mask of uncertainty, this one's all earnestness. I notice his hazel eyes. (Luke jokes that I have a Rain Man–like ability with eyes: I don't process language or directions, but I can tell you anyone's eye color.)

Carlos, the hazel eyes, introduces us to his two friends—Lorenzo, a tall kid who played in a goal, and Campos, a husky guy wearing a sleeveless Arsenal knockoff. While Carlos was a worker who slid up and down the wing, playing like nothing mattered more, Campos walked most of the time, bitching, his hand held up like a chef critiquing fine cuisine.

The trio invites us back to their neck of the villa. At their houses, they grab short stools and drag them outside where it's cooler, the sun beginning to drop beneath the skyscrapers. We drink warm Fanta while Campos tells us how his friend Carlos is one of the unluckiest guys there is: he had a tryout with River Plate, but then (his fingers mime an explosion) he broke his leg. This is a story I'd normally be missing, but Lorenzo's sister Veronica, who is studying English and happy for the chance to use it, sits next to me and fills me in.

They're eager to talk about what soccer means in the villa, especially when they find out we're trying to get the story of *picados* all over the world. (*Picado* literally means "chopped" or "picked off"—which, at first, doesn't sound nearly as beautiful an idea as *pelada*. But Veronica describes it as "your small piece of the game," and yeah, then I love it.)

Inside Campos's house, Ryan and Rebekah record their stories:

"We are very close to each other. We are immigrants from Peru, Bolivia, and Paraguay. You walk around and you know everyone. Like everywhere, there are good people and bad," Campos says. "All boys dream of playing—for Boca or River. Sometimes there's no money for an opportunity. Parents can't pay for club fees, for bus tickets, for cleats. Sometimes clubs discriminate. Your parents do everything they can to get the money to pay and then they tell you, 'No, you're a villa kid, you're a thief.' And there are the older guys. Some had a chance and didn't make it. Now we play here, together, in our neighborhood."

"Fútbol is everything. Nobody can take it away from me," Carlos says. He points to Campos and smiles. "And this fatty kid just plays to try to get in shape."

BEFORE WE LEAVE, we walk as a group to the half-cement, half-rubble field directly beneath the interstate and play in one more *picado*. By now, the workday's over and the slum swells with people who move in waves through our game: a man carrying sheet metal, teenagers with backpacks and headphone wires, a young dad holding a grocery bag in one arm and a baby in another. The ball bangs off a bicycle. (While our game in Nike's alley paused for passing cars and people, this game continues.) One family walks slowly, in no hurry to get out of the action. I study the mom's hot pink tank top and black bra, the way she holds the hand of the man next to her, who holds the hand of the eight-year-old beside him, one tight chain of family.

"You should go before it gets dark. We'll walk you out," Veronica says, once our game has ended. Then she confirms the policeman's story: "Last week, Channel Two came. They stole their cameras, hospitalized them." I wonder if it's foolish to think *fútbol* kept anything from happening to us.

We walk through the corridor, passing a *fútvoleibol* game, homes being constructed, kids on roller skates. At the edge of the villa, we say good-byes. I shake Carlos's hand but then remember that handshakes are American. "Do they kiss in this country?" I ask Luke, beginning the cheek kisses before he says yes. When I reach the end of the circle, I look back at Carlos and realize we did not kiss. I stutter-lean back toward him as everyone laughs and I feel the pang of leaving.

"That way dangerous," Veronica says as she points. "That way safe. Allá . . . no. Allá . . . yes."

AT THE GAS station, sometime after dark, halfway through our drive to Mendoza, the ball rolls out of our rental car. The gas station attendant jogs toward it and juggles it up to his mechanic's jumpsuit-covered thigh. He lobs it back, Luke's foot catches it, and pretty soon we're playing two-on-two under the station's bright lights.

Mendoza is our last stop in Argentina and a setting unlike anyplace we've seen, home to tree-lined hazy lanes, snow-capped mountains, and vineyards that roll out into the horizon. We're staying with two sisters, friends of our friend, who introduce us to a group of winemakers infatuated with *fútbol*. Emilio is a landscape architect and grape consultant, Lucas and Paulo develop vineyards, Antonio constructs bodegas, and Raul is an economist and professor who analyzes wine tourism. (When we ask Raul if he plays soccer like an economist, he says, "I suppose I do. If the probability is good that I will get the ball, I run for it. If chances look bad, I don't.") Some grew up on vineyards, learning the art of wine making from their grandfathers; others came to it on their own. Together, they want to one day make their own wine. For now, they play *fútbol*, have post-game *asados,* and tell us, "It is better to drink wine after the game than before."

On the grassy area outside a bodega where Emilio's sister got married, between the Malbec grapes and the Cabernet Sauvignon, Emilio and Antonio unwind the garden hose into a sideline. Overturned buckets serve as goals. To pick teams, Raul and Emilio line up twenty paces apart and walk toward each other tightrope style, one foot in front of the other. With every step, Raul says, "Pan," and Emilio says, "Queso," their voices echoing each other like a game of Marco Polo. Raul's foot lands on Emilio's, which appears to earn him first pick. "This is our tradition," Lucas says, "what we've always done."

When Luke rockets a ball into the grapes, they joke, "Dont worry, it's only a couple thousand pesos' worth of Malbec."

After the sun sets behind the Andes, we drink wine that's too good for us and eat steak that overwhelms my meat-loving heart. At midnight, everyone, even Ryan, plays *fútbol* in the dark.

GAUCHOS IN THE MIST

MONTEVIDEO—CAN I say it's my favorite? We buy chorizo in the *mercado* by the port and walk the Old City. It is Vienna or Rome or Barcelona, only forgotten about, like everyone moved out, gave up. Now there are wrecks of great buildings. Concrete facades crumbling, exposed brick. Flecks of paint, moss sprouting on the buildings' sides, patches of grass growing in the cracks of balconies. Boarded windows, bricked-over windows, windows that are gaping holes, cockeyed shutters with broken slats. A great gray fog—dirt or soot or ash—stains everything, moving in, taking over. The ghost buildings haunt the streets, shadow reminders of the past. "We meant to be the cultural capital of the world," says Gonzalo, a man whose Flickr photo of a game on the beach inspired us to come here. "But then the bottom fell out." In the eerie quiet, I imagine what might have been.

Not far from the edge of the Old City, there's La Rambla, the stretch of sidewalk that fronts the ocean. That's where the people are. At 5 P.M., hundreds of Uruguayans sit along the cement ledge in front of the beach. "Is there a festival?" I ask as we walk. "Some type of event?"

"No," Gonzalo says, thumbs beneath the strap of his satchel. "This is just our way. At sunset, we come here." They sit, they think. They sip out of silver gourds filled with maté, a tea that looks like the clippings inside a lawn-mower bag. "We are an introspective people," he says. While Luke's spirit seems in harmony with the Brazilians, mine, I decide, is Uruguayan. As I'm looking out at the faces, feeling soothed by all the reflection, Gonzalo says, "Highest suicide rates in South America."

"We are a sad people," he says. "We are highly educated, built to think. But there are no jobs, no opportunities. Our young people leave." The Uruguayans squint their eyes and gaze out at the water.

WHATEVER AURA OF melancholy there might've been on Friday is nowhere around on Saturday: it's all sunshine, wind, and weekend calm. On a sliver of beach, we play with high school seniors who sport highly fashionable haircuts, some opting for the mullet, others for the rattail. They smoke cigarettes and wear 1940s-style swim trunks. (Except for the guy wearing white boxer briefs, made quickly see-through after his postgoal victory plunge into the ocean.) Next we jump into a game on a grassy stretch of lawn in front of the highway. Once, a ball sails out of bounds and toward an oncoming motorcyclist. He barely slows down, lowers his foot, and volleys it back to us. In the Old City, we play in front of a building that is fifteen broken windows wide, four broken windows tall. It's a family game, with people from the tenements on the other side of the court—kids in jean shorts, teenagers in jerseys, fathers with guts, a barefoot mother in a pink tank top standing in goal.

On Monday, we want out of the city and into the country. Victoria, the niece of Luke's uncle's secretary and the woman we're staying with in Montevideo, asks, "But why? There is nothing to see. Only cows and more cows." We tell her we are going in search of gauchos.

"Gauchos?" she exclaims, clapping her hand over her mouth. "But they do not exist. They are only a myth."

Gauchos—South American cowboys who roam the countryside. *Typically dressed in berets or sombreros and baggy pants tucked into boots.* "Our

Old City, Montevideo (Courtesy: Ryan White)

guidebook says we can find them in rural areas," I say, ruffling the pages, aware of how dumb this sounds.

"Ha! Good luck!" Victoria says. "Let me see your little book." She reads over my shoulder, amused by something that claims to have answers, and then looks up. "Fifty years ago, maybe you'd find them, but they shot each other over land disputes. The government made them put up fences. With the fences came the end of a certain type of gaucho. I do not know what you mean by 'gaucho,' but I do not think you will find them."

WE RENT A car. All weekend we've seen old-timey classics parked along the Montevideo gutters. I imagine us taking back roads in an old Peugeot or Fiat. We drive away from the lot in a neon yellow box, something that looks like it should be driven by a cutting-edge clown.

As a kid, I never wanted a car to arrive. On my way to tournaments, I leaned my head against the window and willed there to be more time before I had to get out and go try. Cars felt safe to me: I could just sit there. I stared out at everything, I listened to lyrics, I watched big raindrops swallow small ones on their race across glass. Looking in the windows of other cars, I wondered about the faces moving away from me, finding it hard to grasp that I would never know any of them, that most of the world was out of reach. Pickup changes that: landing in new places, soccer gave us an excuse. It was a reason to talk to the old men playing cards on the corner, to the twenty-year-olds with tatted-up arms, to anyone who looked like they could point us in the direction of a field.

Listening to the CD Anderson burned for us in Guarda, Portuguese covers of melodies we know but can't place, we stare out at cornfields. The map is open on Luke's lap. His finger tracks thin lines. There's Route 5, Route 7, and Route 31. We can go anywhere. Once, the road ends, disappearing into a river. A ferry takes us to the other side—it's the kind of moment that seems extinct and makes us feel lucky. We head north, driving down dirt roads, looking for gauchos. I don't know why. The idea swept us. Men on land, old roads, old ways, open space.

When there is a town, we drive through it—along the tree-lined square, past the church and the school. Every dozen miles there is a field. We see a horse framed by goalposts, cows grazing in the penalty box.

A dusty park offers us a clue—an old man wearing a cowboy hat, wrapping twine around his hand and guiding a slow-moving steer. He looks like proof. He's also pushing ninety. If all gauchos are as old as he is, a game among the gauchos looks unlikely.

We pull up to him, idling down a narrow dirt road. Ferg and Luke roll down their windows. They tag-team Spanish: Ferg talks, Luke listens. The old man will be tough. What do you ask? If he's a gaucho? If he knows any other gauchos? Who happen to play *fútbol*?

Ferg eases her way in. "Do you like fútbol?"

His face is deeply wrinkled, deeply tanned, decades spent outside. When he opens his mouth, his voice is gravely, one word running into another. Ferg and Luke just look at each other.

"Uruguay loves football?" Ferg asks.

The man says again whatever he said before.

Luke says, "I heard, 'The planes told us, the planes.' And 'Copa Mundial.' Maybe they announced the win from the planes?"

In 1930 and then again in 1950, Uruguay won the World Cup; more than fifty years later, those victories are still the pride of the country. I imagine a pilot with a megaphone, calling down the news to the people below, celebration spilling out onto streets.

Ferg tries to move into the present: "Do you know anyone who plays?"

The old man is still smiling and pointing at the trees, at his memory of planes.

AS THE SUN sets, we pull out of town. We're on the outskirts of Sarandí Grande when we see four guys sitting on benches, drinking thermoses of maté.

We drive by, process them—young men, nineteen or twenty, wearing telltale berets, baggy baseball pants, worn-out T-shirts—and then we reverse.

Ferg hangs out the car window and calls out, "Disculpe, ustedes juegan fútbol?"

One guy wears a white beret and a faded blue button-down. He looks like a young, more-rugged Patrick Swayze. He chews on a corn-husk cigarette and surveys us. We're embarrassed of ourselves, our yellow car, our garbled Spanish. He cocks his head behind him. "Aquí."

Twenty minutes later we are in a field—high grass, potholes, unanticipated hills. I'm running, calling out for balls, surveying the play around me—twenty or so strapping young guys throwing berets, playfully trash-talking, plowing into one another. Incredibly, our wandering landed us at the Sarandí Grande Agrarian School: a gaucho training ground.

"Mi amor!" a guy named Francisco calls out when I dribble; "Gringo!" he calls out when Luke dribbles. It starts raining, drops so hard and fast they hurt. We yell, laugh, and play for a while, and then we flee. Standing under the overhang of the school roof, Burro, the Uruguayan Patrick Swayze, tells us to follow them to the farm the next morning.

They point us to the one place in town to stay, rooms above a bar. It looks like an orphanage out of a film—high ceilings, wooden walls, a dozen cots, and great old windows that leak water into Ryan's bed. We read, the rain beating down on the roof above us.

THE PINK SUN rises out of a misty fog as we arrive at the school the next morning. Gauchos wearing old sweaters lean against a cement wall, one leg up, sipping maté, fog circling them. They look like a cologne ad.

They push-start an old-school Mercedes work truck, five men on each side, grunting, driving it forward with their legs. When the engine kicks up and the truck starts rolling down the slope, they run to catch it and hurl themselves in.

Ten guys sit in the back, watching our car take the punishment of big rocks as we follow them deeper into the country. The fog hides everything except for the truck in front of us.

A half hour later, outside a red barn, we lean against a wooden post and watch the gauchos: they bound forward, swinging strong arms. Making a teeth-sucking whine, they lunge toward sheep, herding them into a pen. Occasionally a sheep jumps, all four legs lifting up, air-bound by fright.

The sheep assembly line continues: channeled into a troughlike canal, a long pole dunks them into soapy water. Wet and clean, they bump up against one another in the pen. It's hot inside the barn, and the chorus of *bah*s and the vacuumlike sound of the razors make it feel hotter. Sweat drips off the gauchos' foreheads as they plunge razors into sheep wool.

The curls tumble down, white bellies exposed. When skin's knicked, blood spurts.

Then they pass the razor to me. It rumbles powerfully in my hand. "Whoah," I say, fighting to keep it steady as it shears through wool. "Whoah."

Occasionally a sheep makes a break for it, turning suddenly and scampering in the wrong direction. Ferg and I lean against the wall and root for it secretly. *Go, go! You can make it!*

FOR LUNCH, WE eat lamb chops. They're fresh. Hundreds of sheep stare at us as we eat.

We play four against four in the pasture by the barn. Chickens peck their way through the game; herds of sheep pass behind the water-pail goalposts. Francisco makes the same teeth-sucking sound he made while herding sheep. Sometimes berets fall off. Chests gleam out of unbuttoned shirts. One corner of the field is matted with sand burrs. Burro sits midgame and uses a knife with a three-inch blade to dig at the spines in his foot. Francisco lies down with his face in the grass every time he misses. One guy takes off his slipperlike shoe, sniffs it, and chucks it over his shoulder. Like yesterday, it's power-your-way-through-the-mess fútbol. "Fuerte, muy fuerte," Burro says, describing his style. *Forceful, very forceful.*

Our goalkeeper, Alfonso, is the embodiment of the gaucho legend—the fifty-something-year-old who knows the sheep, fattens the pigs, and teaches the younger guys how to work the land. Like the old man in the park, his face is dark and lined. He wears a sombrero and an unbuttoned flannel shirt, belly out. His pants, tucked into his leather boots, have rips up both sides, exposing strong quad muscles. At the end of the day, when we're talking about Montevideo, Ferg asks him if he likes it. From his spot leaning against a tree stump, he says, "Montevideo, you wear a necktie, tight pants. It's claustrophobic, like a bird in a cage. I like my freedom, my horse, waking up early, the air, the sun, the wind, the country, the working. . . . I like my freedom. Montevideo, no . . . for me, no."

When each sheep has been washed, shaved, and let out naked into the pasture, we return to Sarandí Grande. Three gauchos ride with Ryan in our yellow car, and Ferg, Luke, and I ride in the back of the classic truck, leaning against the side. I drink the maté Francisco passes me, bits of leaves in my mouth. Burro's yelling to Luke that he looks like Bill Clinton, which is kind of true, so everyone is nodding and laughing, the wind swallowing our sound. Holding my whipping hair in my hand, watching two feet of sunset and farmland fly through the wooden slats of the rattling truck, I feel pretty carried away—because of where we are, and because soccer, which Burro calls *fúte* (what an intimate little word), is what got us here.

300 FRUITCAKES

1.

WHEN I MOVED to Slidell, Louisiana, in first grade, everyone but me knew how to read. Ms. Carlan wrote LOOK on the board, drew eyeballs in the *Os* and said, "*Surely* you know this one." I did not. After school, I sat down with my mom and the index of my textbook and studied columns of words. At first I read because I didn't like being the dumb one, but later I read because it was a chance to be inside someone else's life, a chance to go anywhere. In college and grad school, I'd pick an isolated desk in the library stacks, open up a book, transport myself. But those were trips of the imagination, and there's a safety to that. Most of the time I prefer it that way, reading about adventures instead of having them. Sometimes, though, book open in front of me, I feel a small surge of bravery and want my own. That's how I ended up on that boat in Mexico; that's how I ended up spending the summer in Brazil; and that probably has to do with how we end up inside a prison in La Paz.

. . .

THE NIGHT BEFORE our flight to Bolivia, we sleep in the airport, on the air vents in front of the window, the only space besides the floor long enough to lay down on. A woman in old clothes periodically leans over us and shouts, "Americanos! Peligroso!" *Danger!* This wakes us up, as does the cold air blowing into us. We open the bags under our heads and pile T-shirts on top of us. When the sun rises around 5 A.M., filling the window, Ferg and I sit up and lean against the glass. "Peligroso!" the old lady warns.

One day later, we stand in the Santa Cruz home of Jorge Molina, a Colombian who placed seventh in skeet shooting in the 1984 Olympics. Six feet or so and barrel-chested, it's not hard to imagine him winning competitions that involve guns. "Welcome," he says, shaking our hands. "A friend of my daughter is a friend of mine."

I wonder if he knows I've never met his daughter. Daniela is a friend of my friend Stephanie Peel. (I grew up in Pensacola, Florida. Peel is from Plano, Texas. We met at Olympic Development tryouts in Montevallo, Alabama. She eventually moved to Pennsylvania, where she coached Daniela, a Colombian whose family now lives in Bolivia. I'm awed by the way football can web itself across the world . . . but it doesn't seem like the moment to reflect on this awe of reach with Jorge, champion marksman and one intimidating guy.) Daniela had written to us: "Go to Bolivia. My family has a dove-hunting lodge and a cattle ranch in the Amazon. In and around both places, everyone but my father plays fútbol."

In the foyer, I stare at a picture of seven-year-old Daniela petting a jaguar. Next to it, there's a photo of her five-year-old brother standing inside a giant grouper that Jorge caught while free diving in the Amazon. These pictures set a tone.

CHICHITO, JORGE'S BEST friend, is a dark-skinned, stocky guy with a big laugh. "He knows fútbol better than I do," Jorge tells us. "He's the man to show you the country."

Chichito keeps coca leaves, the raw material used to make cocaine, in a plastic Baggie in the center console of his Land Cruiser. They say coca, a local trademark, isn't nearly the same as cocaine, but combined with the ashes of the quinoa plant, it still curbs fatigue, hunger, thirst, altitude sickness—pretty much anything. And the entire time we're chewing it in Bolivia, I feel a whole lot like I might be on drugs, like Chichito is on drugs, like I'm a passenger on a trip with Hunter S. Thompson at the wheel.

We're in the middle of the Amazon—water buffalo cross in front of our car—on our way to a straw-thatched village near the Molina's cattle ranch. It's rained for two days, the narrow dirt roads now mud. Our Land Cruiser fishtails from side to side. Chichito doesn't take it easy, racing along roads he built himself. My gums and tongue are numb, my head is light from either the altitude or the coca, and Chichito keeps wadding more and more leaves into his mouth as he guns the engine, turning backward in his seat to raise his eyebrows and grin at Ferg and me, seemingly pleased our car is slipping from side to side. ("Haven't you guys done doughnuts before?" Luke asks as Ferg and I clutch our hands around the car seat. "Swerving around in a car isn't usually a girl's rite of passage," Ferg says. Our trip offers a multitude of alliances: Luke and me, the couple; Ryan and Ferg, the singles; Luke and Ferg, the language speakers; Luke and Ryan, the boys. This one is Ferg and me, the girls.)

When the sun comes out, Ryan climbs onto the roof to film tracking shots through the jungle. We drive slowly at first, but after twenty minutes, Chichito picks up speed. In another ten, we hit a stretch of sitting water and hydroplane off the road. On the roof, we hear a solid thump.

The car leans against brush. "Ai yi yi. *Ryan*," Chichito says, putting his hands to his head. "Me olvidé!" *I forgot.* He hurries out of the car, steps up on the foot rail, and peers up top: "Hermano, estás bien?"

"I think so, sí," we hear Ryan say, voice full of wonder.

For the next two hours, Chichito periodically reaches into the backseat to pat Ryan's head.

On our way into the village, we slow up as giant black beetles land on and depart from our windshield. The field is the center of the village, the straw-thatched roofed homes built in a circle surrounding it. A horse is tied to a goalpost. A giant oak tree shades the women, kids, and old men who sit close together on a long bench and watch our sunset game. Women dip coffee mugs into a utility bucket full of corn water and hand them to the players coming off the field. As I drink my corn water, vaguely wondering if I'll regret drinking it later, five small girls sit on their heels and smile at me.

AT THE MOLINA'S cattle ranch, an hour outside the village, we drink warm milk delivered from the barn to our table in a tin bucket. We don't shiver as we swallow clumps because we're all on the same page: do not be wussies. We want to be like Chichito. We are fearless, blasé. All in. ("All in": the phrase our defenders wrote with a Sharpie on one another's wrists, which meant you were laying everything you had out on the field. Now in my head about milk, soccer lingo infiltrating . . . will it always do that? Will I be somebody who speaks in sports metaphors, who sees the whole world as a field?)

We head out on horseback to round up cows in the jungle.

I climb on a white spotted horse. I haven't ridden a horse since I was a twelve-year-old going on a twenty-dollar tour in the Smoky Mountains. (My horse ended up in the bushes, all my coaxing ineffectual.) That's it, the extent of my horseback experience.

"Chichito says that's the wild horse," Ferg calls out from behind me. "You OK with that?" I nod, glad to ride a real horse instead of the kind that are child approved.

He trots fast, in the lead, Ferg's horse behind mine. Showing off her comfort level around horses, she makes the kissing sound that means "go faster." Her horse doesn't respond; mine does, bolting, full gallop forward.

I bounce violently on top of him. With every stride, every foot of air off the saddle, I think, *I'm going to fall, I'm going to die.* I want to pull the reins tighter—I know I'm supposed to—but any additional movement seems like it will send me right over the side. A gate appears in front of us, and I'm sure he'll go for the leap and that will be it, my end, but instead he rears up and slows down, the horse and my panic coming to a halt.

An hour later, around a murky lagoon, while everyone else is actively rounding up cows, I sit on my horse in a light rain, staring blankly ahead, still fairly stupefied. When Chichito sidles up to me and holds up his rifle—asking me if I want a shot—I look at him for a second, and then I say, "Why yes, I do." I dismount and cock the gun. Chichito points the muzzle toward the crocodile floating in the water. I pull the trigger. The force rocks me. The barrel of the gun sweeps up toward the trees, the parrots in greater danger than any reptile in the lagoon.

The sound echoes; my hands vibrate. "Wow," I say to Chichito. "Wow."

LATE IN THE afternoon we take off again in the Land Cruiser, this time heading for the dove-hunting lodge. At dusk, the downpour starts. Chichito is not laughing. By eight, we see how dark a road can look when there is nothing around. Our headlights are a tiny glow, doing almost nothing against the rain. We can't see anything. The car hydroplanes again and again no matter how slow we drive. Chichito wipes sweat off his brow as we make turns into the blackness, one tiny road after another. At midnight, a tiny wooden sign—LAS PALOMAS LOUNGE—lights up in our headlights. "Es un milagro," Chichito says.

The cattle ranch was rugged, bare bones. That's what we're expecting when we run out of the rain and into the hunting lodge. We stand in the entrance with our duffel bags by our side and stare: high wooden beams, terra-cotta-tiled floor, hand-carved furniture made out of varnished teak. A large crocodile skull sits in the stone fireplace. Fifteen-foot anaconda skins stretch across the walls. Bright hammocks knit by a tribe in Colombia hang from the beams. Jorge greets us: "Welcome to the lodge."

WHEN DANIELA WROTE to us about Bolivia, she described playing in games with Mennonites in a jungle clearing near the lodge. Once, in Indiana, I ran into a family of Mennonites at a gas station in the middle of the night. Three teenage boys stood in the candy-bar aisle and stared at me, eyes darting back and forth from the floor to my face. I was confused: I thought Mennonites swore off modern ease, including cars, so I didn't expect to see them under fluorescent station lights at midnight.

Indiana, rural Bolivia—Mennonites pick far-flung pockets of the world on purpose, isolation a way of guarding themselves from influence and distraction. In the morning, we pull up to one of the farms in the colony of Mennonites who settled here fifty years ago. It's odd to see a family of fifteen people with blue eyes and blond hair in the Bolivian jungle. The father and sons, who wear trucker hats, overalls, and long-sleeve collared shirts, come out to the barn and stand around us. While the men talk, I pass the ball with one of the teenage sons, his big toe hanging out of his split boot.

The women watch us from fifteen yards away, standing in an outdoor foyer. The mother and daughters wear high-neck floral-print dresses that remind me of old photographs. The youngest, three or four, wears a bonnet with a blue satin sash. One teenage daughter washes her very long hair in a water basin. As she rings out the water, twisting it tightly, she stares at Ryan. Then she brushes it, stroke by stroke, still staring.

They don't play football and they don't know anyone who does.

We try one more farm. This family is smaller—an old man with a Canadian accent and three sons, one of them nine or ten years old, two of them about our age. All three are handsome and tan. They come in from hauling hay, wiping sweat off warm faces. The sons don't speak English or Spanish, only the traditional Low German. The oldest leans against the fence, thumbs beneath his suspenders, eyes on the ground.

"No," the old man says in Canadian-accented English, smiling, his blue eyes twinkling in the sunlight. "We don't play ball here. Our farm keeps us busy. We work from sunrise to sunset—we are too tired for games. No, I don't think you'll find any around here."

I hear the sound of the ball and look behind me to see Luke and one of the sons in the high grass to our right. They stand ten feet apart. Luke tosses him the ball and he heads it back. It's a good header, strong. The ten-year-old sits on the fence, and the older son leans against it. Every time their brother heads the ball, they laugh, a shy sound, the kind of laugh that sneaks into you and spreads out.

THAT NIGHT SIX of the guys who work at the hunting lodge pile into a motorcycle cart. Two guys ride the bumper of our car, hanging on to the rack up top. Ryan is back on the roof. When we get to the dirt field, we see three giant puddles—more puddle than there is field.

The game revolves around two objectives: 1) score goals, and 2) do everything you can to avoid the mud puddles. There is much sliding, skirting, and screaming, but there is only one total capsize into the mud. It happens to the most macho of them all—a man with brushed-back curly hair, a button-down navy blue shirt, jeans, and cowboy boots. He was up, then he is down, caked in mud, cursing while the rest of us are bent over, laughing, gasping, hands on our knees.

As the sun sets and the lightning bugs come out, I see the dust of a Mennonite cart on the road beside the field. The man holds the horse reins with one hand and shields his eyes from the sun with the other, neck craned backward, looking out at the field, at the sound, at the people who are playing.

2.

Ryan has seen pictures of the Uyuni Salt Flats. "We're going," he says, his finger running down bus routes out of Santa Cruz. We book a twenty-six-hour bus to Uyuni, with a one-hour layover in Sucre. The city of Sucre, however, goes on strike. Jorge will not let his daughter's friends head for danger. So we take an all-night double-decker bus to Cochabamba. There is no air-conditioning. We pick the front seats on the top deck (thinking how great it'd be to look out the front windshield). The windows do not open. It is pass-out hot. We are soaked with sweat. Ferg ate a bad empanada and keeps throwing up. Then we drive into a storm. All night we watch the lightning. At midnight, Luke squeezes my thigh and whispers, "Happy birthday." I am twenty-five. A quarter of a century old.

In the morning, we arrive in Oruru. Now we've got to find a bus to Uyuni. We walk through the wide hallway of the station, studying the large-font promises of travel posters. A jukebox plays Enya followed by Ja Rule. We dodge hard sales, men cutting off our walking lane, waving brochures in our faces. We reach a booth run by two women who smile at us with the eager friendliness of two kids manning a lemonade stand. Ryan reaches beneath his T-shirt collar and pulls out a hanging pouch-wallet (which has a distinct fanny-pack-like vibe), what he's worn ever since the incident on the Subte. He takes out cash, buys us four tickets to Uyuni, and stuffs his necklace-purse back under his shirt.

Now we have ten hours to kill. Oruru is tiny. A one-screen movie theater runs what we hope will be a subtitled version of the Steve Carell flick *Evan Almighty*. It is dubbed. I leave fifteen minutes in and sit by myself in the park.

All trip, I've carried the 240-page printout of my book about my brother folded in my deceptively big purse, tucked beneath my cleats. I thought I would work on it. I haven't touched it.

I lean against the park bench and look at the old couple across from me throwing birdseed, crows pecking the sidewalk.

I pick up my purse, unearth my sheaf of papers, flip back twenty pages or so, and just start reading from the middle.

I feel hands on my shoulders. I reach backward, my hands climbing up wrists and arms: Luke, leaning over me.

"Hi," I say, grateful to be disrupted.

"Thought I'd come look for you," he says, sitting down next to me. He pulls a paperback out of his sweatshirt pocket. He reads; I cross out sentences.

I think about the scene in Michael Chabon's *Wonder Boys* where the main character watches the wind blow away the pages of the novel he's never going to finish.

. . .

AT 10 P.M., we arrive back at the station. We see only one bus; it's not the one listed on our tickets. We sit on the curb and wait. Rebekah has nuts in one hand, boarding passes in the other, when our lady from the booth, who is no longer smiling, plucks the tickets out of Ferg's hand and replaces them with new ones.

The bus tour companies have consolidated. We take off for an all-night ride with ten people standing in the aisle, headed to the city described as "climatically challenged" in our guidebook, temperatures below zero at night . . . without heat and with the sudden realization that the window in front of us is broken and won't close. We clutch the jackets we bought at a secondhand market in Santa Cruz around our throats and pull our hand-woven beanies down over our faces. Ferg, Luke, and I pile on top of one another and try not to die.

Ryan sits one row up. "Frío?" the older woman next to him asks, touching his cold cheek. She pulls his face into her chest, wrapping him in her llama-hair blankets, draping her legs across him.

At 3 A.M., the bus deposits us in Uyuni. It's black outside. No one is around (even though the women at the booth told us there would be plenty of people to show us where to go). It doesn't seem like anyone else has a place to go, either: the Bolivians stand with us in the lit lobby of the bus station until we're all kicked out. Then everyone stands across the street, staring at the lights, feeling sorry for ourselves in that primal way that happens when you are very cold. Sleep feels like it's dripping in a wave down my head. People disperse gradually, walking into darkness.

Wind howling, we walk through empty streets until we find the center of town. We knock on the door of a hostel. No one answers. We knock on the door of another hostel. Five minutes pass. Ferg and I sit down, bags strapped across us. Ryan knocks one more time—his knock slow and haunted sounding—and the door swings open, a man rubbing at his eyes.

. . .

AT NINE, AFTER we've slept for several hours, we head to the square with the tour operators. We choose the first company we walk into, having learned yesterday that careful deliberation doesn't always help.

An hour later, our Land Cruiser makes a hissing noise as we fly across salt. Out our windows, it looks like the world got erased—nothing but white. We take funny pictures in this nonspace. You lose depth perception—nothing to track size with. So when I walk a hundred yards backward and stick out my foot, I am a tiny pixie with my foot in the ear of Luke-the-Giant. A miniature Ryan can stand in the palm of Ferg's hand. The ball can be as big as a planet, while we are tiny specks on top of it.

Volcanoes, geysers, islands, and lagoons are scattered across the miles and miles of reflective white sheet.

A Bolivian tour bus stops at the same mountain rising inexplicably out of salt that we do. We stare at the possible teammates as we chew on our sandwiches. "Ustedes quieren jugar?" Luke asks.

"Sí," the Bolivian responds.

We use empty water bottles as goalposts, the ball skipping along the salt. When the ball is shot wide, it rolls forever.

LAGUNA COLORADA, OUR last stop, is a red lagoon. If I read that in a travel guide, I'd be skeptical in the same way I am when a novelist writes about gray eyes. But this isn't just red when the sun hits it at a certain angle. It's red-red, butting up against other water that is fluorescent teal. There's an explanation for all the color, something about algae and sulfur and sediment, but I don't want to hear the science behind it, I just want to stare at it. Hundreds of pink flamingos burrow in the warm water, their reflections rippling.

At night the winds pick up, nothing in the salt to break down the gales. The place where we stay doesn't have heat. We wear alpaca caps and scarves, our Bolivian flea-market jackets, and six layers of T-shirts, huddled together around a table, trying to lay out our film while the wind moans around us. The plan is to have Luke and me be the through-line, a way of holding the other stories together so that the film doesn't feel like a giant montage. But who knew how that would work. Brazil's painful to think about—Rua de Lazer, Família Valão, Ronaldinha, the waiters, Nenê, the old men. Too much. Argentina, Uruguay, Bolivia—it's tough to imagine how any of it will fit. But sitting there, rubbing our hands against our cold cheeks, we feel conviction. As we stare across the salt, thinking about everyone we've played with, we are silent, awed by the game.

ON THE BUS ride to La Paz, we pass around the Lonely Planet, *South America on a Shoestring,* reading about revolutions, conflicts, and customs, dog-earing pages of neighborhoods and markets where we want to go, signature dishes we want to eat. We read each other interesting facts. "La Paz is nearly four kilometers above sea level," Luke announces over the rattle of the bus. "The city's buildings cling to the sides of the canyon and spill spectacularly downwards."

I reach for the book and flip through the pages, my eyes landing on a bolded subset: San Pedro Prison. One of the most infamous prisons in the world. In the 1990s backpackers used to bribe their way in for drugs, large quanties of cheap cocaine produced in makeshift labs within the grounds. It's no longer possible to get inside.

Combing the Internet for clues of where to go and whom to play with, we'd encountered snippets about South American prison soccer. "It makes sense right?" Luke said. "They have nothing to do but play." In the scheming stage, when we sat around a table and wrote anything we wanted on legal pads, a game in a prison sounded like a perfect story.

But out on the road, a game in a prison sounds extraordinarily farfetched. Would we wander up to the gate, our backpacks stuffed with cameras, put our hands on the bars, and say, "Can we come in?"

Pickup games are spontaneous. Our mode of traveling is spontaneous: we show up, we wander streets. That's not how prisons work. There's bureaucracy. We probably needed to obtain permission months in advance. Even if we had that kind of time, where would we start? Do we send an e-mail to a prison? Do we use our twenty-minute college docs to convince prison administrators that we are credible, worthwhile journalists?

Still, it's hard not to linger on the San Pedro page of the Lonely Planet. If it was once possible to bribe your way in for drugs, doesn't that mean there is a chance we could bribe our way in for soccer?

We arrive in La Paz. We hail a cab to the first hostel listed in the Lonely Planet. We put down our bags. We stand in the foyer. We look out the window. "San Pedro," Luke says, pointing. Ryan, Ferg, and I look out across the courtyard, eyes landing on a wide, squat building surrounded by guards. Our hostel is one hundred yards away from the prison.

WE EAT AT a cubbyhole restaurant down the street. In La Paz, three dollars gets you a big bowl of soup, trout, potatoes, and dessert, which makes us like the city right away, especially because we're running out of money. At the checker-cloth table, we slurp *chairo* and look out at the Bolivian families eating on all sides of us. I study people for signs of *fútbol,* registering every jersey, every scuffed Adidas shoe.

At a neighboring Internet café, we google "San Pedro soccer." "There are tournaments," I report from my computer. "Every cell block has a team. They bet lots of money on games."

On a dated travel forum, we find a phone number; apparently you can just dial it up and get a prisoner on the other end. After putting it off for twenty minutes, Ferg retreats into a phone booth.

"She's speaking English," Ryan says as we try to read her lips. "Could we have lucked upon an English-speaking prisoner in Bolivia?"

Red faced and smiling, Ferg emerges. "I'm sorry. I look excited. I shouldn't. Nothing happened," she says. "It's just, I mean, I was talking to a prisoner. A South African busted for drugs. It's kind of nuts. But since we want to film, he can't help us."

We spend another three hours in the otherwise empty café, stalking San Pedro.

. . .

AT THE SQUARE in front of the prison, couples lean over a fountain, kids chase soccer balls in the grass, and women set up stands for the Thursday-through-Sunday bread market. We sit on a bench, staring at the cement walls of San Pedro and the guards who surround it.

Here's what we know: the inmates are in charge. Though the guards patrol the outside, they do not enter the inside. Within the high walls, San Pedro inmates run their own society. Prisoners' wives and children may live on the inside, free to come and go. Men sell ice cream, toy trinkets, and cocaine. Like in the outside world, you need money to get by. Even cells must be bought: if you have no money, you have no place to sleep. There's an average of four deaths a month.

It's hard to find the nuances of language to convince an armed guard to unlock the gates and let us wander in with our video camera. Ferg's holding our shiny postcard—on one side, a picture of a child's hand resting on a beat-up ball, a description of our movie on the other. We made them while fund-raising, hoping they'd make us seem more legit. Now we hope the picture will once again help us convince someone we are credible.

Ryan and I wait and watch while Rebekah and Luke walk up to the men with green uniforms and guns. Rebekah keeps pointing to the postcard and tucking her hair behind her ear; Luke makes wide gestures, like the more actively he moves his hands the more he'll be understood.

A guard points to the left, and Luke and Rebekah disappear around the corner. Ryan and I get up from the bench and tail them from a distance. They stop in front of a side door bearing a gold placard: DIRECTOR. A man steps out and shoos Luke and Ferg away with his hands.

"Did you hear him say something about the U.S. Embassy?" Ferg asks Luke as they walk back to us.

"I think maybe we're supposed to go there," Luke says.

This sounds unpromising. "I imagine they won't be into the idea of four Americans opting to get locked inside a prison," Ryan says as we hail a cab to the embassy.

We watch numbers on the meter climb higher and higher as our errand feels more and more pointless.

As soon as the cab driver drops us on the sidewalk and pulls away, we notice a lack of movement or sound. A CLOSED sign is wedged in front of the blinds.

While things are often closed on Saturdays and Sundays, sometimes even Mondays or Fridays, nothing is ever closed on a Wednesday . . . except for the U.S. Embassy. "I guess if you lose your passport or have your child abducted," Ryan says as we stand in front of the empty building, "you just have to wait until Thursday."

WE RETURN TO the Internet place next to our hostel, and the owner greets us like old friends, shaking our hands, pleased with how much time we spend with his computers.

Before we make our way back to our seats, we ask him if he has any idea how we might play *fútbol* inside the prison. He stands up, walks to the doorway, and whistles to some men in uniform walking along the sidewalk.

Five minutes later, soldiers escort us to the prison director's office, the same office Rebekah and Luke got quickly kicked out of yesterday. This time we're led up narrow stairs to a small dank room with a brown vinyl desk and two orange chairs, what I imagine a 1970s insurance office would look like.

A bald man with eyeglasses sits down at the desk without speaking to us. He writes out directions on a pink sheet of paper. "Go to the Bolivian Ministry of Prisons," he says. "You must speak to Alejandro. If he gives you permission, you may talk to the prisoners." He stands up and shakes our hands. "It is difficult, but not impossible."

At eight the next morning we sit at a conference table. Alejandro has a scar running the length of his face. Everything's in Spanish. I stare at Luke and Rebekah, who have found their Spanish-speaking groove. I swivel in my chair, floored by their ability to understand the sounds that fly out of Alejandro. Even Ryan seems to have stepped up his comprehension, nodding every few sentences. Then we are shaking hands, then we are standing, then we are leaving.

"So?" I ask, as we get on the elevator. "Did we get it? Permission?"

"The prisoners are the ones who ultimately decide," Luke says, pulling up the hood on his sweatshirt as though preparing for covert operations.

WE CAN'T ALL go talk to the prisoners. Rebekah can speak Spanish, Luke can understand Spanish—they're the ones who go. Ryan and I stay at the hostel. I try to read, staring at pages of Kazou Ishiguro's *Never Let Me Go* but thinking about Luke and Ferg in the prison.

When they get back, I hear them immediately, talking fast in the foyer. I jump out of bed and into the hallway, leaning over the balcony to listen to their conversational ping-pong.

"What? What?" I ask.

"We should get Ryan," Ferg says.

The four of us sit on the bed.

Luke and Ferg relay the story, alternating sentences.

"We explained the film—" Luke says.

"They listened with, like, rapt attention," Ferg says.

"They were enthusiastic—got it right away. Made all these insightful comments about 'the connectivity of the world's game.'"

"And then they said, 'Now for the painful part . . . what it's going to cost you.'"

"'You must bring fruitcakes for one-fourth of the prison.'"

"That took us a second. Panetónes. Is he saying 'fruitcake'? Could he really be saying 'fruitcake'? So we had them explain it, and yeah, they wanted fruitcakes. Fruitcakes."

"Then we had to do the math, trying to figure out how many fruit-cakes that was. We asked, 'How will we carry three hundred fruit-cakes?'"

"That's when they said, 'No, no. You give us the money. We buy the fruitcakes.'"

So by "fruitcakes" they meant cash. This is how San Pedro works.

On the hostel notepad, Ferg starts doing the math. It'll cost us about four hundred U.S. dollars.

Ryan is in charge of money. I can see him tallying expenses in his head. But we all know we're doing it. You don't turn down this kind of chance. We're going to play with Bolivian prisoners. I'm trying to imagine it, when Luke turns to me and says, "But they say you can't play. No women. They seemed pretty adamant."

I lean back against my pillow and just look at him.

AT THE ATM machine at the bank next to the hostel, Luke takes out three thousand bolivianos. We film lots of close-ups of the money, of the ATM spitting out the bills, partly because we are trying to make sure we have all the pieces we'll need to tell the story, partly because we are nervous and stalling.

The bread market is in full swing at San Pedro Plaza. Women wearing bowler hats and long skirts stand behind tables spread with loaves of sourdough. A band plays Andean music, men in ponchos strumming guitars as we prepare to walk up to the gates. (Whistling at the favela, guitar at the prison—we have musical accompaniment whenever we're going somewhere intense.)

As we walk up to the gate, Ryan films us from behind.

"Courte," a policeman says, making finger-scissors.

"Cut it," Luke says. Ryan turns off the camera while Luke explains to the guards that we have an arrangement with the prisoners.

We're ushered into the purgatory-like space between the outside world and the men who are locked away from it. The prisoners hang their arms through the bars of the gate, looking at us. One guy chewing on something looks me up and down. There are jeers and catcalls and men making faces. One guy in a red jacket that reminds me of my mother's old skiing jacket recognizes Luke from the other day. They grin at each other, shaking hands through the bars. The prisoner, as though he's the man with the pull on the inside of a club, giving the bouncer the go-ahead, talks to the guard and points at Luke.

The guard fumbles with a big ring of keys, and suddenly there's a crack and Luke is sliding through it and into prison, gate clanging behind him.

The guard turns back and sees me still standing there. I use my pointer finger to signal that I'd like to go in, too. Eyebrows raised, he says something, and even though I don't speak Spanish, I know he's saying, "You too?" I nod as though I know for sure that I want to go in there.

The gate opens and I step through, let into prison. The guy in the ski jacket is ready to sweep us off to some place specific, and Luke is ready to follow, but I'm there to say wait and hold on to his arm until Ryan and Ferg pop through the gate in the same way we did.

There's too much to process. I look out at a festering, crumbling fountain, children crouched on the ledge, dipping coffee mugs into murky water. A clothesline extends across the square, T-shirts puffed in the wind. People appear to wear whatever they want: I see satin soccer jerseys, baseball caps, more puffy jackets worn over bare chests. Men mill, nothing to do, standing with hands in pockets. My brother spent two years in prison, and while this looks nothing like the place where I visited him—no washed-out county scrubs, no hospital-like sterility, no patrolling of order—there is the same pervasive feeling of waiting, of being trapped.

We follow two men up a flight of stairs and into a room of prisoners who have been elected as delegates; they are the prisoners in charge, the men with whom Luke and Ferg have made an arrangement. A calendar featuring a big-breasted woman in a bikini hangs between a poster of Jesus and a framed picture of Simón Bolívar, founder of Bolivia. Winnie the Pooh decals are pasted onto the sides of a computer in the back corner of the room. A man writes down notes on a pocket-size pad covered with sparkly red hearts. Another man stands in front of the barred window, staring at the world outside.

Luke and I sit down on a beat-up green couch. I rest my teeth on my fingernail. Luke hands them an envelope of cash and says in Spanish, "Here is the first part."

Here is the first part: we have this idea, formed from watching action movies, that we'd split up the cash, give them half of it up front, half once we're out safe.

I watch the thick gold rings on Teófilo's fingers as he thumbs through the money. We wait for him to realize it is only half of what we said we'd bring. He finishes counting and looks up at Luke.

Luke clears his throat and tries to explain our offer. His voice trails off.

I sink back into the couch, wowed. Had we really thought we were going to go into a prison and call the shots?

"No," Teófilo says. "Give us all of it now."

Luke doesn't hesitate: he hands over the second envelope.

The total of both envelopes is still less than they'd asked for. There are fifteen hundred prisoners; they wanted fruitcakes for one-fourth of the prison—375 fruitcakes, which cost ten bolivianos each, amounting to about five hundred U.S. dollars. We brought four hundred dollars. We gambled that there was so much math involved we could just play dumb, acting like that was the number we calculated. This makes me nervous. I watch Teófilo licking his thumb as he fans through bills.

"Tres mil bolivianos," he calls out, tapping the stack of money against the table like you would a deck of cards.

He looks to the man sitting across the room, who grants approval with one nod of his head.

"OK," Teófilo says.

Then it is silent, and I don't know why. We appear to be waiting on something. I try to make small talk. "Panetónes?" I ask.

"Sí," Teófilo says.

He reaches under the desk and pulls out a yellow fruitcake carton.

I stare, surprised by it, wondering how long it's been there, if they whip it out as proof every time they're making a deal. Maybe they are telling the truth; maybe they give every prisoner a Christmastime fruitcake.

"Es interesante," Luke says, still sounding like he's choking every time he tries to talk.

"Hasta la cancha," Teófilo says and stands. (*Cancha*, "field," is an expression I know, mainly because last time I tried to say it, I was notified that I was saying something else entirely, something I would definitely not want to be saying to prisoners.)

We walk out of the office and into the sound. Inmates yell, "Hola, gringos!" Throngs of men send up a chorus of low whistles. "I knew I should've walked in front of you," Luke says, leaning toward me.

A prisoner grabs Luke's ass. We keep walking. A man with a box strapped around his neck is selling popcorn like a vendor at a baseball game. To my left, I see a man with a six-inch gash in his side. It looks fresh. He catches my eyes and holds open his jean jacket so that I can see the gush of blood. I keep walking. I look back at Luke to see if he saw it, too, but he's looking in the other direction, at two men playing foosball on the side of the alley. Even though we walk at a pretty normal pace, it feels like we're flying, sight after sight racing by us. I see a man standing in the tiniest concession stand in the world, hardly any room to move his arms, looking like Zoltar, the fortune-teller in the box from the movie *Big*.

We walk out of a narrow corridor and into a triangle-shaped court-yard that serves as the field, one goal easier to defend than the other. A giant tiger outfitted in a soccer uniform is painted on the back wall, the words *Bienvenidos a la Cancha* ribboned around him. Cells line the sides of the court. We sit beneath the tiger and watch the prisoners play. The soccer looks hard and fast and intimidating.

A guard stands next to us (and by "guard," I mean prisoner who's acting as a guard). He swats at a stray ball with his billy club.

When the whistle signals the end of the game, Luke and the prisoner-guard walk across the court to the cluster of players. I stay seated beneath the tiger, watching as Luke talks to the men.

"When can we get on?" he asks, his hands flowering out and then lacing back together again.

"Early tomorrow," the guy says—knowing we're not spending the night.

He laughs, clasps his hand on Luke's shoulder. "Just kidding, just kidding."

Luke laughs, too, loudly.

"You can play with us," the guy says. "Of course."

As I sit and look out, I see white handouts, the kind you see pinned to a bulletin board in a school hallway, which say CELL FOR SALE. Up top, two men sit on the roof of the prison with their legs crossed, laundry spread out around them, drying in the sun. Above a Coca-Cola umbrella, bars divide a window like a tic-tac-toe board, and I probably wouldn't have noticed the window at all if it weren't for the head popping through the center square.

"Gwenny, you can play," Luke says, walking back up to me, squeezing my shoulder before heading back toward his new friend.

I walk slowly over there. Crossing the court, it feels like the whole prison is watching me.

When I get to the other side, the men are gathered into team huddles, figuring out positions, who's playing next. Luke points me over to a group of guys perched on a double row of steps. They sit with their elbows on their knees, just looking out in front of them. One guy has a giant stick, and he's turning it over in his hands like he's thinking about what he's going to do with it.

Another guy's standing a little off to the side, hand on his hips but not aggressively. He's the one I walk up to. "Cómo se llama?" I ask.

"Juan," he says, guarded, short.

"I'm Gwendolyn," I say, touching my chest.

"Wendy?" he asks.

I shrug, nod. "Sí."

I reach to shake his hand. When he walks away, the men on the stairs break into whistles and applause. He kicks them softly in the shins, like something a shy boy would do at the school playground.

People start filling in, coming to see. Men crowd the rail of the balconies overlooking the court.

The ball is the size of a cannonball. It's heavier and harder than a normal ball, more set on staying flat on the ground.

Every game has its own set of rules—you can't score from your own half, no corner kicks, that wall's in-bounds but the garden is out—so Luke tries to find out about this game: "Cuáles son las reglas?" *What are the rules?*

"Anything goes," a prisoner says, cackling, like he knows how ominous that sounds, like he's trying to screw with us.

I don't do anything the first five minutes. I can't find a way to get a touch on the ball. Luke's team controls the play, knocking the ball from player to player while I chase, sprinting in frantic diagonals.

We are twelve thousand feet up in the air—about two miles above sea level. The guidebook had warned that the high elevation makes it hard for foreigners to breathe. We had whole conversations about FIFA banning World Cup games in Bolivia. Luke told us the Bolivian president, Evo Morales, had protested by trekking to the top of a mountain to play in a pickup game at the highest point in his country, to say, *Look, anybody can play up here.*

But at first, when I'm focused on the prisoners I'm playing against and the ball I'm chasing, I'm not thinking about altitude. I'm just wondering what the hell's happening to me, why I can't breathe. I'm gasping for air but not finding any. Which is puzzling, troubling, like the thing I can count on is being taken away.

In my head, I'm telling myself to get it together, because even though the prison is spinning, there's no way I'm going to ask for a sub, no way I'm going to be the American girl too soft to play.

When the ball flies out-of-bounds and into someone's cell, Ryan, who can hear me gasping, asks from behind the camera, "You OK?"

Right as I'm telling him, "Haven't touched the ball, can't breathe," the keeper is hurling the ball at my feet. I take one quick touch and send it forward into space, where Juan runs on to it, rifling a shot that may or may not go in. The referee, who's wearing a button-up sweater (pretty much the last thing I would've imagined a prison referee to wear) wags his finger, shakes his head—no goal. Juan darts up to the netless goal, aggressively waving his hands through what would be the side netting if there were any side netting. The ref, whistle in lips, points his finger and takes one threatening step toward Juan.

My team's down two goals. I feel a flush in my face: any time my team is losing, as the girl, I feel it, I care. I don't want anybody thinking it's because of me.

I get the ball again next play, and this time I don't pass it off as quickly. I want to, but first I have to excavate it out of the mess, dribbling it around ensuing defenders before I can find a passing window. I find the window and pass the ball; I am two for two.

Then the ball's loose in the middle of the field, or not loose really, but far enough away from the guy's foot that I think I can strip it off him. I go for it at the same time he reaches to reel it back in.

Later we will interview him in front of a barred window. I'll learn he's in for murder. He'll tell us he's "a well-known criminal here in Bolivia." But right now he's just a guy who looks graceful and strong. I look at him and think of a ballerina, his neck long, his quads sharply defined, his toes pointed, his face blank.

We hit the ball at the same time. I catch him off-balance. He falls and I stay up. I don't often hear sound in a game, but I can hear this sound, coming from up top, both balconies shaking. Finger whistles, rough voices hollering as I move up the court and the guy scoops himself off the ground.

When the game ends, the sun's beating on my face, there's salt along the corners of my eyes and the line of my jaw, and my chest's still screaming from the thin air, from my tackle. I won the ball, I stole it from him, and the charge I feel—it shoots me back in time. The competition, the fear, the feeling of being almost not good enough, and then the floaty satisfaction of having played well—I just stand there and relive all of it.

A prisoner with tattoos of a heart and barbwire on his forearm crouches down and pours warm Fanta into a pink plastic cup that looks straight out of a little girl's tea set. Luke drinks it and rubs his red face. He jokes,

"No soy Evo Morales." A child waddles toward them; the guy boosts her into the air and passes her to the man on the other side of Luke. "I've been here for two years," the guy says. "Every day we play, every day."

ALWAYS AFTER A game people are open. There's an understanding that you love the same thing. But here in a prison, our interactions feel even more personal than usual. I remember this honesty from visiting my brother—the guys on both sides of him and the women sitting across from them just telling me everything, like they figure they're here, you already know the worst, there's nothing to hide.

First we talk with Juan, the man who called me Wendy, along with two other inmates sitting on the steps, older guys with seasoned faces who are in for murder. They tell us that with the plainness of distance, the fact they've had decades to think about, the fact that's defined their whole lives. The two men treat Juan protectively, like a kid brother, explaining his story for him: he's in for manslaughter—*accidente de velo*. They act like he's different from them, in here more out of bad luck than bad choices.

Fernando, the guy who joked with Luke about coming back tomorrow, invites us into his cell: teal walls, striped blankets, a stack of dirty dishes at the end of the bed, a pan with leftover beans resting on a portable burner. Fernando's handsome, wavy hair, dark brown eyes, olive skin, and he moves easy, confident, sliding the dishes off the bed, gesturing for us to come in. He has a warm, ringing laugh—I could see women falling for him without bothering to fight it. He sits down on the bed and tells his story: "I've been here for two years. Before, my life was . . . a disaster . . . ," he says, shaking his head, rubbing his legs, his smile helpless. "Traficando."

A knock sounds against his cell door. "Here is my daughter," he says as he reaches for her, a two-year-old in a pink shirt holding a toy cell phone up to her ear.

I stand outside the cell, it not being big enough to hold all of us. From the doorway, I watch Fernando kiss his daughter's cheek. "Ahh, mi amor. Besos," he says. "Besitos."

Later, when people find out we played in a prison, sometimes we'll hear,

"Are you guys out of your minds?" They say it like we locked ourselves in there with monsters. We didn't meet any monsters. I know there are people who lack goodness; visiting my brother, one guy's wobbly eyes and sick grin scared me. But mostly, there and here, it's people who didn't start with a whole lot of luck, and people who can't stop letting themselves down.

The man I tackled, the well-known criminal, is striped by the sunlight coming in the barred window. He wears a sleeveless Chicago Bears jersey with #54 stitched in the corner. I wonder what Brian Urlacher would think knowing his jersey had made it all the way to a prison in Bolivia. The prisoner has a steady, quiet voice, the sounds of the game below threatening to drown him out. Usually you can tell whether the person talking is saying something strong even if you can't understand what their words mean: you can see it in their face, hear it in the rise and fall of their voice. But I can't tell with the Urlacher fan. His voice is so soft it's like the quieter he talks the more he can say. "I sold furniture, I sold cars. . . . Accidents happen, mistakes were made. That's why we're here. We're not saints."

At the end, he says, "Here we have nothing. Our life is to play."

Wherever we go, men talk about *fútbol*'s great power to take you away.

GIANT

THE COVER OF our Lonely Planet guide has a picture of a woman in traditional Peruvian clothing—bowler hat, layered scarves, long thick skirt—charging after a soccer ball. According to a small paragraph in the Peru chapter, up in the highlands, women who herd sheep during the day can be found playing *fútbol* by night.

We ride a half-empty bus through the sprawling plains of the Alto Plano on a Saturday morning. We're chattering across the aisle about what Ryan found last night while logging prison footage: Ferg, who had wandered away from the game to get an establishing shot of the La Paz mountains backdropping the prison, directed her camera upward, and the guard tower happened to come into her frame. Ryan was jotting down "various shots of pigeons and mountains," when, out of nowhere—a man with a rifle, aiming it directly at the lens. From behind the camera, Ferg took a half second to realize that what she was looking at was the barrel of a gun. She whipped the camera away. In the last bits of streaking footage, as the guard sees Ferg's suprise at discovering him, he cackles with laughter from the heights of his tower.

Ryan had put the camera down on the bed. "Ferg," he said, "how could you not have told us someone pretended like he was going to shoot you?"

For some reason, even this morning on the bus, she's maintaining it was no big deal: "He was just kidding around."

"Kidding with his gun," Ryan says. "Funny."

"Different culture," Luke says. "Different sense of humor?"

When we get off the bus in Andahuaylillas, a small town in the highlands, the first thing we see is a big grass field, people all over it. This keeps happening. All my life I've participated in conversations about the unimaginable popularity of the world's game, but I am still shocked every time we wander blindly into a place and find it right away.

It's a Saturday tournament, one of the big takeaways from this continent: we saw this at Villa 31, in Montevideo, all over Santa Cruz, in the village in the Amazon. The whole neighborhood comes out to the field. There's music, food, kids waddling about, families spread out on picnic blankets, families banging their feet against bleachers. Men with sweaty faces come and kiss wives' necks.

What's different about this game in El Alto Plano is that the players warming up on the field are women. They don't look like the cover of Lonely Planet—no skirts or hats or scarves, just uniforms that look ten sizes too big, jerseys hanging down to their knees.

Before I know it, I'm drafted onto a team and am wearing one of those jerseys, although on me it's not gigantic. I am at least half a foot taller than everyone else. I tower. This is an all-new experience for me. I'm not even five feet six. The women look at me and giggle, hands up to their mouths, their eyes moving from my feet to the top of my head.

I experience the advantage I've always wondered about, what it would be like to have strides twice as long as everyone else. I keep toppling women. "Lo siento, lo siento, lo siento," I say, helping them up.

When we take our team picture at the end of the game, arms wrapped around one another, I am Yao Ming, I am Shaq, I am Crouch, I am the giant.

Andahuaylillas, Peru (Courtesy: Rebekah Fergusson)

ALL THE WORLD

IN TRINIDAD, IF we mentioned our worldwide search for pickup soccer, we got asked, "How many countries have you been to?" Then we had to admit it was our first. You could see in the nod of the person's head that they didn't believe we'd do it. We weren't sure we believed it ourselves. South America was one thing—once you find the six hundred dollars for a plane ticket, you can bus yourself to any country in the continent for forty or fifty bucks—but getting ourselves to the rest of the world? No amount of letter writing would raise enough to take us around Europe and Africa and Asia and the Middle East. We'd need an investor. It was a hard concept for me to believe in: we were going to find somebody willing to give us hundreds of thousands of dollars?

Right before we left for South America, Luke's mom wrote to her hometown newspaper about what we were doing. A man from Pasadena happened to be passing through a Starbucks in Orange County on the morning *The Orange County Register* ran our story. A day later, the reporter called us. "There's this guy named Les with a Scottish accent who saw your story in the paper. He told me, 'I want to make this happen for these kids'—and he sounds like he might mean it." An hour later Luke was on the phone with him. The Scot told us to go ahead with South America, make a cut, and if he liked what he saw, he'd fund the rest of the film.

Lots of times talk puffs away to nothing. We try to guard ourselves against rocketlike hope. But we all believe Les is our shot. When we come back to Durham, we know we have to shape our two hundred hours of South American footage into an hour-long cut that could make him think *This is a movie that must be made.*

The Center for Documentary Studies at Duke gives us keys to the building, and we edit around the clock, two of us on day shift, two of us on night. We eat vegetable-platter leftovers from the center's events, sleep at friends' houses, and experience what it's like to see the idea in our heads become something real in front of us. When our cut is finished, Ryan flies to California to sit down with Les and his film-industry friend in front of a flat-screen television. From the couch, Ryan studies their reactions. Two hours later he calls. The connection is bad and his voice is muffled, but we can still hear him say, "He wants to fund the film." (What if he hadn't gotten Starbucks that morning? Then what?) I sink into the booth in the hallway of CDS and feel dizzy with luck.

It happens quickly after that. We race against the seasons, wanting to be in Africa when the weather is mild and pickup games are prevalent, wanting to be in Europe during the 2008 European Championship that will put soccer at the front of every European's conscience. We discover we know almost no one in Europe, no one in Africa. We e-mail everyone looking for someone who does. We construct an itinerary, make a tentative storyboard, book plane tickets, and think, *Holy hell, we are doing this.*

BUT I'M AFRAID of Europe. How could it live up to South America? We played twelve thousand feet up in the air in a prison we bribed our way into. A shaman guided us through paradise to a beach where Fabio-like men played games at sunset. We drank caipirinhas made with hail and hydroplaned across mud roads in the Amazon. I shot a rifle at an alligator. None of that was going to happen in Europe.

On the plane ride to Paris, I listen to the French podcast Luke down-loaded onto my iPod—*Je voudrais un croissant, s'il vous plait; J'aime chocolat*—and I worry. You go to Europe to read novels in cafés and buy flowers in markets. But soccer in the street? Do Europeans do that? I could picture it in the 1940s—games on cobblestone, men with grins, an operatic Italian voice and radio static escaping out an open window. But in 2008? Now there were club teams and systems and tiers and syn-thetic turf. Maybe pickup would be gone.

OUR FIRST DAY in Paris, we take a train to the Métro to the basement-level apartment we are renting that is close enough to the sights to be convenient and far enough away to feel like we are seeing the Parisians' Paris. We drop off our bags, buy bread and cheese from the *supermarché,* and force ourselves onto the street, even though we are each thinking, *At home, it is 3:30 A.M., and what I want most is to lay down in bed.*

When we get to the Champ de Mars, the grass stretching out from the Eiffel Tower, where we heard there are games, we see white ropes and a small sign in both French and English: MAIN LAWN CLOSED FOR REPAIRS.

We try to talk to the maintenance men. They ask Ferg out for coffee but know nothing about *le football.* A swarm of French seven-year-olds on an Eiffel Tower field trip play on the side lawn. Luke and I lean back against the bench and watch while Ferg films, in case this is the only soc-cer we find in France. An occasional game ruiner snatches the ball up with his hands and makes a break for it, the other kids tailing him until someone is able to knock it back down to feet.

One drunk man with a Polaroid camera wants to juggle the ball and kiss our cheeks, but we opt out of a game with him. The only people left are either dozing or fondling lovers beneath umbrellas. Luke rolls the ball out in the grass and waits to see if anyone will take the bait. No one does.

The beauty of pickup is that it can happen anywhere, with anyone, at any time. This is also what makes it hard to find. When you plan your trip, you go off the things you hear, looking for the places where people tell you they've seen games, but when you arrive, there's no guarantee that the Mennonites still play in the Bolivian jungle or that the lawn of the Eiffel Tower won't be temporarily closed.

In the rain, we walk six or seven miles home, wet but warm, passing the Musée d'Orsay, the Champs-Élysées, and the Louvre. For dinner, we head to a restaurant Antoine, the man whose basement we are renting, recommended: "It is good, cheap, and you will like it." Photographs of tombstones hang on stone walls, illuminated by soft light. The tables are close together, and the menu is written on a rotatable chalkboard. We order two entrées to split—*bœuf bordeaux* and some sort of very good fish. As we wait for the food, I pull out my notebook and attempt to write out sentences in French that I think we'll need: *Où est le football? Peuvons-nous jouer football avec toi?*

When Fabrice, one of the brothers who owns the restaurant, comes over to fill up our water glasses, he sits down with my notebook and re-conjugates my verbs, changes my articles, adds accent marks. The people at the tables next to us brainstorm places for us to go. (The man to our right spends half his year in Chicago and half his year in Paris. "You are very lucky to have found this restaurant," he tells us. "It is my favorite in the city.")

Fabrice sighs and sits down. "But Paris is like a museum. You cannot play football inside a museum. I think you will need to go somewhere else, more working-class. Like Marseille."

We're already planning on Marseille; we only gave ourselves two days in Paris so that we'd have more time in the old seaport the travel forums describe as "gritty." Marseille is an immigrant city, people from everywhere— Algeria, Italy, Tunisia, Morocco, Armenia, the Comoros Islands. Ryan's heard about the music scene. And Luke declared it "the City of Zidane, the City of Drogba." We had to see the place that could grow both of them.

BEFORE WE LEAVE Paris, we go back one more time to the Eiffel Tower. That first day all I saw were swarming tourists, a gray sky, and a giant metal structure around which no one played soccer. On try two, we walk to the other end of the Champ de Mars. I scan the lawn for prospective players, wondering if we'll always have to round people up in order to get a game in Europe. I'm turning in a circle, in a defeated way, like I'm confirming that I've seen everything there is to see. I'm hearing Fabrice and thinking of Paris as a display window meant only to be looked at, when my combing eyes land on a soccer court. Nestled behind a patch of trees. Goals, players, just waiting there, on the land beside the global icon. (This takes me aback. You mean it was here all along and we missed it? Does this happen a lot? Do we often look to one side while something great is happening on the other?)

How quickly that court changes my mind. I look admiringly at all 1,063 feet of the tower. Now it's spectacular, now it's the center of Paris, the City of Light.

Court in front of the Eiffel Tower (Courtesy: Rebekah Fergusson)

On the court, it's five against five. If you win, you stay on. There are teenage schoolboys with shaggy haircuts and backpacks who look straight out of the textbook-supplement videos we watched in French class— kids with names like Jerome and Jean Paul. A Mexican exchange student tells us he plays here every day. Several Algerian-French guys are the holders of the court, no one able to beat them. I can't stop staring at one guy's quad muscles. They brim with power. I'm excited as I play; everyone is. I wonder if it's Eiffel Tower–inspired. When a thing like that soars up behind you, do you try to rise to its greatness?

Hours later when we leave the court, three other games are happening on the dirt in front of the École Militaire. Wives and girlfriends read novels on the grass just beyond. A fifty-year-old scores a goal and raises his arms over his head. From my angle, it looks like he's catching the Eiffel Tower between his hands. The sky is pink, the sun having fallen directly beneath the tower, making it look lit from within. Luke comes up behind me, arms circling my waist, and together we look out at the people living and playing within the museum of Paris.

On our way back to the apartment, a well-dressed Frenchman mistakes us for Parisians (a mistake that makes any tourist happy) and asks us for directions. I say, "Je ne parle pas français," the one sentence I've really mastered. We continue walking. One hundred yards later he is still behind us, headed the same way we are. He asks us where we are from and why we are here, and we tell him about our chase for football.

"Ah?" he says. "You watch this." He takes the ball from Luke's hands. In his gray sweater-vest, knit pants, and black shiny shoes, he starts juggling in the shadows of the cobblestone street.

WE RAIL DOWN to Marseille, staring at the small French towns and vineyards and hills that fly by the window. For the rest of the continent, Luke will spend train rides briefing Ferg and me about football. He does not want to be tripping around town with people who don't know the local legends. He quizzes us about which player belongs to which team

and informs us of all the facts he believes every person who calls themselves a lover of football should know.

I did not grow up watching. I'd never heard of the European Championship or Manchester United. The Fox Soccer channel didn't exist. I
watched the World Cup, the only soccer that was televised. I was fifteen.
Those games stunned me. I set my alarm for 5:45 every morning, sat directly in front of the television, watched all three games in a row. Then I
went to the field, for the first time playing with an understanding of what
was out there. Before the final, the network made a montage of signature
moments. In English class that year, we wrote research papers on a word of
our choosing; I picked "passion." This—men lying with their faces flat on
the ground, men crumpled and crying—was the most I'd witnessed.
Before I left for any tournament or game, I watched the recorded montage and felt something in my throat.

Zidane and Drogba, my favorites of the 2006 World Cup, are two of
the few players Luke doesn't need to tell me about. A sucker for under-
dogs, the Ivory Coast was my team. I looked at the agony and hope on
Drogba's face and thought: *love*. And Zidane—that headbutt. "Zidane
has tarnished his entire career," the announcer had declared, but as I
watched Zidane walk out to the tunnel by himself, I couldn't think the
announcer possibly meant it. Feeling that cannot be contained—that
may be the whole reason I watch.

But, no, I didn't know about their Marseille ties. Once I find out, I go
read all the stories, articles, and profiles that Luke has already read. Zidane,
the youngest of five children born to Algerian parents, grew up in La
Castellane, a housing project in the northern finger of Marseille. His
whole family still lives there, his brother coach of the local club team, of
which Zidane is "lifetime president." (One of the team's players told a
reporter, "When you say you're from La Castellane, people are usually
afraid. Then when you point out you play for a team led by Zidane, they
suddenly show you respect.") When, for a 2004 *Guardian* profile, Zidane
was asked where he felt most at home, he said, "I am first of all from La

Castellane and Marseille. I love Madrid. I am happy to be here. I have been here three years and hope to be here longer. But I am proud of where I come from and never forget the people I grew up with. Wherever I go, La Castellane is where I want to go back to. It is still my home. . . . It is true that it is still a difficult area, what is called in French a quartier difficile. But I think there is also a special culture there . . . very vibrant and very tough. . . . My passion for the game comes from the city of Marseille itself."

Drogba only lived in Marseille for one year, but he loved the city and the city loved him. He spoke of being friends with the managers, with the trainers, "with the baker on the corner." He scored twenty-nine goals for Olympique de Marseille and took them deep into the Champions League. José Mourinho, the soon-to-be manager of Chelsea, went to watch him: "I had hardly sat down and this giant wearing a No. 11 shirt had already scored," wrote Mourinho in the foreward to Drogba's memoir. "I can still see him celebrating that goal as if it was his last, and transforming a crowd into a great ball of fire. . . ." At the end of the season, Chelsea offered Olympique de Marseille a then-record sum of twenty-four million pounds, but Drogba didn't want to leave. "I wanted to do a Maldini," Drogba said in a documentary about his life. (Luke has to explain to me who Maldini is—the player who spent all twenty-five seasons of his career playing for Milan.) When OM accepted Chelsea's offer, an amount the club felt they couldn't refuse, Drogba cried. The city hung his jersey in Notre-Dame de la Garde Basilica. In the 2009 Champions League, when Chelsea played OM, the Marseille fans gave Drogba a standing ovation. Drogba still talks about how much he misses the city. "In Marseille," he says. "I played with my heart."

THE TAXI WE hailed at the train station drops us off in the center of a large square in the Old Port. Terra-cotta-roofed buildings in sun-bleached peaches and pinks face one another. Boys ride bikes through a fountain. Women sit around the plastic patio tables of a neighborhood bar, drinking the five-dollar wine advertised on the propped-up chalkboard. Gristly fishermen with crossed legs smoke cigars and drink pastis while pigeons dive-bomb from window to window.

Serge, the man renting us our apartment, says, "Your room is up there by the pigeons." He points to the top of a building as beautiful as any French building, only run-down and weathered, which is how all the streets' buildings look. The shutters on the rows of the windows, beaten by mistrals, hang crooked, their paint peeling, dirt in every slat: they look like the keepers of thousands of years of secrets.

"And tonight," Serge says, "you come to neighborhood party. It is a birthday."

We haul our bags up a skinny staircase that winds round and round until we're at the top, seven stories up. We open our shutters and take turns leaning out the window, craning left and looking out at the masts of sailboats, hundreds of them docked at the Old Port.

At eight, we walk along the water to a small fishing harbor carved into the side of a white cliff. Street lamps reflect off the water, rowboats bumping up against one another. The neighbors kiss our cheeks and feed us goat cheese, tabbouleh, and birthday cake. A man in a blue-and-white-striped shirt that looks like what a gondolier would wear, tells us about his city: "In Marseille, we have the music, the football, and the fish. And we have all the people of the world—you will see every culture walking down the street."

BY THE END of the night, I have two pages of scribbled names. While it's very clear to me at the time which name refers to a large grass park, which name refers to a neighborhood with ethnic food, and which name refers to a beach, it's all less clear as I look at the scribbled notes the following morning.

There is one accompanying sketch: it looks like someone started a game of hangman in my notebook, but when I show it to a taxi driver, he reads it as a street map and drops us off at a large stretch of grass along the water.

We stare into the Mediterranean. It is deep blue, none of that crystal-clear stuff we do along the Gulf of Mexico. This water says *sea*. And the fishermen look like fishermen. Salt-stained ball caps, lined faces with bloodshot eyes, knotted hands. A dozen of them stand along the rock jetty. (Luke's dad was a lobster fisherman, ran boats off the San Clemente pier in California. He died before Luke was born, but if he were still alive, he'd be in his eighties, even older than the men standing on the rocks.)

Luke's only been fishing once, with my dad in South Carolina. It was the wrong time of year. The bait guy wouldn't sell us anything. Luke stuck Velveeta we bought at the Citgo on the end of his line just for the hell of it, and three minutes later he had his hands around a giant bass. My dad and I looked at each other, our eyes saying fate caught him that fish. (Then Luke dropped it. The fish tumbled back into the depths of the lake. I wasn't sure what to make of that.)

I look out at the bobbing poles. "Luke, remember when you caught the fish?" I say. "Did you think it meant anything?"

"I was fishing. I caught a fish. Isn't that what you're supposed to do?"

We walk out along the rocks. Three younger guys crouch over a tackle box at the end of the jetty. I eye them for a while as Ferg and Ryan film shots of sunbursts and sea. "Tu joue le football?" I call out, partly because they are athletic looking, partly because I'm still feeling out my powers of communication.

"Le football?" a guy with slicked black hair and designer sunglasses asks.

"Oui," I say.

"Oui?"

"Oui."

"Attendre ici." He wedges his fishing pole between the rocks and takes off. We watch him hop from boulder to boulder until he disappears into the parking lot.

When he comes back, his hands work at the bow tie of a plastic bag, unearthing a long-sleeve OM jersey. He flips it around. "Chemise de Drogba," he says, voice quiet with gravity.

"C'est vrai," the man says. "Real." He lets me hold it. I run my hands over Drogba's name.

On our way back to the grass, Luke and I argue about what "real" means.

"The guy just meant it was an official jersey," Luke says. "Drogba didn't actually wear it."

That hadn't occurred to me. Do you do that with a jersey that came from a store, carry it around with you all the time? Tiptoe down rocks so that you can show it to strangers? I guess you might. That consumed look on his face—shirt in his hands, he could hear the stadium and see the field.

Five or six games stretch across the park. We stand there watching, weighing, still wondering whether or not the jersey once belonged to Drogba. A ball skips toward us. Luke takes off after it and volleys it back. He's quiet for a second. Then he says, "When the ball comes toward me, I consider the game beckoning me—the game wants me."

Luke acts like I'm a sap. No, catching a fish when the bait guy says you can't isn't a sign. No, that jersey couldn't be the one Drogba actually wore. But then a thought like that sneaks out and gives him away: he's a romantic, despite whatever he may tell you. We follow Luke's volley across the grass. I slide off my flip-flops and walk into the game. In South America, you don't wear shoes unless you're playing on concrete. In France, I feel a hand on my shoulder. "Madame," a distressed-looking man says, "tes pieds."

SOMETIMES I'M AFRAID to watch men play soccer. When they are fully absorbed in a game, they're at the height of their power, at ease in a way that every woman wants. The first time I saw Luke play, he had me right away. I looked out at that calm and felt risk.

But watching men play can also be seeing them at their worst. The first ten minutes of our grass game in Marseille feel like one man's ego vying against another's. Guys take on three players at once, trying to relive old glory. Then when they're hammered, they cry out and grab ankles, faces stretched into whines. They bitch as if their individual greatness is being thwarted by everyone else's inadequacies. Grumpiness spreads, infects everyone.

A guy wearing a shirt the color of a highlighter, who dribbles and dribbles and dribbles, flashes me smiles you can tell he thinks are smoldering. He's got greased-back curls and facial scruff. When the game dies off, he reaches for my hand and whispers in my ear, "Where are you from?"

"United States."

"But you aren't fat. I thought American women were fat," he says, smiling. "Sorry we're not passing you the ball more. We are French. We are selfish." I laugh at him and shake his hand, and then he wanders away.

Luke's found his own conversation on the other side of the field, talking with two of the younger players from the game who didn't play with the same petulant irritability as the rest of us.

"We're going to a rap studio," Luke tells me as I walk up to them.

"You have to see the music," says a guy wearing a wifebeater and long basketball shorts. He has big brown eyes and skin that is kind of dark, kind of light. He shakes my hand. "My name is Fares. I'm Algerian, like Zidane."

MAYBE I'M JUST copying Zidane, copying Drogba, like a kid who learns her hero loves something and decides to love it too, but Marseille is beginning to feel mind-blowingly special. There are the buildings—grand but neglected, like the ones I loved in Montevideo. And then there was the goat cheese, the birthday cake, the tinkling sound of boats in a harbor. Then the man with the magic jersey on the rock jetty. And now we're piled into a white Fiat with Fares and a kid named Lamin, a Gambian immigrant who just met Fares on the field. I'm sitting on top of Luke, my head hitting the sagging ceiling fabric, camera bag wedged under my chin, on my way to a rap studio.

There was a story in *The New York Times* about the rap scene in Marseille. (This story is probably also part of why I love this place—the writing was so good it made you wish it was your city they were talking about.) Two months before we arrived in France, race riots rocked Paris and Toulouse, but not Marseille, and, according to the *Times* piece, music may have had something to do with this. When 130 conservatives from the French parliament brought suit on twelve rap groups for "causing" riots and "anti-French sentiment," none of those groups were from Marseille. Marseille hip-hop can be plenty angry—lyrics confronting the city's high unemployment rates, the conflict of having two homes, and the prejudice the French are known for—but, as the lead rapper of popular group IAM explained, "Marseille rap never integrated violence the way Paris did." And this, he says, is because of the local pride you don't necessarily find in the rest of France. The immigrant poor don't live in isolated concrete blocks far away from the center of the city like they do in Paris; the poorer neighborhoods are scattered throughout Marseille, all within city limits. "So residents feel that they belong to Marseille, because they do," reporter Michael Kimmelman wrote, "and in turn they feel that Marseille belongs to them." Songwriters pen odes to their local neighborhoods and the streets where they first proved themselves. Musicians sell their CDs on their own block. The big-time rappers help out the small ones. The city converted a tobacco warehouse in the center of town into a music studio for youth, encouraging artistic expression. Marseille's hip-hop takes cues from flamenco, jazz, blues, and American rap—as much a fusion of cultures as the city itself.

Fares turns up the volume on the hip-hop station. Lamin, eighteen, has only been in France for one year, but he's already learned enough French to talk fast back and forth with Fares. He wants to be a rapper—he's got notebooks full of verses in English and French—and for him, this trip to the studio is a chance.

Two rappers are sitting outside on the steps when we pull up. Fares bumps shoulders with both of them and then gestures toward us. The only word I can make out is "football."

"Yeah?" the guy in a big red hoodie says in English. "In Marseille, when the football is good, the people are happy."

He exhales smoke. "Here football and music are closely related. Both give you a chance to say something," he says. "Kids get here from all over the world. Songs let you show where you come from, who you are, what you have to prove."

He snubs out his cigarette and holds open the door. We walk up the stairs into a real music studio. I've never been in one and I'm impressed by it. The soundboard is full of shiny levers and knobs. There's a glass wall that feels important. You go on the other side of it when you're ready to make a song you want people to hear.

The rappers, part of the label Street Skillz, once opened for Soprano, the most famous rapper in France, but their faces are still eager to please. "We'll freestyle you a song," the guy in the hoodie says.

They put on headphones and go behind the mics. The main singer, a short thin guy with dark skin, grabs a ball from the corner of the room and juggles while he raps. His right foot in full command of the ball, his shoulders move side to side in sync with the beat of his song.

After, I see Lamin talking to the ball juggler in the corner of the room. He walks back over to us. "They gonna let me hang around," he says. "Maybe give me a job a couple days a week."

In the studio, we play an impromptu game of two against two. In the way they scoot out the chairs, and their nonchalance when the ceiling panels get dislodged, you can tell this is part of a routine, like soccer is how they get inspired to play music. Which is funny to me, fascinating— the inverse of what I'm familiar with: listening to music to get inspired to play soccer.

When I was twelve, I tried out for the Florida Olympic Development team, safety-pinning number 1566 to the right leg of my red Adidas shorts. I wore a pedantic T-shirt that said IF YOU DON'T PRACTICE, YOU DON'T DE-SERVE TO DREAM, and I listened on my headphones to "I'm Your Baby Tonight," by Whitney Houston, pushing the words down in my chest: *"Whatever you want from me/I'm givin' you everything."*

I didn't make it. I watched the kids with bright pink congratulations

handouts skip across the grass as I sat Indian-style, listening to the coach
tell the rest of us, "You've got to walk away from here thinking we made
a mistake," even though his tone said they didn't make mistakes.

When I talked to him, when I stood in his shadow and looked up,
trying to mumble out, "How can I get better?" without crying, he said,
"Your run is just too awkward for this level." He probably said other
things too, nicer things, but that's what I remembered.

I came home and kept hearing him say in that lying, pitying voice:
You've got to think we made a mistake. I spent half an hour every day dribbling around trash cans while I listened on my headphones to my brother's
Eminem (Whitney Houston now banned). I walked to the track with my
dad and worked on extending my stride. I practiced with my team, with
my brother's team, and I called up the high school team and asked if
I could train with them too. On the days I doubled up on practices, I
dragged the trash cans beneath the street lamps and dribbled in the dark.

I THINK A little about the name Street Skillz. *Skill—the ability, coming
from one's knowledge, practice, aptitude, etc., to do something well.* I banked
on skill. I was a social disaster, the type of twelve-year-old who wanted
friends too badly to have any, but as long as I knew how to play, nothing
mattered. "Every player's got to have a bag of tricks," my coach told us,
his Trinidadian accent thick. A real orator, he knew when to pause, how to
set a spell. Sometimes parents couldn't understand him, but we always did.
"Magic you may summon at any moment. I'm talking the *su*-per-natural.
These tricks are your signature, your specialty, your armor."

A coach can't know which speech will be the one that lands, but this
bag-of-tricks idea—I absorbed it instantly. When we stumble upon our
last game in Marseille, those are the words I'm hearing.

At first, it's just sixteen- and seventeen-year-olds lounging on a court,
taking turns chipping the ball at the crossbar, the same thing Luke and I
grew up doing on the other side of the world. (How does this happen? Did
we all come to it on our own—think, *What if we try to hit the crossbar?*)

They are teenagers with swagger. Collars popped, cologne strong. Faces from all over—first- and second-generation immigrants. One kid wears giant faux-diamond earrings. They push one another, steal one another's shots, talk in rapid French. Three of them circle a cell phone blaring rap, bouncing to the beat. The way they populate the court—some sitting, some standing, some dancing, some shooting, some lying down with their heads on backpacks—you can tell they're here for the long run, until the lights go out.

Then they start playing. The frequency with which they hit the crossbar should have been a sign, but their tricks still take me aback. A little of the flash we've seen before—the rainbows, the windmills, the bend-down-and-pretend-you're-tying-your-shoe-but-nudge-the-ball-forward-instead—but most is so original the four of us will go back to our apartment and try to reenact it later that night, in our socks, on the wooden floor, going through it piece by piece. They call for the ball with a lot of angry *icis*—"here," said with a level of demand and feeling that goes way beyond the *icis* I heard in French class. One kid playfully headbutts another kid's stomach. They throw out English expressions: "Oh my goodness," they shout whenever somebody beats somebody else. "Yes, lady!" they call when I have the ball. One of them—a guy wearing shades and smoking a cigarette while playing—tells me, "Zidane, he played here, ici, on this court."

"Really?" I say. "Vraiment?"

"No," he says, grinning.

The kid with the diamonds—he's the world standout so far. No one moves like he does. Later, after the game, the other guys make him dance to a beat on someone's cell phone. We watch as one fist hits into the other, his whole body coiling and then uncoiling, the best dancing I've seen in my life. The guys bear-hug him and holler as he finishes, rubbing his head and burying him in the crowd. "It's a kind of African dancing—they always bringing new stuff over," a kid with cornrows explains to us. "Dancing is how he expresses himself. That's why he loves to dance on the field, with the ball."

The diamond wearer points to God, to his earrings, to his heart, and says in English: "I LOVE YOU, DANCE."

Other guys dance, too, and then the dancing bleeds into freestyle rapping, one act followed by another.

When the first kid goes, the only line I understand—a line that makes them all jump up and down and scream—is "Prisonnier de ma passion / appelle moi Ingrid Betancourt." *Captive of my passion, Call me Ingrid Betancourt.* Ingrid Betancourt—a woman who ran for president of Colombia, taken hostage for 2,321 days, a nationalized French citizen . . . in the songs of teenage boys rapping on a football court.

Yassar, an Armenian kid, goes next, messing with his silver chain as he waits for the cell phone accompaniment. "For my family in Marseille," he says. Once he starts, you can tell from his face and from the faces watching him that whatever he's saying is strong, packed with the feeling of a teenager and the rhythm of someone with a gift.

Later, we'll find someone who translates it for us:

Lost between the street and the school benches
different cores
I have often heard that I am messing between rights and duties
Color Blank
Lost in this racism
For them, inferior you are if elsewhere are your roots
Dreams are my nightmares
Given that my dreams are killed
Lost as defeat
which satisfies them
Often you must take again
the luck you have to take
Lost because my passion exceeds
the simple level of pleasure
Well-defined goals
hurried ambitions

Lost because they criticize me, not enough or too present
I am going to the snow
I stand for me
Lost in what I am becoming
My teenage crises . . .

I'm moved by him. And the rhythm is so good we're wondering if maybe it's a popular song that he's just memorized. Could he really have just come up with that on the spot? Why is it so hard for us to believe things are real?

WHILE I WANT to stay at that court forever, we are late for dinner with Fares's family. His mother cooks roasted chicken, fried dough filled with goat cheese, homemade Algerian bread, French pastries—the best meal any of us can remember. We sit on the balcony, candles flickering on the

Marseille, France (Courtesy: Ryan White)

table as we talk about the countries we came from and the country where we are now. When we thank them, they say, "This is how we are in Marseille. Everyone is welcome."

I lean on their ledge and peer out at the lights of Marseille. Our game is still going in my head. (That's one of the best parts of playing: you can take games with you, mental recordings of feeling to go over again and again.) At the end, when the sun made streaks across the court, a kid snapped his fingers and yelled out, "Le foot ct la fiesta!" He threw his arms around the two pairs of shoulders next to him and pointed around the circle. "He's Robinho, he's Zidane, he's Drogba, I am Eto'o. We are all the world."

BIG FIELDS AND
SMALL ONES

1.

ROME—WE WALK past women with high heels wedged in cobblestones and priests who fly by on mopeds, robes billowing. We want to play in the Vatican. We have the slightly illogical rationale that if we can get a game with Bolivian prisoners, we should be able to get one with clergymen.

This desire sprang from the discovery of the Clericus Cup, where priests-in-training from all over the world play one another on a field overlooking St. Peter's Basilica. For weeks now, Luke has been reading up on these player-priests. "Cardinal Bertone—the Vatican's secretary of state—is a *calcio* devotee. He just bought a Serie C team," he tells us during our standard briefing session on the train. "He hopes one day to have a professional team representing the Vatican . . . the world's smallest country."

Though Luke sent e-mails to everyone from the info desk to the pope himself, when we arrive in Rome, no one has responded. The possibility that somewhere within the walled city the clergymen play pickup raises a host of questions in our minds: Do they play peacefully, or do they exalt in their one opportunity to let loose? Are there dirty tackles, cheap shots? How competitive do the men of God get?

Pigeons circle as we wander around the Vatican, soccer ball in hand, asking any sprightly looking priest, "Mi scusi, padre, lei gioca a calcio?" We also talk to policemen wearing berets and red turtlenecks (looking way more *GQ* than American officers) and Swiss Guards outfitted in puffy suits made out of what looks like the blue and yellow fabric of a carnival tent. While one priest dribbles the ball with his hand like you would a basketball, while telling us how much he loves football, everyone's clear about one thing: we've got no chance of playing inside the Vatican. A Swiss Guard fingers his sword and tells us with a small smile, "It is quite impossible."

Redirected to the seminary schools, we find someone to show us to the field. We arrive at a large dirt area with several accompanying bulldozers. The old grass is being replaced with turf. "This is Italy," the seminarian tells us. "It will take a long, long time."

PRIESTS, WE LEARN, aren't the only occupational groups to form teams in Italy. Betsy Whitaker, a 1984 Duke alum, tells us that there are teams for singers, teams for lawyers, teams for politicians. Her town is home to Cristiano Cavina, a bestselling author who plays on the national writers team. After another two days getting shut out at the Vatican, we take off to Casola Valsenio to see the writer.

Driving through the Tuscan countryside, it's good to be outside the city and away from our failure. I look out at hills blanketed with red wildflowers and wonder what a profession can say about you. In *Soccer in Sun and Shadow,* Eduardo Galeano wrote, "Tell me how you play and I'll tell you who you are." I love that line. What happens when you add chosen jobs into the mix? Could you look at a singer on the field and detect flamboyancy, confidence, stage presence? Would Mick Jagger have a different football style than John Lennon? Would a lawyer argue every call? Could you tell whether or not a politician is a crook by the way he plays defense? Would a writer overthink every play?

In South Bend, I was on the English graduate intramural team. Our captain e-mailed us inspirational quatrains from Greek mythology. We hadn't won a game in ten years. Once, after our spectacle-wearing defender tried to head the ball, the referee had to stop the game while everyone scoured the grass for his missing lens, exactly the type of moment you'd expect from a team full of literature lovers.

OUR TIME IN Casola is a romance-movie montage: we drive in through the Apennine Mountains, passing cyclists pedaling so slowly they look like they'll tip right over. On cobblestone streets in the town's center, old men stand under arched doorways of buildings that are centuries old. Betsy, a petitely muscular, high-energy woman who treats Ryan, Ferg, Luke, and me like we are longtime friends, sits us down with her three daughters at the kitchen table in her apartment, feeding us wine and pasta as the wind whips the tree limbs outside the window. A storm pours on us as we pick cherries on a hillside and watch the lightning in the distance. Hiding in a barn, we listen to the sound of the rain pummeling the tin roof, Luke blowing hot air onto the back of my neck. We shower in the claw-foot bathtub of a seven-hundred-year-old stone-walled apartment that belongs to a man named Biaggio, whom Betsy tells us is in a cave somewhere spelunking. The room looks like it belongs to a wizard: towers of ancient books; black-and-white photos from the time Biaggio invented a flying bicycle, the whole town gathering to watch the test drive; paintings incorporating every kind of material, from twisted roots to mummified cats; hundreds of knives gouging the fortress-looking wooden door.

In the evening, the eight of us stroll down streets empty of cars. Ernie, Betsy's blond ten-year-old who is fluent in Italian, has a music recital. We sit in old, creaking seats and watch people of all ages run through numbers—some piano, some tuba, some singing. Two men who have no previous singing experience perform a duet on stage. Wincing and out of key, the men look like they feel extraordinarily silly. They plow bravely through the song anyway. I sit with my knees against the seats, fully drawn into the experience of witnessing first efforts. How different it is than what I do, clutching tightly to the one thing I know.

AFTER THE RECITAL, we meet Cristiano, the writer, at the pizzeria. He's behind the counter and he's got a large knife in his hands, chopping hard and fast, blade slamming down on peppers and onions. He's not the Italian with gelled hair and fancy shoes; he looks grizzly—buzzed head, face shadowed with stubble. He glances up at us and nods at Betsy but keeps going on with his pizza, thumbs now mashing at dough. I can see the heat of the brick oven on his face as he takes pans in and out.

After Cristiano has closed the pizzeria and swept the floors, six of us— Cristiano, Ryan, Ferg, Luke, me, and Emma, Betsy's teenage daughter— sit together on the patio, a pitcher of beer on the wrought-iron table in front of us. "I don't see myself as a writer—I am a narrator. I record the stories of this place," Cristiano says. "I never want to be somebody other than a pizzaiola. When I don't make pizza, I write. When I don't write, I make pizza."

He speaks in a gruff voice, English words thrown out with some defiance, like he's thinking, *This is not my language, and I cannot do what I want with it, but I will talk it anyway.* Bare bulb glaring down on him, he rubs at his eyebrow ring, smoking cigarette after cigarette. "I grew up in the story. I am like my characters. Only child, no father, poor. We lived in a housing project in town," he says. "We played calcio from six A.M. to eight P.M. in a gravel lot. Our entire time. The lot was beside a vine that is older than your country. I'll show you."

Cristiano takes us through the quiet streets. The clocktower is lit up in the moonlight. Lanterns hang from pastel-colored stone buildings. "Here is the spot," he says, standing in the middle of an empty lot. He kicks gravel, shells flying. "And here is the vine." It is knobbed, gnarly, twisted, and tall. He slings one arm around it like it's an old friend, witness to the same games, town, and lives that he is.

. . .

WE PLAY WITH Cristiano on Sunday, not in the gravel where he played as a kid but at a field that looks dropped between two mountains. I don't know what happened to the people he used to play with, but I get the idea that he's the only one left. The players on the field with us are the fifteen-year-olds who live there now. "It is not the same. They do not play the way we used to," he tell us, waving his hands at them. "They are chic, soft. They have video games, motorcycles. For us—it was the only thing."

Cristiano's wearing a T-shirt with the sleeves cut off (which isn't normally a look I like, but on him it just seems like he ripped them off because they were in his way), along with dark gray sweatpants, one leg rolled up gangster-style. I study this pant leg, wondering if this is part of some effort to combat the fussiness of a writer's life. The running in the morning, the playing, the pizza making—physical, honest things he latched on to in order to balance his hours spent holed up in his head.

The game is OK—a little too quiet, like we all know soccer can be more than this. The fifteen-year-olds have Nike cleats, gelled hair. I say to Cristiano, "I thought Italians were loud, expressive. . . ."

"The silence is because of you," he says. "Italians don't play with women." Which seems true—the teenagers look uncomfortable, faint grimaces—but I also think it's because of him. They act self-conscious, like they can see themselves in Cristiano's eyes and have a sudden desire to eschew everything and spend the rest of their teenage lives no place else but on the field.

Cristiano stalks the wing, grumpy, taking touches that are crude but good, accomplishing what he needs them to. He swipes the ball away from the young guys, shoots the shit out of it, moves like someone who does not grapple with hesitation. At 5 P.M., he leaves the game early, smoking a cigarette in one hand, holding an apple-juice jug in the other, walking toward his uncle's pizzeria.

THAT NIGHT, WE meet Cristiano at his apartment so that we can record the man who records. Like most Italians, he still lives with his mother. When I watch him swoop down and kiss the cheek of his mom, whose hands are white with the flour she is rolling pasta in, I wonder if we should all live with our mothers. "Cappelletti, best pasta in the world," he says, squeezing her shoulder as she cuts dough on the kitchen table.

Cristiano takes his book off the shelf in the living room and sits down on the chair in front of the table. "I read the end," he says, flipping to the last few pages. "I am not a mystery writer—I don't care."

He reads in nearly the same rough voice in which he speaks, his Italian only a little softer and slower. Then he closes the book. "Finito . . . the end."

He pours us grappa and translates the meaning, hands gesturing. "It is a story about an old man who imagines what he'll say to his grandson . . . that there is a god for the soccer fields, a kind of magic. Not the big ones—the small ones in the provinces." Head cocked to the side, he smiles, shyly, like he's telling us something personal, emotional: "Soccer will give you much more than you can give it."

That sentence hits me. I drink down my grappa—god-awful stuff—and wonder why I took so long to see something so easily true.

In every game I've been in since college, there's some play that's made me feel momentarily gifted. I stand there on the field, asking myself, *Could you have been great?* But no matter how far I could've gone, I never would've left as big an impression on the game as it left on me. Standing in that kitchen, all unfulfilled wondering leaves me completely.

SO I GUESS it's easy to predict that a day later, while I'm sitting next to a five-gallon glass jug of Chianti (filled up at this amazingly cool gas-station-style wine pump), feeling 100 percent content, I would open an e-mail from Stephanie Peel, who's now playing in Sweden: "Have you heard the U.S. pro league is coming back? Do you think you're going to try out?"

Luke, who's noticed me frozen, comes up behind me, messing with my hair as he reads over my shoulder. I eye the computer. A chance, right when I decided I didn't need one. I feel irritated, elated, panicked.

2.

FOUR YEARS AGO, Ruud van Nistelrooy—star forward for the Netherlands and Manchester United—took a vacation along the Blue Ridge Parkway in North Carolina. The weather was bad—dark sky, poor visibility. Unappealing road trip conditions. So when he saw a sign for Holiday Inn Drive, he pulled off the highway and opted to wait out the weather.

While hauling his bag out of the car, he noticed a small white placard: ASHEVILLE INDOOR SOCCER CENTER.

The Asheville Indoor Soccer Center is not easy to find. You must drive down Holiday Inn Drive through the hotel parking lot until you reach a winding, poorly lit road that takes you to a vinyl-sided warehouse one would think was abandoned were it not for the small, easily missed sign with an arrow allegedly pointing toward a soccer field. If you are Bobby Somerville, indoor center manager, there is no chance an international superstar is going to arrive in your foyer.

When the tall brown-haired man with a strong nose walked into the indoor center and explained that he was on holiday and had been driving for a long time and wanted to bang the ball around a bit to stretch out his legs, Bobby was getting ready to go home. Because Bobby doesn't like to let people down, and not because he thought he might be talking to Ruud van Nistelrooy, he agreed to keep the field open for another half hour.

Ruud's first strike banged off the ceiling lights. Bobby stood up from his desk and raised his arms, like, *I let you in and now you're destroying my field?* Ruud ducked his shoulders and waved in sheepish apology.

Five minutes later, Mike Rottjakob, a local coach, walked in. "Who is that guy?"

"No idea."

Mike walked out of the office and back to the field, watching for several minutes before returning to Bobby's desk. "I think that's Ruud van Nistelrooy."

They leaned over the walls of the indoor field and tried to decide if it was possible that one of the top goal-scorers in the world could be playing right there in front of them, in Asheville, North Carolina.

"Ruud?" they called. "Ruud van Nistelrooy?"

As I filed team registrations, the main task of my part-time job at the indoor center, I'd make Bobby repeat the story: "He was very coy. Never answered us directly. He'd smack a volley, saying in jest, 'Who could hit a volley like that?'"

Half an hour later, after Mike and Bobby had called every soccer player they knew, Ruud van Nistelrooy was playing in a pickup game with anyone who wanted to join.

Because of this story, and my subsequent fondness for Ruud van Nistelrooy, when Ryan, Luke, Ferg, and I are putting ten dollars on a team in the 2008 European Championship, I choose the Dutch.

Ferg bets on the Germans; Luke opts for the French (which he blames on the boys of Marseille, who effectively convinced him of their greatness even though they'd be missing Zidane); and Ryan goes with the Italians. I don't hold Ryan's pick against him. Primarily a tennis player, he must not know the Italians are the team you love to hate—theatrical dives and pouty faces, nothing you would knowingly choose to support. I haven't forgiven them for the dramatics that brought on the questionable penalty kick that robbed the Aussies in the Round of 16 at the 2006 World Cup, nor the questionable penalty kick against the United States in group play, nor the way Materazzi insulted Zizou's sister and then crumbled to the ground. Some countries teach the dive as a part of the game, and some countries don't.

Of course, when we're inside a room full of Italians, I keep this perspective to myself.

We arrive in Arezzo and discover that the art school where we're spending the night has no working television. We drop off our bags and hop in the rental car, scouring streets for a TV, which is usually easy to find when the national team is playing. But downtown is not accessible by car. It's a twenty-minute walk we don't have time for. The one bar on the outskirts of town is closed, garage door all the way down. But coming from inside, we can hear sound.

Ferg and Luke bang on the aluminum. Someone cranks the door halfway up. "Game?" Luke asks.

Now we are surrounded by Italian men who have closed the bar in order to fully focus on the game. It is a very loud room, but not a happy, loud room, because the Italians are already down 2–0.

With my team's two-goal lead, I'm able to keep my reactions fairly neutral. It is not until the Netherlands scores their third goal that Rebekah, Luke, and I give ourselves away with one clap of our hands. The four men to our left slowly turn their eyes on us, a new awareness in their faces: they have given their beer and their food to the enemy.

A large man in the back row rises from his seat and makes several trips to the bathroom, cupping water in his hands and flicking it at us, as though we are the curse in the room that he must clear.

FOUR DAYS LATER, wanting to see a Euro game up close, we rail to Innsbruck, Austria, where Sweden will take on Spain.

Three hours before kickoff: Swedes cloaked in the blue and gold flag, Swedes hanging off traffic signals. Swedes wearing the gold crown of a Nordic victor, Swedes wearing moose antlers. Old lady Swedes, blonde-beauty Swedes with their hair wrapped into Princess Leia buns, and one guy in a yellow wig wearing what looks like makeshift lederhosen (Swedish national team shorts hitched up high with blue-and-yellow suspenders), half-waddles, half-folk-dances through the masses.

And then the Spaniards. Men dressed as red-and-yellow versions of Bozo the Clown, men dressed as female flamenco dancers. Faces sectioned into the red-and-yellow stripes of the flag. Four men in costumes that are part Superman, part Zorro: red hat, yellow mask, red spandex bodysuit, yellow bikini, red tights, Spain flags tied like capes around their necks. The chanting, the jumping, the beer mugs, the jerseys everywhere. All moving together, one wave takes over streets.

I'm holding a cardboard sign: WE NEED TICKETS.

One Swedish Viking and three Spanish Zorros at Euro 2008, Innsbruck,
Austria (Courtesy: Luke Boughen)

"Ha!" a man wearing a red fedora says, thumping Luke's shoulder.
"Don't we all!"

A middle-aged couple, sort of American looking—khaki shorts, polo
shirts, sunglasses—asks us how much we're willing to pay.

"Two hundred?" I venture.

He makes some sort of cry and claps his hands to his head. He doesn't
bother responding, just walks away.

One man—shady looking, quiet, secretive voice—puts his chin against
his chest, looks at the ground, and mumbles, "Seven hundred?" Euros. As
in eleven hundred U.S. dollars.

You hear a number like that and you give up. We have no shot. I lower
the cardboard sign.

Luke buys a big-bottled beer for three euros from the man standing
on the corner and takes the sign from me. He keeps it propped above his

shoulder as we let ourselves get pushed toward the stadium, the sounds of horns, chants, drums, and shuffling all around us.

A man wearing a Peter Pan hat and a Spain jersey signals to us. Luke sees a gap in the crowd and jogs through it. Peter Pan pulls two tickets out of his back pocket and explains that his friends have an extra ticket and he wants to sit with them. He's got two tickets to sell, and since it's already almost game time, he'll sell them for two hundred euros apiece.

We waffle, standing in the center of the street, weighing the positive—getting to go to a once-in-a-lifetime Euro game—against the negative, the staggering amount it would cost us.

Peter Pan drifts farther away from us, not wanting to get separated from his friends. Compared to seven hundred euros, two hundred euros is a steal—it's hard to pass up. "All right," I say, "let's do it." We run through the streets, bumping into Swedes in chicken costumes and Spaniards in polyester jumpsuits, trying to find him, eyes searching for that little green hat. Ten minutes later, we slow to a walk. He's gone, nowhere.

But one hundred yards out from the stadium, through dumb luck, the flow of our crowd pushes us into the flow of his, the green of his hat popping against the dark brown hair of the heads surrounding him. "We found you!" I say, grabbing his shoulder and whirling him around. He smiles, recognizing me. "Sí, sí," I say, pointing to the stadium. Luke explains: we want those tickets.

We tuck beneath an archway, moving away from the press of the crowd. We hand the four hundred euros to him; he hands the tickets to us. I squeeze the man's forearm and say, "Thank you so, so much."

WE ROLL TOWARD the stadium, the game-buzz feeling even better now that we are going. I have on an almost-Sweden-blue T-shirt and Luke's wearing his Spain-red sweatshirt. We find yellow face paint lying on the ground and smear it across our cheekbones. We party with drunk Swedes and drunk Spaniards who hang their arms around our necks and yell chants into our camera. All the cheering is in my ears. We saw the Sweden national team bus drive in earlier, everybody beating at its sides, at all the players who made it.

As a fat Swede with a blond mustache clamps his arm around me and bounces, I think about my brushes with national teams. In my sophomore year of college the coach of another school had said to me, "Congratulations!" I waited to hear what for.

"The under-twenty national team. You *made* it."

"Nope, not me," I said, smiling, marveling at the cruelty of hearing the thing I'd always wanted to hear and it not being true.

"I'm sure of it. Alyssa told me. She saw your name—Oxenham."

Standing in the soccer office, I put my hands up to the straps of my backpack and concentrated on keeping my hopes down. I walked to my truck, goose bumps on my arms. Even though I told myself not to believe it, some part of me grasped on and wouldn't let go. She called later that night to say she'd made a mistake.

It wasn't my first time getting faked out. The spring of my freshman year I had made the under-eighteen roster. Oxenham, my name, in the middle of the United States national team list: I stared at it all that morning and went to a doctor's appointment that afternoon. I floated there, hardly aware what the appointment was for, hardly remembering the nagging pain in my foot. I listened to the doctor tell me about the torn ligament—that if I kept playing my foot would collapse, that the sooner I had surgery the better.

"You'll get another chance," my coach had said, but it was crutches and a screw for six months and then another two years before I was any good again. Then I graduated, the same year the pro league folded.

"That was it"—a worldwide refrain. Each place we go, players who came close tell us about broken legs, bad timing, unexpected folds in fate. Some tell us right away: they want us to know. Other guys tell us later, with their eyes down, embarrassed of the pride and self-pity they can hear in their own voices.

"The victory will be ours!" a Spaniard now shouts into my ear, holding one corner of a room-size flag that billows like a parachute over the top of us. "España, España, España!"

A dozen turnstiles and ticket takers ring the stadium. We say our good-byes to Ryan and Ferg. We are going and they are staying, which I feel bad about. The group logic is that at some point, we might want a shot of Luke and me in a stadium. So Ferg packs the handheld camera into my purse, gives me last-minute instructions, and then we're off, walking up to the stadium gates.

We've shaken off our leave-Ryan-and-Ferg-behind guilt and are smiling at one another when the woman in the Euro 2008 visor who takes our tickets says, "Just a minute." At first, there's no panic—waiting is a part of being in lines, a part of getting let in. But then the waiting seems personal, like only we are waiting.

The woman speaks rapid German into her walkie-talkie. Luke and I raise our eyebrows at each other. Then she turns toward us, running her fingers over our tickets. "You see, these are thick, too thick." She points to some very small print. "And here—it should say 'Coke Side of Life.' Yours say '*Cake* Side of Life.' These are quite fake." She laughs lightly, like this is quite funny.

Luke and I are thinking of our euros and the game that will happen without us . . . when we see a fleet of stout Austrian police officers coming our way. That's when it occurs to us that scalping tickets isn't entirely legal. We're not sure which part of the process is against the law—the buying or the selling—but when we ask if we are in trouble, the officer says, "Oh yes," as though she is surprised we didn't already know.

The stadium music sounds Disneyland-themed, xylophone pings and organ chimes meant to convey magical enchantment. This is what we hear as we walk through the gate, past the game, to the police office.

In the station, slumped against Luke, I hold my yellow-painted face in my hands. I'm trying to think if there is a way to make our story sound innocent, minor. My racing mind comes up with nothing. A lady with thick mascara is looking at us and waiting, so we just tell her what happened. Luke's saying, "A Spaniard in a Peter Pan hat," when I see Ryan and Ferg, who apparently witnessed our incident, walk through the door . . . here to save us.

"How did you get in?" I whisper to Ferg.

"We told them we have Peter Pan on tape."

Apparently, Austria dispatched hundreds of undercover cops who blended themselves into the crowd, carrying cardboard signs similar to our own, trying to catch the men who prey on naive idiots like us. All day they'd come up with nothing, so the footage of me profusely thanking Peter Pan is highly coveted.

The footage is analyzed on a high-tech computer program. He double clicks on the Spaniard's face, blows it up—bingo, the man they are looking for. Now there are only sixty thousand–plus people to search through.

As we're escorted out the back of the stadium, we hear the roar of fans ballooning larger and larger and then the comedown, the letting out of air. Luke and I catch eyes, looking at each other but seeing the field, imagining the source behind the sound—maybe a missed breakaway, maybe a Xavi to Torres through-ball. We walk out the gate and I glance back. "So close," I say. And so far away.

WHAT HAPPENS NEXT feels like a sign. We're being escorted out, walking along a back alley, a service road to the stadium. There's a chain-link fence, a grassy field, sounds of playing. We walk up and look out: to the left, thirty ambulances and firetrucks parked in a row; to the right, men and women in paramedic and firefighter attire—fluorescent jackets with reflective stripes—playing soccer, scampering downfield, laughing and screaming. A hundred yards away, Spain plays against Sweden. Until their walkie-talkies summon them out to rescue an injured player or drunken fan, they sprint across the field in heavy black boots.

We stare through the chain-link fence at a small game we never would have seen had we not been turned away from the big one.

Outside the stadium (Courtesy: Luke Boughen)

3.

"THAT WOULD ONLY happen to an American," says Erich Braun, a German who played with Luke in college, after we tell him our fake-ticket story on the ride from the train station to his house in Rödermark, a suburb of Frankfurt. "Only an American wouldn't know to watch out for that."

"The font was small, very small," Luke says, putting his hands over his eyes. "But, they caught the guy—thanks to that green hat. We got our money back."

That night, we barbecue sausages and drink Franziskaners as Luke and Braun rehash memories: how upperclassman Braun liked his bag of balls rock hard, sending freshman Luke back to the locker room to repump the bag; how the Notre Dame team fined one another two dollars for public displays of affection, guys hiding in the bushes to catch unsuspecting teammates with their girlfriends. "My girlfriend was already suspicious—me being thousands of miles away at American college," Braun says. "And then she comes to visit and I won't hold her hand in public."

At eight, we watch Germany play against Turkey in the Euro 2008 semifinal. "Big rivalry—we've got a huge Turkish population," Braun says. "It's probably similar to the U.S. relationship with Mexico."

Braun pours himself another beer. "There are guys that I played with who are on the national team, playing in these great tournaments, playing in front of all these people," he says. "I ask myself, Why are they on TV? While I'm sitting here?"

Braun's fate-bemoaning is familiar. Maybe every player wonders what happened; it's always hard to know whether you ran out of talent or belief.

"The plan was to play for two years at Notre Dame and then go pro—remember how fit I was in college?" He adds with a smile, "I mean, fit for me." (Braun was the typical star forward: always wants the ball, scores all the goals, and runs as little as possible.) He picks at the label on his beer bottle. "You know, I lost speed, got injured. I was the best and then I didn't make it, and now I don't know."

"Have you given up hopes of playing pro?" I ask, listening as though his answer can inform my own.

Braun shakes his head, his jaw loose. "I'm too old—it's impossible. My body hurts. I'm happy where I am. I play on a team. Even forty pounds overweight, in this league, I'm good enough," he says. "But you guys . . . how old are you? Twenty-five, twenty-six?"

We nod; he nods. "See, you're at the hump where you've got to decide whether you're going to keep trying. But I'm twenty-nine, getting to the time where I ask myself, Do I hang up my boots? Because I can't do what I used to. I'm watching myself get worse and wondering, Do I keep playing for the fun of it or just let it be?"

On the TV, Turkey scores first, Germany equalizes and then goes ahead, Turkey ties it up. Germany wins in overtime. After each team scores, we hear people celebrate—chanting and car horns ringing out Braun's window.

. . .

WHEN WE TAKE off for the field the next day, Braun is deep inside a nostalgic fog. "We used to play every day after school—get home, throw down our backpacks, head to the field," he says as we walk along a brick road lined with cottages with fresh paint and flower boxes, like a pretend neighborhood out of fables. Braun has a twine vegetable sack slung over his shoulder, tinged with old-fashioned charm that a black Nike gym bag won't ever have.

"The barber lived there," he says, pointing to the cottage to our right. "And that was Jimmy's house. I'd knock on his door, he'd call out to his mom, then we were gone." Now Braun's not walking diagonally across lawns to find teammates; he's pushing buttons on his cell phone, texting directions to his friends Toby, Til, and Kelvin.

"Man, I'm excited. I haven't done this in forever," Braun says when we reach the field. "Nowadays they keep all the fields locked up. I had to get a key."

The gate scrapes against the driveway as it opens. We walk out on lush grass. Braun and Luke haul the goals out to the endlines. "Last time we were here," Braun says, "first touch I took? Strained myself."

I sit down on a bench and lace up my Asics, watching the guys trade jokes and also cursing myself for my decision to leave my cleats at home. In South America, they occupied key backpack space and never got used. But had I really thought it would be like that in Germany? I try to imagine Braun and the other Germans going barefoot, scampering around on the perfect grass. It doesn't fit. They belong in the cleats they are tightly lacing.

I bend down, pull at the tongues of my shoes, realize that I'm nervous. Braun's friends all played somewhere: Kelvin, a tall black guy who drove up in a Mercedes, played first division in Germany. There are only six of us, which means there will be nowhere to hide, and if I'm not good enough, it won't take long to find out.

I'm not sure I'm looking forward to this brand of soccer. I try to keep my mind from making blanket statements about a country's style—the

Brazilians are creative, the Germans are efficient—but I do sort of think that. On the field, the Brazilians and I loved the same thing—surprise. (So much so that they seemed almost distracted, too amused to remember to go for the kill.) Germans don't seem as into surprises. I thought all the things the announcers said on TV during World Cup games would be true: they'd be good at the long ball, at passing, at free kicks, at work rate, at hard tackles.

"Welcome to Germany," Braun says, after he lays out Luke on the first play.

All game, they engage in man-battle: they grunt, they shove, they grab shorts, they exalt in the flare up of the old competitive streak that runs through any athlete. Braun's shorts rip halfway through the game. When he runs, there's a white flutter of nylon, exposed white leg.

Passing—triangles, overlaps, square balls—frustrates me. If no one goes for the dribble, my chances of stripping balls off people is significantly reduced. Normally that's my pickup game MO: I take it from people who hold on to it too long. (In college, I taped a *Sports Illustrated* quote about two linebackers to the inside of my locker: "What they had in common was the maniacal way in which they pursued the ball.") But here Braun and his friends just play the ball forward. When Luke does go for something a little more elaborate, Braun says, "Boughen, stop with that jambalaya stuff." And when the ball comes to me, I don't go for a move, unwilling to take a chance in a game where no one else does.

"First to three?" Braun calls, once the sun starts to dip beneath the houses.

Braun backs up into Luke and calls for the ball. "I'm going to end this right now," he says as he receives it. He slams a volley off the post. Til retrieves it and comes toward me. When he takes a second touch, I pounce, swooping down upon him. I take the ball, charge forward, shoot the ball early. I don't normally shoot early; I don't normally shoot at all. But Luke keeps teasing me about my tendency to dribble myself into a corner, to lay it off when it makes more sense to shoot, to do anything but take a crack at it myself. So I shoot and I score and the game ends.

Braun hits his hand against the crossbar, vibrating metal echoing. He stalks off to the empty grass behind the goal to fume by himself, pacing back and forth, shaking his hands in the air.

"Even though it doesn't matter, I still care," he says on our walk home. "As long as I play, I care." He's silent for a second. "I'm kind of mad at Til. You can be surprised by a girl playing ball once, maybe twice, maybe three times, but not for two hours. Do something, trip her, do anything." He hitches his twine sack higher up on his back. "You know, I have this theory: the fatter I get, the better I play. I can't do all the fancy stuff. I have to stick to the basics. Get the ball, pass it off, and finish when you can."

THERE IS A God for the small fields. I hear Cristiano's words when we are walking away from Braun's field, and I hear them again when we're staying with Balint and Butter in a 250-person town in Hungary. Balint and his mother first came here when they were hiding out from the Communist regime.

We drink homemade wine and look out at the Hungarian countryside—like Tuscany, only secret—while Balint tells us about the game that's happened here for the last thirty years.

On Thursdays, the three local villages—Szentbékkálla, Mindszentkálla, Köveskál—meet at the largest grass field, although it gets smaller as players get older, goalposts moved in five yards every year.

There are grandfathers whose faces look as ancient as the one I pictured in Gabriel García Márquez's *A Very Old Man with Enormous Wings.* There are also teenagers: six climb out of an old VW bug with a patched paint job, techno music blasting out of open windows. Plus there's the kid, an eight-year-old wearing a Cristiano Ronaldo jersey. Like in Trinidad, like in Brazil, one generation passes the game down to the next.

At sunset, I notice Ryan hiding in the bushes with his elbows mashed against his rib cage, his technique for keeping the camera still. I wander over to see what he's found and look out at four players headed into the dusk. Three walk along the road that slopes upward, while one rides a bike slowly, his hand on the backpack of the kid to his left. I witness a chain of shoves, the kid on the end pushing the kid in the middle, who pushes the kid on the bike, who teeters off the road and into the high grass before righting himself back onto the road. Two wearing imitation Brazil jerseys adopt fleeting jousting positions, topped off with a series of roundhouse kicks, and continue to wander away.

That night we go to sleep in a loft used for drying lavender and almonds, the nuts spread out along the wood near our heads. Luke breathes steadily in my ear as I lay there, seeing the sunset horseplay and the shifting end-lines of small fields.

4.

IN HUNGARY, WE could not pronounce the town name or say hello or good-bye, only thank you (*köszönöm*), because Butter taught us a mne-monic device ("cuss a gnome"). When we get to London, we bask in the ability to eavesdrop on the tube, to read the headlines over people's shoulders, to know what's happening around us.

While Americans jog after work, the British seem to play football. We see the men on the tube, cleats on the their feet, ball in hand, on their way to a "kick about." (The term "pickup" has an entirely different connotation—something you do with women in bars.)

Our first day in London, in Regent's Park, we play in what is by far the most boring game of the trip. No joking or yelling, no anger or enthusi-asm, only an occasional player muttering beneath his breath. The most entertaining moment happens when a guy wearing a T-shirt that says CRAP chases a softball through our field. Having a kick about feels no more joy-ful a thing than riding an elliptical machine.

Luke tells us that Eric Cantona, former Manchester United star, be-lieves the British are the best fans: while the Italians and Spaniards will boo you in hard times, the British will suffer through it with you. To some extent, you can feel this approach in the Monday kick about: they are out there no matter how dull it gets, loyal to the game long after the life has died out.

Leaving the park, we hear shouts coming from the far corner of the grass. Men flail their arms. "If you want to play in an interesting game," says a guy propped up on a bicycle nearby, eyeing us, "this is definitely the one you want."

The players are Iraqis—most of them Kurds, a few of them Sunnis. The brawl apparently involves who will play on which team. The yelling pauses for half a beat, and Luke calls out, "Can we play with you guys?"

This appears to overwhelm them. A man in bright yellow board shorts covers his face with his hands. "No, no," he says, voice full of agony. "We are busy today. You come back tomorrow. Seven P.M."

Coming back tomorrow almost always goes poorly, so we're not surprised when we arrive at 7 P.M. on Tuesday night and no one is there. We make circles around the park, searching every enclave, remembering Paris and how close we came to missing an entire field. We talk to several guys who confirm they do play here, often, toward the end of the daylight hours. We camp out around a tree and wait, surveying some mild, uninspired games that make us more and more sure we want to play with the Iraqis.

I spend the time against the tree trying to imagine a tryout. It feels preposterous. Am I going to safety-pin a number to my shorts the way I did when I was twelve? Pull my hair into a high ponytail? Drop off my pillow and duffel bag in the dorm room? Pack Goldfish and granola bars? Want it so bad all over again?

I'm five years out of college. They'd handed me plaques, patted me on the back, told me to find a new life. And I did: I theorized about literature, went to readings, wore scarves, graded papers, bought coffee every day from the Texaco.

I pick at the twigs around me. I think about the game in Marseille, the game in the favela, the game in the prison. Maybe I've gotten better, developed the vision I never had in college, picked up some of the swagger we've seen everywhere.

I stand up, brush the bark off my butt, and juggle the ball with Luke while a small part of me considers mounting a comeback.

THE NEXT DAY we huddle again around our tree. The Iraqi patch of grass stays empty, but we hear loud British voices coming from another side of the park. We walk to a stretch of grass where we see a mix of pale guys and African immigrants. We get there right as they're being invaded by a softball game. "No wonder England's team is so weak," Dean, a black Londoner, complains. "You can't get any pitch because of all the cricket, the softball. Softball, for God's sake."

We hunt for a new patch of grass. I shiver and make small talk about it being cold.

"It's summertime, baby girl," Dean says. "Where are you from?"

"United States . . . Florida."

"We had an American come out before. Short guy, said his name was Woody. It took a week before anyone recognized him as Woody Harrelson."

"Really?" I say. (I get pretty excited whenever I hear about famous Americans with soccer inclinations.)

"Rode his bicycle up to the pitch every day. Even came when it was pouring. Didn't miss a kick about."

I tell him we call it a pickup game in the U.S., wondering if others are as interested in the variety of terms as I am.

"Pickup?" he says, face greatly skeptical. "Sounds Playboy-esque to me."

Landing in the center of the park, we play high-spirited football. Guys say, "Last goal" . . . and then "One more goal" . . . and then "Final goal" . . . and then we all half walk, half trot to the closest bar to watch Spain play Germany in the finals of Euro 2008. Standing room only, we crane our necks at the TVs in the corner, watching the men whose jerseys we are wearing.

ON FRIDAY, IT is our fifth day at Regent's Park. It's empty, the English presumably celebrating the end of the workweek by loosening their ties at a pub rather than sprinting around in the grass. We are leaning back against our tree when we notice a man juggling a ball in the exact patch of grass where we saw the Iraqis. One after another, they begin to show up.

The wind whips across the flat fields, strong as hell, blowing us forward as we walk toward them. I rub at my arms and bounce in place. A short burly man, who is wearing shin guards without socks and the same bright yellow board shorts he had on when we saw him last, calls out, "Hello! You are back. You want us. Best soccer of your life."

With the exception of one Moroccan, everyone is Iraqi. Like the other day, most are Kurdish, some are Sunni.

Once the game starts, I run by the Moroccan, a guy who looks startlingly similar to Pee-wee Herman. He exclaims, "Madame! Play slowly. Please! I am injured."

Ryan follows him with the camera. He puts his hands on his hips and sighs, speaking into the mic: "She is good. . . . I'm not against women. I like them, I love them actually—that is my problem."

The teams, we discover, are lopsided. "A trade!" the man in board shorts yells, summoning Luke over to his weaker side. "Paid for by Iraqi petroleum!"

A bald guy in his thirties wearing all-white shows up half an hour into it. "Where are you from?" he asks.

Aware that my country is occupying his, I say, "the United States."

"Ha!" he says. "Fallujah versus New York!"

After the final goal is scored, we sit beneath the tree, still warm from the game. Some of the men work in information technology, others in construction. When I ask one of the guys in construction how he can want to come to the field at the end of a long day, he shrugs. "This is my happiness."

Everyone begins to leave, the wind now cold against our wet skin. The Moroccan calls out, "Good-bye, Au revoir, Charra, Fiimaan illaah, Ma'a salaama!"

WE GO TO dinner with Ehman, the man from Fallujah, at an Iraqi restaurant. We talk about Iraq, the United States, and England, broaching the politics not touched on on the field. Of the four of us, I am the one who knows the least. We invaded Iraq in search of weapons of mass destruction, which we did not find. Sunnis, Shiites—I know both sects are fighting to take control now that we'd ousted Saddam. But that's it, all I know, even though my country is in his. Fallujah—I didn't know 60 schools, 65 mosques, and 36,000 of the 50,000 homes were destroyed in the war. Ehman doesn't talk about most of this, saying only, "We are fighting to protect our land," but I read about it later, so that I won't go back on the field and shake hands with men who have fled their country when I am ignorant of my country's role in their nightmare.

On Saturday, our last day in London, we play again with Ehman. A few of the players who were not there on Friday do not want to play against a woman. "It is religion," Ehman explains. While I'd once imagined defying oppressive gender restrictions, I'm feeling less gung ho about trampling on religious beliefs. I nod, I might even say, "Of course"; I watch from the sideline.

Near the end of the game, a curly haired man changes into jeans and red cowboy boots. I stare at the boots. "Ahh? You like these?" he says, rotating his ankle as he belts up his jeans. "Cowboy boots are my love—I own seven different colors. In my country, we don't have them. They make me feel like a different person."

I sit there looking at him, wondering about all the shades of meaning inside those cowboy boots.

TEN-MINUTE GAME

WE ALWAYS LISTEN for yelling. From the Iraqis in London to the old men in Brazil, the best games are marked by a failure to refrain. It's not usually teenagers shouting in one another's faces; they're too conscious of keeping their cool, of portraying to the world that there are more important things ahead. But right around the time you're on the other side of your playing career, there's a certain behavioral abandon. Weeknight games matter as much as or more than anything else in your life, and you've stopped trying to fight it—so yes, you're going to yell your head off if someone says your goal is not a goal or tries to rob you of your final two minutes on the court.

We've heard the yelling in every country, in Hungarian, Italian, French, Portuguese, German, and Spanish, but when we are on a court in Jerusalem and the yelling is between Jews and Arabs, there's a new level of heat.

THREE MAJOR RELIGIONS have roots in the Old City. Everyone walks like they belong. As we drift by tapestries puffed out from the breeze, passing women wearing burkas, nuns in sweeping black habits,

Boys juggling in the Jewish Quarter of the Old City (Courtesy: author)

Hasidic Jews with broad-brimmed hats and ringlets of hair drooping down past their ears, we're conscious of the majesty of history. It feels like we're walking in the place the whole world grew out of.

While space and territory are major issues in the Old City, every quarter has found room for a football court. In the Christian Quarter, kids wearing replica jerseys, from Messi to Van Nistelrooy, play goalie wars on bleached stone. In the Jewish Quarter, guys with yarmulkes pinned to the back of their heads play on a field overlooking the graves on the Mount of Olives. In the Muslim Quarter, players scrimmage on a court lining the fortified wall of the Old City. But it's not until Friday night that we find a game where Jews and Arabs are playing together, though the players are quick to clarify, "We'll play against each other but never with each other."

We're at Gan Sacher Park around ten at night. Here, like our games in Malick, Rio, and Paris, if you win, you stay on. It's first to two goals, or whoever's ahead at the end of ten minutes. The level is high: three of them point to their club-insignia-splashed sweatshirts and tell us they play in the Israeli professional league. Most players are Jewish, many wearing yarmulkes, white-collared shirts, and black pants. There's also a family of ten or so Arabs. They are full of jokes no one else understands. When I get on the court and do any sort of move or run or touch, they clap their hands, whistle loudly, and sing "Olé, Olé, Olé."

Once our team is off, Luke and I sit in the center of the divide, the right side of the court all Jews, the left side, Arabs.

"Do you play here a lot?" I ask a bald Arab with a large stomach, who speaks a little English.

"I am here under doctor's orders," he says, tapping his gut.

Leaning against the concrete wall, the Arabs await their turn to get on, and then they wait past their turn, bumped to the next game. A guy

Boys playing in the Muslim Quarter of the Old City (Courtesy: Ryan White)

with Michael Jackson–like hair pulls out a stopwatch and keeps track of time. He calls out what I imagine is a notification that the ten minutes is almost up.

Once the second goal is scored and the current game ends, the Arabs walk on the court. But so do a group of Jews, who also say they've been waiting. Standing in a tight cluster, faces close together, men scream at one another until the Arabs walk back to the wall, unhappy. They speak into Ferg's camera:

"Tell her that we are the shittiest people wherever we go."

"We are the people of shit . . . the struggling people."

"Be careful, one of them might understand Arabic."

"Maybe they will take us with them."

A skinny teenager wearing glasses and a yarmulke tells Luke that it is always tense on this court. What happened yesterday makes it all the more tense: on the street where we're staying, an Arab took over a bulldozer from a construction site and flipped several vehicles, including a bus. An Israel Border Policeman climbed into the tractor and shot and killed him. "One day after a terrorist attack, it is very hard to play with Arabs," the teenager says. Last night the police had to come.

The Arabs get on the court the next game but lose quickly, beginning once again the cycle of waiting.

NEAR THE END of our night, Luke and I are on a team with three Jewish guys. We're playing against the Arabs.

Two minutes in, Luke slots the ball into goal and turns to walk back to the center of the court. But there are no nets, so it's not always easy to tell whether a goal is a goal. My bald friend does not believe it went in. The Jews believe that it did.

Even though Luke is the scorer of the goal, even though he had gestured back and forth with the bald man, we're not a part of this argument. Maybe we would be if we could speak Hebrew, but we can't, so now we stand there and watch, bystanders to a conflict between Arabs and Jews.

Men flood the court. It looks like a riot—a sea of people coming from the left, a sea of people coming from the right.

Some point within the post. Some point outside. The skinny kid with the glasses yells in the face of the bald man, whose friends hold him back by his shirt. "What the fuck," a Jew yells, although I would not know he's Jewish if he had not whispered to me, "I am *not* Arab." I had not asked.

Sound grows unbelievably loud, the most shouting I've ever heard at once. Crowded in the box, fingers pointed, faces distorted with anger, the men seem like they're arguing about more than this game—like they're also yelling about yesterday's terrorist attack and tomorrow's never-ending mistrust.

On the other hand, we've had the is-it-or-is-it-not-a-goal fight all over the world; it's a sign of being swept up in the game. Maybe there is some relief in arguing about football instead of the overwhelming history of crimes against one another. Right now, they are consumed with the desire to know whether or not the ball went in.

Then comes the realization that we have it on tape. Two separate swarms of men charge Rebekah. In the rest of the world, we fended off similar demands for a replay because rewinding tapes while shooting is asking for disaster. But no one seems to hear Rebekah say no. Their hands are up to the camera as if they are ready to rewind it themselves. "OK," she says.

Heads crowd around the LCD screen until they see it and disperse in continued disagreement: even the replay is unclear.

It's midnight by now. Faces and shoulders sag. "Penalty kick"—two words I can snatch out from the chaos of sound. Both sides take the compromise. A tall Arab walks over to Luke and hands him the ball.

Luke sets it on the white spray-painted dot and walks backward. All the sound has gone quiet. He looks up at the bald man, begins his run up . . . and drills the ball against the post, metal clanging.

The Arabs celebrate. The man with Michael Jackson hair points up to Allah.

Off the court, Ryan and Ferg talk with the players. On the Arab side, a man says, "We're not here to make trouble. The problems that happen outside, we have nothing to do with. We come here as players who play."

On the Jewish side, a man says, "There is only one court in the city center. Arabs are citizens exactly like us. We cannot legally tell them to leave. It may sound nice when Arabs play against Jews and nothing happens, but it is one big bullshit. People act like football is above politics, above all tensions—bullshit."

On the other end of the court, Luke and I lean against the rail. He nudges me, points his chin toward two kids to the side of us, one Arab, one Jewish. They head the ball back and forth, counting how many times they get in a row. The Jews watch this, the Arabs watch this, Luke and I watch this. Maybe the exchange between two kids doesn't mean anything, but I don't think Luke and I are the only ones on the court hoping that it does.

2.

NONE OF US wants to go to Israel without going to Palestine. We take a white van across the border to Ramallah, the closest Palestinian city to Jerusalem. I expect patrols and a checkpoint, forgetting that no one cares about who goes into Palestine, only who comes out. This direction, there's no security, no border check, nothing. We're just all of a sudden in the West Bank.

The first time I heard of Palestine was in seventh-grade geography class. It was the part of the map everyone wanted. *The West Bank*. It sounded regal to me, like the stretch of island where all the big houses are. Then I read a young-adult novel set in the Gaza Strip about a forbidden friendship between an Arab boy and an Israeli girl. Palestine, it turns out, was different than I'd thought. In the book, the country sounded poor and dusty and hot, which is still how I think of it years later. In the smoky images I've seen on TV, everything's the color of sand.

We climb out of the van when everyone else does, stepping into Ramallah's center square. So much is happening it's hard to see anything. Cars and more cars, mufflers not muffling, circle a roundabout, and maybe all that circling is what I notice first. Roundabouts kind of freak me out. Even though every car I see is different, in my mind they become the same set of cars going round and round forever. In the center of the roundabout, a string of colorful, triangular flags, the kind you see at a racetrack, hang from an iron structure that looks like a dinkier version of the Eiffel Tower. At its base, there are four life-size lion statues, two seated and calm, two on their feet, mouths roaring at the people who walk by.

Brightly colored signs and advertisements pop out against the grayish white buildings. Luke points out "Stars & Bucks," green font looking exactly like you'd imagine. Storefronts are crammed on top of one another, each one so tiny it looks like they are getting squeezed smaller and smaller. Vendors sell spices, fabric, shawarma, men's dress shirts, and sunglasses. (Every country's street vendors sell sunglasses, even though Americans are pretty much the only ones who wear them.) The sidewalk is jammed with people. A man wearing a red jumpsuit, pant legs bunched into white boots, has a giant contraption strapped across his back. It looks like a cross between a hookah, a genie's lamp, and a giant golden urn. Yellow flowers stick out the top. A tray holding a stack of big pots and a tower of plastic cups is hooked behind his butt. I watch until my theory is confirmed: in less than ten seconds, he hula-hoops the tray forward, sinks to one knee, unstraps the gold container, and pours hot tea into one of the plastic cups. The attire, the flowers, the ornate structure—I like witnessing tradition that most likely has nothing to do with tourism, considering there are no other tourists anywhere in the square.

Ramallah is, however, listed in our Lonely Planet guide, *Israel*. I just read about the city's beginnings: the first to come to Ramallah were Christian exiles fleeing religious persecution. They set up homes in the remains of old crusader castles and worked as farmers and shepherds. That rural image is hard to imagine as we stand there in the hordes of people. In 1948, when Israel declared itself a state and there was mass exodus of 750,000 Palestinians from the coastal cities, Ramallah became the teeming city it is now.

Many people are on their way to somewhere, but many others just stand and watch the madness. These street witnesses are the ones we think we should talk to. The problem is that we don't speak Arabic. While Luke is normally armed with a sentence about football, he's not this time. The Arabic alphabet is 100 percent indecipherable to us, the Arabic key terms spelled out phonetically in the back of our Lonely Planet guide don't include hunting for football, and although Luke downloaded one of his podcasts, none of the expressions have stuck.

Luke bends toward a row of men, his hand up by the side of his cheek. He hurriedly mumbles hi. It sounds more like "Hhh," his shame over using our language instead of theirs chopping it off. Then he raps his hand against the side of our ball and says, "Football."

THAT'S ALL LUKE said—football. Then we were on our way, following a man in a collared shirt and dress pants through the streets. We walk outside of the city center, down narrow alleys that are quiet except for the sound of construction. Ducking through the doorway of a building that looks pretty much the same as any other, we find ourselves standing in a room with ten or so teenagers clustered around a Ping-Pong table.

"Hello!" a girl calls out, putting down her paddle and walking toward us. "Who are you?"

"I am Sireen," she says, not waiting for our answer as she shakes our hands. She has large brown eyes and long eyelashes. She wears a white veil, a long-sleeve shirt, and black jeans with a gold emblem of a crown on her back pocket. When I say my name, she arches her back and makes a face. "That is very hard."

The man we are with stands behind us but doesn't say anything, probably because he has no explanation for what exactly we are doing here. And this teenage girl, who speaks English in a high-spirited, beautiful voice, seems more capable of figuring it out than he does.

She pours orange soda into five paper cups and then asks, "Why are you here?"

How odd it is to say we came to Palestine to play football. I can't

remember all of a sudden if that is true. It sounds indecent—going anywhere in search of a game. "We'd like to play football," I say.

"Football?" she exclaims. "But I love football!"

"You do?"

"It is such a great love! Oh, let us play." She claps her hands and stands
up, speaking in fast Arabic to the teenagers gathered around us.

The boys follow her out the door. I walk next to her and her friend, a
girl wearing a short-sleeve T-shirt and no veil.

"Will your friend play, too?" I ask.

"Her? No. I am the only girl who plays. I am also the only girl who
wears a veil. I just want to. We are very liberal in Palestine. You can do
whatever you want." She laughs shyly and shakes her head. "I do not
know why the other girls don't play. They think it is for boys or something.
But if I were president, all girls in Palestine would play football. It is so fun."

When I ask her how she learned to speak English so well, she says,
"Why I studied it of course."

Four boys grab large rocks from a wall of piled stones, stacking them
into goalposts on both ends of the parking lot. A semitruck forms one
sideline, the street the other. The man we met in the square plays, as well
as a guy in his twenties whom we assume runs the community center
(and whom I notice is wearing sunglasses, defeating my Americans-only
theory). The rest are kids and teenagers. Sireen's little brother, an eight-
year-old in an orange T-shirt that says SOCCER, is the youngest.

The afternoon heat is the kind that can snuff out any desire to run
around, but no one acknowledges it. It's the dress shoes that are bothering our friend from the square: he points to them and shakes his head,
aggrieved that these shiny black things are what he must play in.

Sireen doesn't bob around like a girl unfamiliar with the game; she's
on a mission to get in the action. She takes the ball and goes, dribbling
instincts strong. When she sees me do my scissors, she gasps and walks up
to me, her fingers circling my wrists. "You must show that to me." I show
her once, and then she's trying it on her little brother in front of the semitruck. "I cannot believe it!" she yells, high-fiving me.

When she scores between the two piles of rubble, she throws her hands over her head. She walks toward me and drapes her arms around my shoulder. "Oh! I like you," she says in my ear. "I do not want you to leave. Tonight, you all must come to my house."

WE SIT ON two perpendicular brown couches, drinking coffee with Sireen's mother and grandparents. We tell them their daughter is very good at football, putting Sireen in the uncomfortable position of having to translate praise back and forth. "My mom says I am good at whatever I try," Sireen says, looking down. "That I am strong and opinionated. In the Arab world it is a surprise."

"Did your mom ever play soccer?" Luke asks.

Sireen's mother, apparently catching the gist of the question, shakes her head and finger aggressively.

"Are you going to have babies soon?" Sireen asks me. "Oh yes, I think you want them right now."

I laugh and ask her what she wants to be when she grows up. She doesn't know, maybe something with computers; maybe she will write poetry. We talk about differences in culture and dress and expectation. "I don't like what you're wearing," she says, pointing at me. I purposely wore jeans and the most conservative shirt I had, sleeves down to my elbows, collar up at my neck. I ask why not. She shrugs, laughs, says she does not know. Ferg tells the family we are going to Egypt next. "You going to take me with you?" Sireen asks. "I want to come. One day I will go all over the world like you. Egypt is very hot. My mom says you will go white, come back black."

She heaves out a sigh. "Probably, you should go to the checkpoint now. It is worse later at night. But don't worry. Tourists have no problem. I know, I know, you do not want to leave my beautiful Palestine."

She walks us up the main street to help us find a cab to the border. By now it is dark. The Dumpster to our right makes a banging noise. Ryan, Ferg, Luke, and I jump. A cat darts past us. Sireen stops walking. She turns and look at us, raising her eyebrows, laughter already escaping out of her. "You people are afraid of a pussycat?"

I laugh with her but then I'm quiet, because even though we all know how unfair life is, sometimes that unfairness hits hard. Like when I overheard the Texan on the other side of a Mendoza café telling the woman trying to sell him a trinket, "I CAN'T understand what you're saying. No, no, NO, I don't want any." Or when Ronaldinha's mother was telling us how she wants her daughter to see the world while we, right then, were seeing it. Or when Nenê was talking about the difference between the opportunities in her life and my own. And now, here in Palestine, while we're walking next to a sixteen-year-old who acts like she has a different scale for fear.

Sireen gives each of us a friendship bracelet, tying them around our wrists: "Now you can remember me." This good-bye feels even harder than most.

At the checkpoint, we wait in line, standing inside a cage of silver bars about the width of a trough, tense people behind us, tense people in front of us. Nobody talks or moves or knows what's happening.

Two hours later, the line begins to move. At midnight, silver turnstiles like the ones you see in front of a stadium pop us back into Jerusalem.

FINAL CALL

OUR FLIGHT TO Cairo leaves Jerusalem at 7:45 A.M. We've heard that the Israelis take security seriously, so we arrive at 4:30 A.M., pleased with our arrival more than three hours before the flight.

The Israeli Defense Forces staff the airport. Brisk, beautiful, twenty-year-old women serving their mandatory duty ask us hard questions.

"How many of you are there?"

"Four."

"Are any of you a couple?"

"We are."

"How many years together?"

Luke says four at the same time I say three. We feel guilty all of a sudden, scrambling to clarify that while we've been a couple for three, we've know each other for four. The soldier looks hard into our faces and slaps a number 2 sticker on the back of our passports.

Ryan and Rebekah fare less well. "You are not a couple?" No. "But you used to be?" No. "But you date?" No. It's apparently a very suspicious thing for a male and female to travel together if they are not romantically connected. The Israeli government does not believe in being just friends.

Ryan and Rebekah's passports receive a number 5 sticker. When they are being frisked for a half an hour, their bags entirely disassembled, we know that it is better to have a number 2.

When it's over, we coast to the carry-on security area, operating under the false impression that we are in the clear. Luke and I thoughtlessly drift to one checkpoint, leaving the suspicious, just-friends number 5s on their own.

We wait for Ryan and Rebekah to emerge. After twenty minutes, we poke our heads back around the corner and see that their carry-ons are now being seriously inspected. Luke and I sit down, watching Jewish kids wearing yarmulkes, backpacks, and Heelies skate by us. After another ten minutes, we check again and discover that Ryan and Rebekah have vanished. A backpacker wearing a MEAT IS ANIMAL MURDER . . . TASTY MURDER T-shirt tells us, "They got sent back to the beginning of security." We're glad we gave ourselves that three hour buffer.

When it gets closer and closer to our boarding time, we head to our gate and tell a woman at the desk that our friends never emerged from security.

"Don't worry, we will not leave without them," she says.

The board is flashing FINAL BOARDING CALL. Luke and I stand on our tiptoes, hoping to see Ryan and Ferg sprinting down the hallway, backpacks bouncing up and down. The ladies speak in Hebrew to each other, and I wait patiently until the woman who promised me everything would be fine says, "OK, I just wanted to close the flight before I let you know what happened to your friends. A bag set off a security alarm and must undergo a twenty-four-hour investigation. You will take a bus to Cairo."

On the other side of the airport, Ryan and Rebekah have spent the last two hours undergoing questioning and getting their carry-ons dumped all over the investigation room. Though we have two identical cameras, only one of them set off an X-ray machine. "Probably, if it went through again, it would not go off," the officials informed Ryan and Ferg. "But now we must check and make sure."

Because our checked bags were already on the plane, and, according to security, could not be retrieved, Ryan and Ferg scrawled out a note to be hand-delivered to us, telling us to board without them. We never received the note. Security then decided there *was* time to off-load our bags. "Would you also like us to off-load your friends?" an airline employee asked. Since we never got word that we were supposed to get on, there was no need for us to be off-loaded.

It is hard for us to grasp that they will not let us on our flight and yet will not put us up in a hotel or get us on another airline or refund our ticket. The X-ray machine made a stray beep, and now we have no way to get out of Israel.

Upon examining the bus route, we discover that we will not be allowed across the border because overland routes require a preexisting visa. All Royal Jordanian flights for the next three days are booked. Unless we can convince security to forgo the twenty-four-hour investigation and let us onto the night flight, we're done for.

"Probably, if you were Jewish, if your security profile was a little different, maybe a number two instead of a number five, you would be on your way," Gabby, a Royal Jordanian flight attendant, tells Ryan. "I think it is very bad what they are doing to you. It does not encourage tourists to come back to our country."

Five or six hours into the process, somebody apparently decides Ryan and Rebekah aren't terrorists after all. Security agrees to an abbreviated investigation and hastily drapes our camera in plastic wrap. "We will return it to you at the gate."

At 5 P.M., we sit at the gate. The board is once again flashing FINAL BOARDING CALL. No one has delivered our camera. Our bags really are on this flight, so Luke and I go ahead and board.

"All right folks," the pilot announces. "We are all ready to go, just waiting for two passengers who got held up in security." Another ten minutes go by. Luke and I stare out the window, willing them to appear. We see a black SUV peel around the corner, spinning to a stop. Ryan and Ferg hurl open the passenger car doors and run toward the plane.

"Gabby was doing everything he could to get our camera, racing back and forth, his comb-over billowing in the wind," Ryan says as he collapses down in his seat. "Our car was racing through the airport . . . we almost took out a median . . . squealing tires. It was like a scene out of *Courage Under Fire*."

The flight attendant hands him a cold orange juice, pats him on the shoulder, and says, "Time to relax."

WE DO EGYPT poorly. We are again staying with a friend of a friend, but this time the friend of the friend has just been divorced and is fully occupied with the chaos of that. He apologizes to us as he drops us off at midnight outside a vacant apartment property on the outskirts of Cairo. When we walk in, flying roaches dive-bomb across the room. I'm from northwest Florida—I can kill a palmetto bug without thinking twice, but this isn't one or two bugs sneaking out from the shadows. This is an infestation. There are too many to see at once. They haunt the corners of our eyes. We bat our hands around our faces, shut each window, and launch our attack. Fifteen minutes later, we realize we cannot keep the windows shut. It's over a hundred degrees outside. We have no AC or fans. Windows shut, we're baking ourselves.

Windows reopened, the mosquitoes come in droves. All night they buzz in our ears. We sleep on a bare mattress pad in warm-up pants and sweatshirts, scrunching the hoods as tightly as we can so that only our eyelids are feastable. I wake up soaking wet with sweat, scratching the bites that are somehow covering my cheeks, brushing a roach off my leg. I hear the sound of vomiting coming from the bathroom. I look to my left and see that Luke is no longer next to me.

I put my hand on his back as he hurls in the shower. When he collapses onto the mattress an hour later, I go into the kitchen and see four bowls—three filled with cabbage, one of them empty. "Maggot," he says, "in the cabbage."

The water isn't running, the toilet doesn't work, and the whole apartment smells like vomit. Around noon, we set off to the center of the city in search of a bathroom. We've come at an unseasonable time, too hot for pleasure, so we are the only tourists around. Vendors flock toward us, fighting one another off, needing our money in order to make their living.

"A toilet, that is what you are looking for?" a man in a white turban asks. "Follow me."

He leads us to a quiet corridor a few streets away. "First," he says, "let me show you my perfume shop."

We are desperate for a bathroom. "Thank you, anyway," I say, "but I must go in search of a bathroom." I am speaking in stilted phrases, I guess replicating the polite, formal English of the Egyptian man who has led us through the streets.

"Oh, OK," he says. "You may use mine, no problem."

"I think we'll just go find a public bathroom," Ryan says.

"Why? You will have to pay. You may use mine for free, my friend."

Ryan, Luke, and I are wary, but Ferg follows him. And if she's using it, we might as well, too.

"Feel better my friends?" he asks.

"Thank you very much," we say.

"Now. Come see my perfume shop. It is very beautiful."

Luke is still ghastly looking, and I'm all of a sudden not feeling too hot either. Clammy, nauseous—my stomach can't handle the idea of going into a room full of floral scents.

But Ferg feels bad. This man brought us to a bathroom. She ducks into his shop. We reluctantly follow.

Pretty glass bottles line the walls. "One hundred percent natural oils," he says. He pulls bottles off the shelves, unscrewing eyedroppers. "Sit down, sit down. May I get you a cola?" he asks.

"No, thank you," I say.

"Madam," he says, holding his hand up to his chest. "Please. You are insulting me. You are guest in my shop. Please sit down."

I sink down into the couch, head pounding. He rubs his wrists against Luke's neck. His hands clap Ryan's cheeks. He smears drops across Ferg's cheekbones. I evade his hands, but the fragrant oil is still in my nose and I am not feeling good, not feeling good at all.

"Now then, how many will you buy?" he says.

Ferg's shoulders sink as she looks at the rest of us. "How much are they?"

"Fifteen U.S. dollars," he says. "Twenty-five for two."

"I'll buy one," she says.

"Buy three, buy four—take them as souvenirs for your friends and family."

"I'll just take one."

He frowns, reaches for her credit card, charges her twenty-five dollars.

"I only bought one. You said it was fifteen dollars."

"I will throw in an extra."

"But I said I only wanted one."

"Madam, they are very beautiful oils."

WE ONLY HAD three days in Egypt, having worked it in as a layover between Israel and Kenya, and our ten-hour airport detainment means we are already down a day. The bathroom hunt took up another half day. And we've somehow managed to lose our Lonely Planet, *Africa on a Shoestring*. While we don't like to think we're dependent on a guide-book, we are. We don't know the names of anything. We can't say please or thank you. We don't even know where the pyramids are. But "pyra-mid" is one English word the driver knows. "Football" is another.

Our nausea, our petty aggravation over the perfume, our exhaustion from the sleepless night—none of it matters when we pull up to a game backdropped by the Great Pyramids of Giza.

As we play, thick dust rises up from our feet. Our shins are the color of charcoal. On corner kicks, when many of us are gathered in the box, the dust cloud rises so high I can't see through it. The Egyptian players are quiet and focused, the pounding of our feet on dirt the loudest sound. They play a brand of soccer that is clean, strong, and technical. On the sideline, fifteen boys sit on a rail. A man in a mint green robe watches from the endline. Beside him, a kid flies a kite. (Kite flying is on our list of things found round the world, along with stray dogs, Fanta, and old men playing cards.)

One game, that's it, that's all we're going to play in Egypt. But the pyramids are behind us and the sun is setting. Sounds of techno music filter out from a party tent to the left of the field, dust rises around us, and strands of white lights glow behind the goal—again, we feel lucky.

IN THE CAB, on our way to the Cairo airport, Ferg rifles through the contents of first the camera bag and then her purse, more and more aggressively. "I don't see the plane tickets," she says.

We made a folder for all of them—tickets from Egypt to Kenya, Kenya to South Africa, South Africa to Ghana—which we kept in the insert of the large camera bag. The folder is no longer there.

They are not electronic tickets. They are paper tickets. We triple-search backpacks, camera bags, Ziplocs, and purses. We look in the sides of the cab door, run our hands along the carpet in the trunk when we get to the airport. I don't want the cab to go; I feel like I'm watching our chances of finding them drive away. I sink down to the curb, incredible heat in my face.

How many times have I patted myself down, checked once again that my ID is where I think it is, opened zipped pockets to make sure my boarding pass is still there, left for the airport hours early just to be safe— possessed by a constant fear that something will happen. It's like I knew, like all that airport-edginess was a premonition of this moment in Cairo, when I am facing, or trying to face, the disappearance of plane tickets for the entire continent of Africa.

In the airport now, Ryan, Luke, and Rebekah are at the counter. The attendant who can speak English keeps saying the same thing: "I am sorry. I can see your reservation right here in the computer, but unfortunately, without your paper tickets, I cannot let you on the flight." Luke's voice gets louder as he repeats, "But you can see our reservation—you can see we paid for the tickets," and I'm looking at him, holding his wrist, thinking, *So this is what he looks like when he finally loses his calm.* Next to him, Rebekah's face is still. Ryan's at the counter now, passing the credit card to the man in front of him.

We board our flight to Nairobi. No one speaks. The scope of this financial loss is bigger than any of us know how to comprehend.

A DAY LATER, Ryan stands in the office of Kenya Airways, where a woman whom he will later describe as "the nicest lady in the world" will overlook the rules, reissue our tickets, and begin the paperwork that will eventually result in the refund of our Egypt-to-Kenya flight. Our luck, our relief—we feel it in our legs.

AUSTIN'S FIELD

I AM IN the backseat of a taxi with a camera bag and a pillow on my lap when I see my first *matatu*. It's a fuchsia pink minibus with a giant picture of Mariah Carey above the taillights. It's thumping loud music, and there appears to be some kind of strobe light. A man hangs outside the door; he periodically jumps off the still-moving vehicle, thrusting out a hand to those trying to leap on board, then shoving them safely down the aisle. He hits the side of the bus and the driver takes off.

In the next seven days, under the gray, muggy skies of a Kenyan winter, we stand in the dust clouds and wait on *matatus*. Most have a name. We see Jay-Z, Beyoncé, Sir Alex, Messi, and Luke's favorite: WESYDE written in huge letters across the front, AM THE FATHER OF THIS GANGSTA SH** written in huge letters across the back.

Some of the designs take on a collage format—pictures arrayed haphazardly across the back. We see Jesus alongside 50 Cent. Wayne Rooney, the British soccer star, is pasted over an American flag. The *matatu* emblazoned PIRATES OF THE CARIBBEAN has a plastic skull and crossbones attached to the front grill. We watch with wonder and appreciation until a number 32 or 41 pulls up, and then we make a run for it.

Once we're tightly packed inside, we pass our fifteen shillings forward and stare out the window as our insides vibrate to Kanye West. Nairobi has an estimated two million slum dwellers, roughly 65 percent of the city's population living on 5 percent of the land. We're getting dropped in Mathare Valley, the oldest slum in Africa.

BY 3 P.M., it's raining hard and we're camped out in the one-room house of a guy named Bonfas. Unlike most of the slum, he's got electricity and a television. We're sprawled on his bed watching *Terry*, a made-for-TV movie about a guy who lost his legs to cancer but ran across the country anyway.

When George, Tito, and Kepha swing through the curtain door, they smile and do the Kenyan handshake around the room. It's a multidirectional handclasp, followed by a fist pound. (Women don't do the fist pound, but I don't know that; the Kenyans just smile as I bump my fist against theirs.) We know this group of guys through Ryan's best friend JB, who spent a year here on a photography Fulbright. The picture on the front of our postcard that we used at the prison—a kid's hand resting on a well-worn ball—came from Mathare.

George shakes the rain off his knit cap. I ask, "Will you practice in this?"

"It's one thing to be out there and it starts raining," he says, sinking down into the couch. "It's another thing to go out into the rain."

Kepha, who's slouched across the bed, long legs sticking off the end, stands up and pulls back the wet curtain, watching three kids kick an orange across the mud. "Come on," he says, "I haven't gotten to play in forever." Kepha was the best in the slum and once hoped to be the first guy from Mathare to make the national team. Now he works at the Inter-Continental Hotel and doesn't get home until after dark.

George sighs and rubs his head, smiling reluctantly at his friend. He claps his hands softly against his legs. "All right."

LUKE AND I follow George and Kepha out to the field in the rain. The big day for Mathare football will be Saturday; today is Thursday and we're headed to a practice for the local team that George plays on. Kepha drops in whenever he's not working.

Nobody is talking. We don't know one another that well. I want to skip this part, the acquaintance silence. Maybe I get it from my mom. She puts herself out, filling discomfort with chatter, things she doesn't even mean to say. It's not that the silences bother her; she's just afraid they bother everybody else.

So as we walk, I throw out some filler question, something like, "Boy, isn't it wet today?" Then I walk with my face feeling hot, regretting my quiet-filling and promising myself to lose that habit. But I'm lucky, because Kepha mishears me completely.

"Nah," he says, "George is the star now."

I think about this and what he must have thought I asked. I say, "Do you miss playing?"

"Yes," he says, almost before I've finished asking. He smiles at me, the same unsubstantial smile I hand out to people when they ask me the same thing.

George is watching Kepha. "Football is in our blood," he says, cocking his head to the side. "It's not easy to quit."

We walk by corrugated-tin homes. Trash is everywhere, some of it pressed down into the ground, some of it heaped outside the homes. A young girl in an oversized Sunday dress, ornate, old-fashioned, and faded, something that looks like it should be on a ghost, grabs my hand and skips alongside me. Drunk men run obliquely toward Luke and me, calling us *mzungus* and putting their arms around our shoulders. They're too far gone to be threatening. They wobble side to side. "Chang'aa," George says. "It makes the brain go blank." *Chang'aa*—moonshine—is the illegal alcohol brewed at the base of the river. It's the largest industry in the slum, but most of the money goes to bribing the police.

There's only one bridge across the river. It's off to the right and the field is off to the left, so George and Kepha lead us down to the bank and start rock-jumping their way to the other side. The rocks are not close together. George offers me a hand. I'm leaping from one small, unsteady rock to another. It's not the water I'm afraid of falling into, it's what's in the water, all the waste of the slum draining down to the river.

Once we are safely across, Luke asks what I'm thinking: "Does anyone ever fall in?"

"Fall in? We used to swim in this river."

We're glad to reach the field, something we have in common. The men are able to strip down right then and there—bare legs and boxers—but they point me over to an abandoned shack. It's dark when I go inside, and I try to figure out the best way to change as fast as possible while touching my surroundings as little as possible. I'm tugging my clothes on and hopping on one flip-flopped foot as I try to put my Asic on my other foot, when I fall sideways, my hand landing in something soft. I hold my hand up to my face and see that someone's shit is all over my fingers.

I'm not going to come out of the shack and tell them the white girl needs to wash her hands. Plus I know the only faucet in the slum is a fifteen-minute walk away. I've seen the women hiking over to it, washing clothes and babies while standing in the mud and filling jugs to haul over to their homes on the other side of the valley. I wipe my fingers against the ground, breathe deeply, and head out to the field.

They call it the Red Carpet, the clay the color of a baseball infield. "The surface is better when it rains," George says. "Packs down the loose dirt."

We walk toward the team, clay gritty beneath our feet. I don't miss practices nearly as much as games. I'm unable to get lost in them. You have to cater to rules, cones, touch restrictions. We start with a passing tunnel. It's such an easy thing—pass the ball, run to the other line—and it's that easiness that can unnerve you.

I want the ball to stay flat on the ground, but the clay makes it bounce, and I send a few bad passes, jetting it knee-high at the player across from me. Eventually I settle down and fall into a rhythm, remembering the satisfaction of doing something you know how to do over and over again.

The coach gathers everybody up in the center of the field and gives instructions, but I've got no idea what they are. English-as-official-language does not mean it's the language people actually speak. I think he's speaking Swahili but will discover later that most people actually speak Sheng, a mix of English, Swahili, and the forty-odd tribal languages found in Mathare.

The coach throws me a yellow pinny. I backpedal over to the wing. An outside mid, it's my tendency to float to the side. I know the other team is shooting on the big goal, but I can't figure out where my team is supposed to score. There are cones bookending the half, and most likely my team can score between them, but nobody seems to be trying to do that. "George," I say, quietly, "do we score between the cones?"

He doesn't hear me. I take off anyway, rushing toward the other team and the ball. They knock it around and I'm chasing. Each player's on the move. Ever since our plane landed in Kenya's still-dark sky, we've seen the runners—silhouetted against the horizon, running to work or wherever they needed to go—and the long-haul mentality carries over to their football: they sprint continuously, and there's the feeling they could keep this pace forever.

Like so many times before, the playing ends when the sun goes down. The coach calls everybody in for a postpractice huddle, and standing there I feel disoriented, shot back into the past, remembering postpractice and postgame huddles in Pensacola, in Durham, on hot soccer fields across the South. This huddle's in Nairobi, and he's speaking a mash of languages, but it feels the same as any huddle—the emphatic hand gestures and stern face, the sense of getting ready for whatever's next. He tacks on a few sentences in English at the end—come out strong, win at home: it's the same.

WE START THE walk home in a downpour. I'm trying to keep up but I'm also trying not to fall. There are no lights, it's hard to see, and the three guys are ahead of me. We follow the narrow trench of open sewage. I'm trying to walk alongside the gully and not in it, but it's overflowing because of the rain. It's just a chute of blackness, human waste, and mud, rushing down the valley to the river. I'm slipping every third step, looking like someone who's ice-skating for the first time. When we head into the deepest part of the slum, where it's impossible to pick out my steps, Kepha slows up and grins at me. I grab on to his extended arm while he slings me onto the bank of packed-down trash.

We wind our way through the maze until we pop out at the top of Mathare, next to the main road. George and Kepha wait with us as we try to hail down a *matatu*. But with the time of night and the rain, they're full. We're waving at 32 and 41, but none of them stop. "Sorry," I say, as the fifteenth *matatu* flies by. "You guys don't have to wait."

"Nah, we'll wait."

The *matatus* hurtle down the road, beams of headlights and snatches of music washing over us as they sail into the dark.

"Will we play on the Red Carpet on Saturday?" I ask.

"Nah, the tournament's on Austin's Field."

"Who is Austin?"

"He's the one who's always there."

A 32 *matatu* brakes in the mud, and the four of us start running for it. There are bodies spilling out the door, but George and Kepha help push us on. I see a small sign that says 12-PERSON MAXIMUM, but its letters are faded, a faint reminder of rules nobody expects to follow. My face is in a man's chest, my back is up against the aluminum side, and it's the first time I can visualize how people get crushed to death. But there's a thrill to it, peels of laughter escaping down the aisle as more and more people climb on. Nobody acts put off when we stop; nobody wants to leave a mother out in the rain. A woman gets immediately wedged between two men. We catch eyes, exchange smiles. The music is loud and the doorman is dancing side to side as he throws bodies aboard. I figure this is probably the ride of my life.

Luke and I get off at what we hope is the right area. There aren't lights or signs. We are in the dark. We wander down one street and then another, no idea where we are or what we'll do when we don't find Tito's apartment. We turn back, try new streets, and feel shocked when his building appears ahead of us.

. . .

AT EIGHT ON Saturday morning, we see Austin up against the goal-post, twenty or so kids playing barefoot in the dirt around him. His long, thick dreads are packed beneath a beige knit cap, his face handsome in a soft, thoughtful kind of way. He's wearing brown cords and a green warm-up jacket zipped all the way to the top.

It's a couple hours before the tournament will start. It's cold outside. I didn't know it could be cold in Kenya. I stand shivering in my T-shirt watching Austin gently pick a kid up by the collar. I move close enough to hear his unraised voice. I know from Tito and George that Austin spends all day at the field, even though he does not get paid.

Austin taps a kid on the back of the head, a gesture that makes me think of my own coach. Initially, when the dad at his pickup game had asked him to take the team of under-ten girls, Coach laughed and said no. But he went to watch the first practice, grumbled, "Man's out there doing a bunch of junk," took the bag of balls, and was on the field for the next ten years. Like Austin, Coach didn't make a living off soccer; he took only enough to cover his gas and tournament hotel rooms, and if your family couldn't afford to contribute, you didn't. His day job changed over the years—delivering packages, working as a nurse practitioner, driving school buses—before coming to practice. We trained three days a week and usually called him up on the other two, wanting him to meet us at the field. He never said no. It's hard for me to grasp how much he changed our lives.

It's harder still to grasp Austin's impact. He's coached every kid in the slum under the age of twenty-five. "You know, these are kids who have nowhere else to go," George said. "So they just come together to play. And he is there, coaching them."

The kids' faces tilt up toward Austin's. The practice has ended, but they're reluctant to leave him. They scatter to the side but nobody goes home. A few notice the men are beginning to line the field. They skip toward the bag of chalk and plunge their hands into the powder.

An eighteen-year-old named Henry, who will referee the tournament, hands me a stick-and-twine spool and points me over to the corner of the field.

The field hasn't always been a field: first it was a string of tin homes burned down in a land dispute, then it was the garbage dump. Shattered glass, candy wrappers, and bits of green plastic bags emerge from the dirt. "No matter how often we clear it," Henry says as he lines up my twine, "the trash still floats to the top."

The field is also where most of them voted just six months ago, standing in long lines in the dirt, the election having prompted the largest turnout in history. "Three days after we voted, the results were supposed to be announced," George had said. "They had not been announced. That's when all hell broke loose." When President Mwai Kibaki, a Kikuyu, was announced the winner of the election despite most of the country believing Mr. Odinga, a Luo, earned the most votes, riots raged all over Kenya. Mathare, where dozens of different tribes have lived side by side for the past forty years, was hit the worst.

I crouch down like a catcher, holding my line as I watch goats chewing on vegetable scraps. The side of the field is lined with homes—sheets of rusted tin nailed together, large rocks holding down the pieces forming the roof. SWEET BEEF BUTCHERY is painted on the tin shack behind the goal; HOTEL NOW OPEN is painted on the shack beside it. Behind the other goal, there's the brick wall of a real building, painted into an advertisement: VEGETABLE FAT, THE HEART OF EVERY MEAL.

As I keep the twine low, tight, and straight, guys take turns tossing down chalk. They clasp their hands together, delicately, like they're holding baby birds. Luke is slower than everybody else and he makes funny unsure sounds as he scatters the chalk side to side, a little drivel of whiteness that the kids who come behind him thicken out and extend. A layer of chalk has coated Luke's legs and arms, making him look even whiter than he is.

I laugh up at him, already feeling keyed up for the football.

It's tournament-style—everyone puts in twenty shillings and you play, the winner taking home the loser's shillings. It's only about thirty-five cents a person, but it makes it so that you are playing for something instead of nothing. Many of the men brew the *chang'aa*, earning about six dollars a day, and playing means they give up a day's wages. But if they win the tournament, they stand to make up what they lost.

BY 10 A.M., guys start showing up to the field, sorting themselves onto teams. It's still cool outside, the kind of weather you can run forever in. Players jiggle their legs loose as they count off their coins. Each team is spreading out a crumpled piece of paper across someone's back as they take turn writing down their names. George, Tito, Bonfas, and Luke are all playing together. I've been taken by another team: a small teenager tapped me on the shoulder, looked hard into my face, and said, "You be with us."

In the huddle, my very young team is speaking in Sheng. One is hitting his hand against his other hand, saying what I imagine to be *Let's do this* or *Play hard* or *Give it everything you have*. The same kid who tapped me earlier pulls up the sleeves of his green jersey and hastily offers me some words in English: "You're a forward—we're on."

The sidelines are full. People look for work Monday through Friday but not on Saturdays, so there's no reason not to stop and watch. The field's at the top of the slum, along the main road, so all of the coming and going moves around the field and sometimes through it, the occasional person walking defiantly with his or her head held high through the middle of a game. People are stacked up along the sideline like they've been posed for a picture, kids crouched in front, women in the middle, tall men in the back. If you look at just the clothes, you could think you are standing on the sideline of a field in small-town America twenty years ago: there are snowflake sweaters and Gap sweatshirts and T-shirts that say things like CK1 and HARRY'S PLACE. Kids perch on roofs and sit on shoulders, piggybacking their way to a view of the game.

When the whistle blows, it feels like a small earthquake—the rumble of twelve men stuffed into a rectangle, waist-high clouds of dust and smoke, short explosions of sprints.

I check back to the center of the field and catch a ricochet on my chest, taking it down to the ground and sending it up the field to the fifteen-year-old. I hit three one-time passes in a row, playing the ball as soon as it comes to me. I want to dribble, but as in Brazil, I know I have to wait until I've earned the right to gamble.

I get the ball twice in a row at the top of the box and shoot early. The first ball is a sloppy volley and the second I hit wide. But the speed of the game is fast enough that I know I'm lucky just to get off the shots.

"I thought you played well," Luke says, once the ten-minute half is over. He squeezes my shoulder and heads to the center of the field.

I find a place on the sideline and watch as the men gather together, arms draped over one another's shoulders. George has told me that they never lose, and I figure this is part of why their faces look tight. They've got a lot to defend. They grew up here as a pack of tight friends and are now in various stages of making their way out of the slum. They're the guys everybody looks to, and they know it.

Tito came to the field in his dress clothes—orange V-neck sweater, stiff white-collared shirt, dark jeans, and a fedora hat—not changing until right before the game. Now he's wearing cleats and a shiny green jersey with his collar popped. He's speaking intently—the stern face, emphatic hands. I scan the huddle; they all know just by looking at one another what tribe they come from, but it's hard for me to tell.

Tito kicks the ball off. I move near Ryan, who's crouched down over the camera. It's a different kind of filming than the games you watch on TV: you don't have to keep the whole field in the frame or worry about missing some of the action. You can let the camera linger on a face long after the ball is gone, catching somebody when they're swept up in playing, no idea anybody is watching. I look out at the field, wondering what private moments Ryan will find in this game. Luke looks more nervous than I've seen him look in any other game. He toe-pokes the ball over the head of the approaching defender, and the crowd responds, but then he slips in the dust, falls down, and the other team scores on a counterattack.

After that, I forget to watch. I'm looking out, but there's too much going on along the sideline: goats butting heads, women scrubbing laundry, three boys exactly the same height with arms around one another's shoulders like they will protect each other for life. I forget about the soccer. I tune in for pieces—seeing the other team score a goal, hearing Tito yell, "You put in twenty shillings, now protect it."

By the end it's 3–0 and Tito, George, Bonfas, and Luke go sit off to the side, their faces like stone. I sit down next to Luke and say, "That's the worst I've seen you play," thinking it's no different than telling someone he took a bad picture, implying that in real life, he's more than that.

But his face looks stricken. "I didn't play bad," he says, staring at me. His shoulders turn from side to side like he doesn't know where to go, and then he says, "I'm done here." He disappears into the sea of people.

Sitting down with my arms draped over my knees, I feel bad. One, for hurting his feelings, and two, for not even knowing if I was right. The only thing I'd seen him do was fall down, which is easy to do in the dust.

I jog to catch him and push his shoulder. "I'm sorry," I say, and he looks into my face, accepting my apology but still knowing I'd thought he played badly.

THERE'S ANOTHER GIRL on the field. Vinique, who is Henry's sister, has high cheekbones, smooth skin, and long, styled extensions. I watch her along the sideline, the easy way she folds into the scene. A teammate's talking in her ear. Her hands in the pockets of her Nike warm-up jacket, she's rocking back on her heels and laughing. I know from George that Austin coached her, that she's gotten to play on a school team and has traveled to Sweden, that she's a star of the slum.

When her team goes on, the game's too much of a mess to get many touches on the ball, but you could still see that Vinique is scrappy. Maybe playing with guys breeds that kind of player. Lacking some of the size and speed, you throw yourself at everything.

She's playing against one of Austin's teams, a group of older teenagers. Most of the time Austin just coaches from the sideline, but once they're up by two goals, he takes a pinny and heads onto the field. The kids watching scream and point, thrilled by the chance to critique the man who usually critiques them. He has a slow, graceful gait. When he launches the ball over the top of the VEGETABLE FAT wall, everybody laughs. But he rockets a volley off the crossbar, sinks a few passes, does enough to give us an idea of what he used to be, before he stopped being a player and became the person who made the players.

The small teenager tugs on my T-shirt sleeve, telling me my team is almost on. We gather in a huddle. They throw me enough sentences in English to understand we're playing somebody who is better than us. We're packing everyone in the back. The kid tells me, "You're the lone striker."

I DON'T REALIZE how lucky I got in my first game until I play my second. It's more like an elite-level game of Ping-Pong than a football match, fast volleys from one end to the other. The ball never stays flat on the ground. Dribbling is an impossibility, passing a far-fetched idea. It's all reflex, rushing to the ball, which bounces in the opposite direction of my anticipation. The Kenyans do a better job reading it. "We know the dips and the hills and how it will hit off the slope," Henry tells me. "Where the clay is loose and where you can keep your feet." The strategy is just to get whatever you can on the ball and send it downfield. Goalkeepers know it's more effective to just punt it to the other end, but the last line of defense heads it right back across, while the rest of us turn from side to side in the middle. It's the ugliest high-level game I've played in. Everyone's good: I'd seen George and Kepha move with the ball; they're smooth, fluid. But the field changes the game.

Every time I cut, my feet slide out in the dust. I never beat anyone to the ball. I misjudge divots and read bounces wrong. When it's over, I lean up against a shack. I think about what the fifteen-year-old kid said to me before the first half started: "You're the lone striker." It sounded romantic, like someone who should be in the woods or in novels. I'm not a lone striker. Maybe I used to be: in my junior year of high school I scored sixty-six goals in one season. I saw nobody else, heard nobody else—that's a lone striker.

I lost the gift completely, but I can still recognize the quality in other people's faces—the ability to rage yourself into grace. Standing on the sideline, I can see it in James, the old brother of Henry and Vinique, one of the guys I'd juggled with while waiting for things to start. His body is hard muscle, and his short dreadlocks fly upward when he moves. I know he's a brewer: he spends all day down by the river. George and Tito had told me about him over Tusker beers. It feels weird to know details about his life even though I've never talked with him; we'd only thrown smiles at each other as we lobbed the ball back and forth.

I watch him, the way he stalks the field, his touch on the ball—control like he's about to burst. He scores goals, ugly goals, the ball hitting some bump in the field and ricocheting away from the keeper. He shoves people with an unapologetic matter-of-factness. His shin guards are scrunched down low on his legs. It strikes me as odd that they're there at all, a kick to the shins seeming like something that couldn't possibly hurt him. He's on a quiet rampage out there, in pursuit of the ball. George told us, "Those guys are passionate about their twenty shillings," but watching James, it looks like it's about more than any shillings.

The best part of this trip around the world is witnessing the motivations. Some you hear, in shy postgame explanations, but others you just see on someone's face, too big and too private to put into words.

When James scores, the kids stampede the field, where maybe they'd stay if it weren't for Austin's silent step toward them, which sends them darting back to the sideline.

THREE OF THE five teams will take home sandwich bags full of coins. My team is out of the running. We're still playing, other teams' fates dependent on how badly we lose.

The big game, the one that will determine who's first, second, and third, is between the brewers and the role models. All day the sideline has fluctuated, people moving in and out, but now it's cramped, nobody moving.

Watching the twelve men play, I feel like I'm watching a match from the old days, a game to defend your honor, the brewers playing to show they're more than just brewers, and the role models playing to show they still know this game, this field, and the battle of this slum. It's a high-scoring

Saturday football at Austin's Field, Mathare Valley
(Courtesy: Ryan White)

game, and it's hard for me to keep track of who's ahead and who's behind. The kids are apparently torn, charging the field and cheering no
matter which team scores.

When the ref blows his whistle and the game is over, the brewers and
the role models have tied, putting the brewers over Tito, George, Bonfas,
and Luke in the final standings.

Kepha, dressed in his InterContinental uniform, shows up right as it's
over, holding his playing clothes in his hands. He sees me watching him.
"It's all right," he says, smiling, sticking his hands in his pockets.

The referee passes the team captains their shillings, and it happens so
quickly we don't catch it on camera. Austin's team comes out on top; the
brewers get second; Tito and George get third. It feels anticlimactic, after
the roar of the sidelines and the goal celebrations, to see a man walking
away with a small plastic bag of coins dangling down from his fingers.

• • •

THE NEXT DAY, in the rain, we meet James at the base of the river. Oil drums of moonshine, tilted on their sides, roast over fire pits. Every so often one releases pressure, a firework of fermentation shooting into the sky. The smell of *chang'aa* and sewage is strong. The brewers dot the bank, sweating from the heat of the fires. James and two of the other brewer players know us from the Saturday football and come to shake our hands.

James is a water hauler, filling buckets from the faucet at the top of the slum and carting them through the narrow garbage-paved alleys back down to the riverbank. Bonfas, who's come with us, translates for James: "Brewing isn't work you do because you want to. Most people drink a little to get some steam. It's the only way you can do it. On a day like this, you

Ferg crossing the river as a moonshine barrel releases steam in the background (Courtesy: Luke Boughen)

see what I'm doing . . . this is what I do every day so that at night my wife and son have something to eat. We're paid hardly anything. I wake up at four A.M. and work all day. By five P.M. I am very tired and it's difficult to go play football, but I have to play, I just have to.

"Some people see us pushing water carts and they don't know we're players. When you're down here, everybody thinks you're just another drunkard. But when you get to the field, people are saying, '*Oh,* that person can *play*'."

Most of the brewers watch James talk. One of them turns toward me, his words slightly slurred. "Playing football—you were something." This isn't true, I hardly did anything, but I thank him and shake his hand. He stands over Ryan's shoulder as he films and then he turns to me. "Can I film you—ask you some questions?"

Once we finish talking to James, the brewer turns the camera on me. I have no idea what to expect.

He asks, "What do you think we should do? How can we make this better?

"We don't have water, we don't have sewage, we don't have lights. There's too much drink, too much drugs, we want to change things.

"What do we do?"

He holds his hat to his chest as he asks these questions, eager to listen. His brow is knit, serious, like he truly thinks I will know. I don't.

I say maybe people will see their story in our film. Maybe someone will do something. But we aren't doing anything to change their world. We come here and then we leave.

James wears Copa replicas, the sides blown out, mud sloshing around his bare toes, the cleats digging into the sludge as he disappears down a series of mazes. Sometimes, in an effort to power the cart over potholes, he explodes into a sprint, the rattle of the cart ringing down the alleyway.

WHEN WE GO to find Vinique, she's braiding hair in her sister's beauty shop, a tiny teal shack. She leads us out to a large open space, where dozens of kids are spread out in the high grass.

The kids see the cameras and circle around us to watch. Vinique tries at first to scatter them but then gives up and starts to talk:

"I started playing because of my brothers and sisters. At first, I was really shy and didn't want to kick the ball. Everyone knew how to do it, but I did not and I was too scared to try. But they encouraged me, and now we are the family that plays football.

"I have four sisters. After the elections, we stayed in a displacement camp outside the police station for three weeks. The Kikuyu was the one who won the election, and people didn't like that. Our neighbors came in our house and told us we betrayed them. They knew our house had many girls so they were coming to take us. So we had to pack our things and go, before they came.

"But now, everything is cool, and we play football like normal.

"I play in the back. As a defender, your work is to tackle. I love to tackle.

"Sometimes, later on, men will come up to me while I'm working or just out walking and say, 'I saw you! You were that girl playing football! Let me shake your hand.' They want to buy me a soda just because I can play. It's embarrassing.

"Where I live, there are small young girls, and sometimes they go to the field and say, 'Hey, I'd like to be like you! I'd like to play like you!'"

We close with her intro, in which we ask her to say her name, where she's from, and whatever she wants to say about football. She smiles and says, "My name is Vinique, I'm from Mathare Valley, and I play football at Austin's Field."

WE FIND AUSTIN crouched along the sideline of his field. He's coaching fourteen-year-old girls. Some wear cleats, a couple wear one cleat, some run barefoot. Two wear the same beige knit cap as Austin.

He doles them onto teams, watches for a few minutes, and then comes to us.

It's hard to find quiet in a slum; people and sound are everywhere. We go up on a roof across from the field, where you can only hear a soft buzz from below. As Ryan and Rebekah set up the camera, Austin, Luke, and I lean over the ledge and look down on the practice.

"Who's the best?" I ask.

"That one," Austin says, pointing at a girl moving through the mid-field. She dribbles through two players, slots a through-ball, and walks the wing like someone who finds her calm on the field. Her hand touches her knit cap.

Austin sits down on the ledge. In a quiet voice, he describes Mathare— the lack of electricity or water, the garbage, the sewage, the drug addicts, the drunks. "It's a place where if you're not careful, you lose your life.

"People come here when they have nowhere else to go. I lost everything—my parents and my family.

"I started coaching. At first people didn't know what I was doing. Some people ask me, 'Are you paid?' And when I tell them no, I am not paid, they say, 'Ahhh, then why are you working so hard like that?' I say for the kids. I should just work hard for them. I'm always on the field.

"On Saturdays, we have the tournaments. When there is something like football taking place, people come and watch. And they say, 'Oh, they play like those who are playing on the TV'."

When his voice drifts off, we ask the basics, things we already know but need said in order to put all the pieces together in the end.

"What is the name of the field?'

"Austin's Field."

"Who is Austin?"

He laughs, embarrassed: "I am Austin."

ON MONDAY WE go looking for animals at Nairobi National Park, the only national park within a city limit anywhere in the world. Here you could see giraffes silhouetted in front of skyscrapers.

Ruben, the taxi driver who first picked us up from the airport, swings by Tito's apartment, and we pile in. We pick up George at a butchery close to his house. Though he recently moved outside of Mathare, he's not trying to move past it: he's working toward a degree in social development, and

George and Luke with the giraffes (Courtesy: author)

he spends most of his week back in the slums, trying to help kids give Mathare the same fight he did. "People think Mathare is all drunks and drug addicts," George says as we sit in the traffic of downtown Nairobi. "But that's not all of us."

Like Ryan, Ferg, Luke, and me, George has never seen animals in the wild. When we pull up to the park, there's a smattering of people wearing khaki safari clothes and riding in Land Rovers equipped with tour guides. We wave to them from our station wagon. We buy tickets and a map and they send us off, bouncing down dirt roads, off to see the lions.

It's surreal to stand one minute in a slum trying not to breathe the smell of sewage, and the next to be driving in a pocket of open space flung right into the middle of Nairobi. There's no explanation of rules, no signs instructing you not to pet the animals, so when we see giraffes, George and Luke stride out into the high grass to see them up-close. (Later, as we're leaving the park, we finally see a sign: STAY IN YOUR VEHICLE AT ALL TIMES.)

A strip of wood, a placard that looks like it should lead to the Yellow Brick Road, reads LION CORNER. We see no lions but there is a baboon perched on a rail, the park falling and spreading behind him. He is regal, otherworldly. There's something silent and impressive about him, like he knows the answers to all the unanswerable questions.

We get out of the car to watch him, leaving the doors flung open. Luke takes his picture, and the baboon remains motionless, his eyes not registering our presence . . . until he moves, and he does it so smoothly we all fail to notice that he is, in fact, moving. He hurls himself forward with his strong arms, and Luke is thinking, *What a picture this is going to be— he keeps coming more and more into my frame,* failing to realize this also means he is coming more and more at us. Then the baboon is bounding, bounding fast, and Ruben, George, Luke, Ryan, Ferg, and I are screaming and scattering, half laughing, half scared.

With one leap he is on the roof of the car. When George darts toward him and slams the door shut in an effort to dislodge him, the baboon rears back on his hind legs and lets out a roar that lets us know that he is capable of gouging out our eyes, of crushing us with one blow of his mighty arm.

We're spread out, watching him from a distance. He swings himself into the car. He finds my purse in the passenger seat and fingers through it as though he's handled purses all his life. (He is so humanlike, Ruben is afraid he might actually drive off with the car. This taxi is his livelihood; his father sold his store for it. The baboon filches a muffin, climbs out of the car, peels away the plastic wrapper, shoves our only snack into his mouth, climbs back into the car for a final search, and comes up with a discarded banana peel. He eats it one side at a time. And then he's gone, waddling slowly back into the great beyond. We watch him disappear, and then we drive off into the dust.

SHADOWS AND STADIUM

CAPE TOWN, SOUTH Africa is beautiful but disturbing. While we're staying in an apartment downtown that looks like any fantastic downtown only better, because it's backdropped by mountains and ocean, we also drive by the "townships," the South African word for "ghetto," which look similar to Mathare, incredibly poor, and from what we can tell, the townships are all-black, while the nice streets we walk down are nearly all-white.

We're here because this is the country that will host the continent's first World Cup. There's drama about that. The British newspapers keep writing articles that say there's no way the country will be ready. The stadiums are half constructed, and there are rumors that FIFA is scrambling for an understudy.

At a lookout point on Signal Hill, we stand in clouds that gradually disperse, revealing shoreline, teal water, and the beginnings of Green Point Stadium. We walk down to the construction site, Ryan and Ferg mesmerized by the ballet of cranes.

In our planning, we wrote on the legal pad, "Game with guys building stadiums?" That was our hope. It seemed foolproof—surely there are hundreds of workers, and surely some of them must play—but I experience my familiar crisis of confidence as we actually arrive. Games with stadium workers? Too perfect sounding.

Yellow-suited bodies are strewn across the grass in front of the stadium, helmets resting on faces, hands resting on chests—nap time. The men sleeping on their stomachs reveal numbered backs: 10 emblazoned like a jersey number under the banner TEAM GREEN POINT."

A man laying on his side and eating an apple watches us weave around sprawled limbs. "Hi," I say. "You guys building this thing?" I breathe in, wowed by my ability to ask dumb questions. I plow forward. "Do you play football?"

"No," he says, smiling. "I sleep."

"Do you know anyone who does?"

"Sure."

"Where?"

He points at the stadium. This confuses me. Maybe he doesn't understand. I'm not looking for the stadium. I'm looking for a game outside of it. "I mean, do any of the workers play?"

He smiles again at me, like he's willing to be patient. He points once more to the stadium. "Go to the left."

We walk down a dirt road, listening to loud sounds—beeps and plowing and engine roar. Next to the stadium we don't see much, just a green hill. But men walk up it, so we do, too.

We reach the crest and look out. Below us, men wearing helmets, construction jumpsuits, and heavy work boots juggle the ball between one another. When one of them heads the ball, helmet making a *tink* sound, Luke sputter-laughs. "This. Is. Beautiful."

YELLOW HELMETS, PLACED two feet apart, form goals. Most players are steelworkers. One man, Babs, is an engineer, the only black engineer and the only engineer who plays football on his lunch break. "I've promised management it won't affect production time," Babs says. "We eat all our lunch on our tea break so that at lunch we can play. It's the only time we've got. We do it for love of this game."

Some men are good, not slowed down by their Timberland-looking boots, and some men aren't. One man with a big gut unclips his work suspenders and calls out in Xhosa, one of the native languages of South Africa, what I imagine is something like, "Here I go." There's the sense that this round-cheeked, round-bellied man isn't normally a player but decided for whatever reason to play today. He toe-blows the ball forward, runs, gets tripped up, tumbles down. He lays there in the grass on his stomach. His smile is huge. It contains embarrassment, shyness, surprise, happiness. It doesn't fade as he struggles back to his feet, doesn't fade as he jogs across the field, doesn't fade the whole time we play.

The half-finished stadium shoots up behind us. We are literally playing in its shadow. Great stage right over our shoulder, our game feels like adult pretend. We mimic greatness, our moves outlandish and exaggerated. When a goal is scored, men dogpile on top of one another.

Twenty minutes in, the lunchtime horn sounds and the game ends.

"You going somewhere with all that skill?" Babs says to me, after we've walked off the field.

I laugh and cross one leg over the other, my flamingo stance, what I always do when I feel shy and uncomfortable.

"I mean it—you going somewhere with all that skill?"

I rake my nails through my hair, that tryout in my mind for the first time since we've been in Africa. "What about you?" I say. "I saw you pirouetting out there. Did you ever want to play?"

He waves his hand. "Nah, not since I was small. I knew I wanted to be an engineer." He grins, leans toward me, adds, "But when the ball comes my way, I still see if I can make up lost moves."

I laugh and ask, "So what's it feel like to build a stadium?"

"Normally I build a shopping mall or an apartment building, so to build the home of soccer, my passion, it is exciting."

I figure he's heard all the talk about South Africa not being done in time, so I ask him, "What do you think about the people who say South Africa won't be ready?"

He shrugs. "You have to be in Africa to say that. The guys who are saying that are the people who've only seen Africa on the TV. But we, the actual guys who are here on the battlefield, we know we'll be ready."

We shake each other's hand and wish each other luck. I walk over to where Ryan and Ferg are interviewing one of the steelworkers. "If I can't play for our national team, at least I can tell my son, 'Your father built this stadium.' I am doing something for my country," the man says. "Sometimes I stand in the middle of the pitch and think, Hey, in 2010, people will be sitting right here."

Men around us restrap their suspenders, scoop up helmets, and walk back to the stadium that will hold the greatest sporting event in the world.

VILLAGE CHAMPIONSHIP

I STAND BEHIND fifteen or so teenage boys on the ledge of an abandoned school in Mafi Sasekpe, a rural village of straw-thatched homes in the Volta region of Ghana, looking out at the game happening on the half-grass, half-dirt field. In front of me, three teenage girls balance ice chests on their heads, selling doughnuts, candies, and soft drinks to the packed sideline. Kids wander up and down, waiting to chase errant balls. At the endline, next to the goal, middle-aged women beat on drums and dance—hips, arms, and maracas shaking. The village elders sit beneath a giant oak tree, too far away from the game to actually see it, but close enough to see the spectacle around it.

It's a village championship, the four local villages gathering for football. I don't know how often these championships occur, but the play happening on the field has the intensity of a game you only play once. I move closer to the sideline, trying to find a few inches of space so that I can have an unobstructed view. Players keep getting wrecked. So much so that I start mentally lauding the term: it *does* look like the high-impact hit of one car crashing into another. Twenty minutes later, when I'm subbed in for an outside midfielder, that is what it feels like. I can hear them coming but I don't see them—just a force clapping down on me. Air knocked out, ball gone, I pick myself up, no idea how I'll make up for that.

Ten minutes later, my oversize jersey puffs out like a sail as I make a streaking run. (I'm sort of floored by my audacity the whole time, thinking, *What, do you think you're going to outrun them?*) It's as though everyone else has been paused and I'm given three seconds of free rein to run along alone. I call for the ball and there it is, bouncing across bumpy grass toward me. Here's where I should shoot. Instead, I pretend to shoot and whirl around. (My urge to dribble—I couldn't keep it down.) While the defender I'm in front of lunges to block my fake shot, two other defenders close in on me from behind. I'm quickly stripped of the ball and dispensed.

Luke fares better than I do. His instincts strong, he moves into whatever style of play the game calls for. That's not to say he adopts the physical acrobatics of the Ghanaians, he just turns to his knack for composure: he knows how to stay calm in the fray. The faster the game gets, the more controlled he becomes, receiving the same bouncy balls that gave me hell, threading passes to his streaking teammates.

He plays so smoothly he convinces the Ghanaians that he has the ability to truly see a game . . . and is therefore the ideal man to officiate the final. They hand him a whistle, a yellow card, and a red card, and send him into the center of the field.

Battlefield, war zone, gladiatorial arena, carnage, bloodshed—the war vocab borrowed by announcers, writers, spectators, and players to describe a game—all of it sounds in my head as I watch. Splayed limbs, one forehead banging into another, soaring, cleats-up tackles, flying bodies everywhere. Broken men keep getting carried off the field. Luke sprints up and down, issuing one yellow card after another—nine in total. To say he loses control of the match would imply he at one time had control; he never did. I don't know if anyone could. The sidelines rage. Because we are staying in Mafi Sasekpe and have friends on the team, the other villages believe Luke is biased. Our friends in Mafi Sasekpe aren't satisfied, either. Since every tackle is crunching and violent, Luke doesn't appear

The shoot-out (Courtesy: author)

to have figured out which ones to let go and which ones to call. I feel like how I imagine the mother of a goalkeeper feels: I cannot bear to watch.

When Luke blows the final whistle, the game is tied, which means Luke will now officiate a penalty kick shoot-out. All villages gather around the goal. Players shoo away the roosters that waddle across the field. Kids sit down next to the penalty takers. The women dance and wave batik-print sarongs above their heads like lassos. It ends with the same crumple and explosion of all shoot-outs, and there's Luke, in the middle of the wild celebrations, whistle still in his lips.

ALL THE SOUNDS of the game starkly contrast with the quiet we find later—two boys making a ball.

Step 1. Walk a mile to the store and buy a pack of one hundred "rubbers," the stretchy bags used to hold sugar.

Step 2. Fill up one bag with water. Then blow into it until it inflates like a balloon.

Step 3. Knot the end and turn the stem inside out, covering the ball.

Step 4. Wrap additional plastic bags over the ball, pulling the plastic tightly. Layer as many times as you can, stretching the plastic until it's tight.

Step 5. Find a sock to cover the plastic. Use a machete to cut off the end.

Step 6. With needle and thread, sew the sock shut.

L.A. AND BUST

ONE DAY WE are in Togo—we hadn't made it all the way across the border before we saw our first game, on the beach a hundred yards to our right, in front of churning ocean, fifteen guys against fifteen others, half the players in Togo, half probably still standing in Ghana—and then the next day we're on a plane, headed away from Africa. You're there; then you're not. Always, I'm shocked by the way the present turns into the past.

I lean my head against the plane window, look at the flight attendant as she talks about seat belts and emergencies, and think about Togo. Big umbrellas and beach shacks lined the sand-caked streets. Women carried heavy loads on their heads, a coiled bandana cushioning the ice chest or laundry basket or sewing machine. Men in tank tops sat in plastic patio chairs, calling out in French, ready to sell doughnuts or drive people wherever they need to go. In the cab, games flew past our window, more per street than any country so far. We craned our necks to see farther down each dusty lane. In front of a whitewashed wall, *COCA-COLA* written in faded, cursive letters, something you would see on a 1940s movie set, we played with teenage boys wearing jelly sandals, and a teenage girl wearing a Drogba jersey. A man rode *un moto* through the center of the game. "Bon soir," he called out, his fingers arched up from the handlebars, dirt clouds rising up behind him. Not wanting our time to end, we played until the sun set, inhaling the salt smell, ball whistling against sand.

WHEN WE LAND in Durham, North Carolina, we say good-bye to our professors and the friends who housed us and then we pack up our cars for Los Angeles, where our producers and future await.

Ryan cuts through the center of the country and gets a speeding ticket in Arizona; Ferg takes the southern route and pops a tire coming out of a campground in New Mexico; and Luke and I take our Montana detour and hit the deer.

After ten minutes standing beneath the streetlight staring at the busted car, we get back on the freeway and limp along in the dark at thirty miles an hour. Two hours later we make it to our exit. Driving down some small rural road, only fifteen miles away from Luke's friend's cabin, we see flashing lights in our rearview mirror. I'm scared of all policemen, sure that I'm seconds away from getting caught at some undefined thing. Luke pulls off to the side while I stare at our speedometer to confirm what I already know: there's no possible way we are speeding.

Because our window does not roll down, Luke opens the car door as the officer approaches. "Stay in the car!" the policeman shouts, his whole body tense, hand on his pistol.

"Broken window," Luke explains to the man who is on full alert, unnerved by the creepy car with one headlight driving thirty miles beneath the speed limit at three in the morning.

"What's going on here?" the officer asks, beaming his flashlight into Luke's eyes.

"We hit a deer."

He nods, face loosening. "That'll happen in these parts," he says. "My wife hit three last month." He tells us to take it to Crash & Repair, deer collision specialists in the morning. He pats the side of the car, tells us to be safe, and we finish inching along toward the cabin.

THREE DAYS, SIX hundred dollars, and one windshield later, we are on our way again, driving through desert. We don't know the economy is beginning to tank on our drive across the country. We also don't know our producer is going through a messy divorce.

When we arrive, Les takes us to a fancy lunch at an upscale Mexican restaurant in Pasadena. On our way, I walk along beautiful streets past women wearing expensive things and try not to feel afraid of the glitter and glam of Los Angeles. I was actually born here, in West Covina, which until now was just a random fact about me I used to sound cool as a kid— I'm a California girl—even though we moved before I was old enough to remember anything. Now I cling to this, like maybe it means I could belong here, that this place isn't as strange as it feels. But I feel less at home here than I did anywhere in the world.

At the patio we sit down one table away from where Steve-O from the *Jackass* TV show is celebrating his birthday. We talk quietly about him, eat chips, and until our food arrives, engage in pleasantries with Les about our drive and the California balm.

I am three bites into my wet burrito when Les breaks the news: "Guys, I'm sorry—but I can't fund the rest of your movie."

RYAN, FERG, LUKE, and I walk away from lunch together. In my head it happens in slow motion, like you see in the movies, four characters wearing sunglasses striding toward something. Only we are striding away from something. I hear the voice of the random guy at the end of *Pretty Woman*: "Welcome to Hollywood! What's your dream? Everybody comes here; this is Hollywood, land of dreams. Some dreams come true, some don't; but keep on dreamin'. . . ."

I feel a weird sense of relief. Having an investor—it had always seemed way too lucky.

We process the new reality together, taking turns filling it out: we are in Los Angeles; we have no way to pay rent; we have no editing equipment. Do we drive back across the country? Could our cars make it? How would we get to Asia? The Middle East? How would we finish the film?

FRANCIS, THE PRODUCER that Les had hired to make sure his money was being well spent, stays with us even though Les can't fund the rest of the film. He calls in favors across the city and sneaks us into studios after hours. One friend of his lets us borrow a computer she won't need for another month. We edit and edit and try to figure out what to do now.

Maybe we just won't go anywhere else. We made it to Egypt and Palestine—that could count as the Middle East. Could we leave out Asia? That's what people suggest—scrap it. Franklin Foer, author of *How Soccer Explains the World,* this century's most famous soccer book, didn't make it there. China, the most populated country in the world, rarely qualifies for the World Cup; in 2002 when they did qualify, they failed to score a single goal. When I research the Asian pickup scene, the Internet turns up only one article in *Time* magazine: "Woes in Asia." An excerpt:

> "In Japan, it's often said that we teach too much," says Yahiro Kazama, one of the few Japanese to have played professionally in Europe. Japanese kids—like others in East Asia—participate in organized after-school soccer, but tend to abandon the sport outside regulation time. "They are good at learning," says Japanese soccer commentator Michel Miyazawa. "But if I ask my son to play with a ball, he seems surprised and says 'Really? Here? Now?'"

Near the end, the article states, "Look around Asia, and the goalposts just aren't there." This is discouraging.

We already have too much footage. It's impossible to go to twenty-odd countries without acquiring more fantastic material than you could ever use. I keep staring into the computer screen at moments I love that I know we will cut. William Faulkner's expression about the need to "kill your darlings" is scrawled across a Post-it note on the corner of our desk. Going to Asia would only make it worse.

But we set out to make a movie about pickup soccer around the world—the entire world. Luke watches J-League highlights every week and swears the Japanese are the most enthusiastic fans he's seen anywhere. I too had seen the slew of Asian supporters at the 2006 World Cup. We don't believe they aren't into it.

LOS ANGELES—LAND of famous people. I see three my first month. There was the *Jackass* guy at the restaurant. Then when I'm at the coffee shop on Wilshire Boulevard trying to write a new fund-raising letter, Jason Alexander walks in. The barista yells, "No coffee for you!" George does a good-sport smile and says, "You got me. . . ." And while Luke and I eat an ice cream sandwich at Diddy Riese, a MINI Cooper zooms up to the sidewalk and Britney Spears steps out. Paparazzi with telephoto lenses trample us as they try to get closer to her. Her friend yells, "Watch out for those people!" We are those people. *I just sort of got protected by Britney Spears,* I think to myself as I lick ice cream.

As I stare at her (and the frenzy of men with telephoto lenses stalking her), I make a mental list of famous people who have soccer inclinations. Drew Carey owns an MLS team; Jon Stewart played soccer at William & Mary; Tina Fey wants all daughters to play sports; Kobe Bryant touts himself as Marta's biggest fan; Steve Nash claims to be the NBA's most skilled soccer player. Maybe one of them is the answer.

After we've edited together a rough cut of what we've got so far, Luke and I drive to a Los Angeles Galaxy training session with the intention of handing our cut to Munoz, a guy Luke grew up playing with who is now on the Galaxy's developmental squad. Our hope is that he might pass it on to Beckham. As we pull into the back entrance of the stadium, we see a Bentley pull out. Luke and I look at each other: why not give it to Beckham directly?

Luke flips a U-turn and we take off after him. I rifle through the console in search of a pen and scrawl my phone number across the DVD case.

At the stoplight, I fight to get out of the car. Our door handle still broken, I have to crawl into the backseat, which is currently occupied by a giant old-school ice chest. I squeeze myself into the narrow gap between the chest and the seat and slide out of the car. I run past the black Escalade in front of us—briefly thinking, *Is that Beckham's bodyguard? Is he going to stop me?*—and up to the Bentley, hoping the light won't turn green before I get there.

When I arrive at his rolled-down window, he's turned around, reaching into the backseat to adjust his kids' seat belts. I wait for him to turn back around, his profile returning to the front. His eyes glance left, land on me, and his whole body jumps.

I stick the DVD of our unfinished documentary through his window. "Can you watch this?" I ask, panting from my sprint through traffic.

I've never fawned over handsome stars before, but when I'm a few inches away from Beckham's face, I'm startled, distracted, thinking, *So, this is why people freak out.* I'm staring at his famous eyes when I notice them glancing at my chest.

I realize I have accidentally put my boobs in David Beckham's face. I'm wearing a lowish tank top, bending down into his window, and they are in his direct line of vision. There is nowhere else for him to look.

I back up and blather, "My boyfriend and I are making a movie about pickup soccer around the world."

He smiles and nods and says "OK" and "OK" and possibly "Cool."

The light turns green. I run back to the Camry, push over the ice chest, and throw myself into the backseat.

On our drive back to Luke's cousin's apartment, I torture myself with replays. I go through all the things I should have said. I could have mentioned the prisoners in Bolivia, the moonshine brewers in Kenya, the eighteen-year-old rappers in France. A movie about my boyfriend and me—that's how I'd described it? And in a hot wave I realize I'd said "pickup"—even though the British say "kick about." Beckham might have no idea what I mean by "pickup." And then there's the working title I scrawled across the DVD: *Footplay*, a title I loved and pushed for. I thought it was whimsical, fresh, playful. But when we were taking votes on a title, someone posted, "Ever typed 'footplay' into Google? Think fetishes. . . ." I sit there, still in the backseat, adding this up. Footplay, pickup, and my phone number: in all likelihood, in his eyes, I am a feverish groupie thrusting him a DVD with God knows what.

Beckham never calls. I don't blame him. We can't get ahold of any other famous people, either. Turns out they're hard to track down; none of our brilliant plans for infiltration work out. So we overstay our welcome at friends' apartments, eat peanut butter sandwiches, film weddings, and answer flyers that say things like "Get paid $100 to drink"—all while we figure out how to finish the film.

Ferg is the one who discovers our chance for a big break (that's the way people talk in Los Angeles—"big breaks" and "long shots" and "jackpots"). She was in the MelroscMac store in Hollywood when she saw the advertisement: "Submit a trailer to win $10,000 of Apple merchandise." She brought back the flyer and we sat around a kitchen table and stared at it, feeling first great hope and then great doubt: what is the likelihood of actually winning a contest?

We make the trailer. While we edit, Luke and Ferg sing lyrics from *Team America*: "We're gonna need a montage/Show a lot of things happening at once/Montage."

The places, people, and games collapse together—the Eiffel Tower, the pyramids, the World Cup workers, the bikini-gods on the sandbank, the gauchos, the diamond-wearing dancer in Marseille, Sireen holding on to her hijab in the parking lot, James standing in front of a trash-strewn bank and saying, "Down here, everybody thinks you're just another drunkard. But when you get to the field, people are saying, '*Oh*, that person can *play*.' " We sit four across the bed and watch it over and over, convinced that even if we don't win the contest, we've got to find a way to finish.

We start asking for money again. None of us can muster the gall to revisit those we've already hit up, which is pretty much everyone we know. Ferg buys a book about fund-raising, and we come up with strategies: we send out a Facebook blast, post a plea on our Web site, and make a tier system of donations—twenty dollars means you are a fan; fifty dollars means you are a player; one hundred dollars, a teammate; five hundred dollars, a captain. We receive donations from strangers within the soccer community who say things like, "Show the world America speaks the same language." By March, we raise eleven thousand dollars in donations and a friend loans us another ten. We feel overcome with gratitude.

In March we find out we're one of ten finalists to win the Melrose-Mac competition. The finalist with the most votes wins. I convince an old coach to give me the log-in info for a server that allows you to send an e-mail to every college coach in the country; Luke and I send so many e-mails our Yahoo accounts are turned off for two days. Soon bloggers come across the trailer. When Soccer By Ives, the most popular soccer blog in the country, puts us on his site, our hits go from thirty-something to six hundred–something in two days. Until the voting window closes, all four of us e-mail everyone we've ever met or heard of and ask them to e-mail everyone they've ever met or heard of. Then we wait.

We book the rest of our plane tickets, even though this is foolish. If we don't win, the money we've raised needs to go toward editing equipment. But our instincts say, *Don't think; just go.*

AT THE TOP

WE SAW A picture of a rooftop soccer court in Tokyo, skyline bright in the background, so we've come to Japan to find it. We have one week.

Music is everywhere, whether you're getting on a subway, crossing the street, or walking through a department store. It's soft music, trance music. We walk through the middle of Shibuya Crossing, keyboard notes ruffling our thoughts as thousands of people—women with trendy haircuts, fingerless gloves, and high-heeled boots; teenage boys with skinny jeans and fluorescent high-tops; and businessmen wielding briefcases—swoop past us, and our search for soccer courts begins.

Maybe the "Woes in Asia" writer—the guy who couldn't find the goalposts—just hadn't looked high enough. We stand on the street corners, craning our necks to the sky, as though we can see to the top of the skyscrapers. The Japanese do not label every street, and we have no address to go off of. We often feel like we're on a massive, sometimes embarrassing scavenger hunt, tapping on shoulders and mumbling broken sentences. "What?" they say, frowning, leaning their heads in so the Americans can try again.

In Tokyo, Luke repeats the sentence he has pieced together through language books and podcasts: "Do you know of any rooftop football courts?" He tries different inflections until he sees comprehension light up a face. This is often followed by a vigorous shake of the head: no, no, they know nothing about *sakka* courts.

Luke talks to schoolgirls in uniform, who giggle when he speaks. In front of a row of restaurants, he tries two men wearing sandwich boards that advertise daily specials. Luke hits his syllables, but they just frown at him. "Biergarten?" they ask, as though, in their experience, this is what most tourists are looking for.

Then Luke tries a guy with a mohawk and leather jacket who is selling gold jewelry that glitters with the flash of Tokyo's lights. The man pulls a notepad out of the back pocket of his jeans and starts to make us a sketch. He gives us directions very slowly, using his hands to reinforce the Japanese directional terms that Luke has memorized. We follow the turns as far as we can and then we ask again: "Do you know where there are rooftop courts?"

A businessman in suit and tie smiles at us and says, "Ahh." He points his briefcase up into the air. "Field."

DOWN ON THE street, we weave through the throng to the rotating glass door of a department store. We walk past Prada bags, Chanel counters, and ladies sampling perfume, and then we board an elevator, standing next to tired shoppers who empty out floor by floor until we reach the top.

The doors open to reveal businessmen wearing well-cut suits and deep blue scarves, leaning back against park benches. They're smoking cigarettes, unrolling soccer socks, and slipping off dress shoes. Changing out in the open, they take off their slacks and undo their button-downs, donning long-sleeve replica jerseys, warm-up pants, and winter gloves. They jump up and down to shake out the cold.

Behind them—two *sakka* courts cloaked in netting that prevents the ball from soaring off the edge. The man behind the counter explains it to us: in Tokyo, because space is at a premium, the courts are snuck up onto the rooftops. Men come to play at the top of the city. Surrounded by the peaks of skyscrapers, it's a pocket of quiet up here, the busy crossings and electronic signs a distant blur down on the ground.

It's not cheap to rent a court at the apex of Tokyo, and it's not something the men we play with do every day. There's the special-occasion feeling, like renting a bowling alley or a skating rink for a birthday party. I watch a guy with thinning hair clap his gloved hands together and beam. I think of what a coach once told me: "You need to smile more as you play." He was right—I rarely smiled. When my high school team put "Girls Just Want to Have Fun" on our warm-up tape, I couldn't believe it. I did not just want to have fun.

On the AstroTurf court, my teammates throw their heads back and laugh at mistakes. They laugh when they score; they laugh when someone else scores. There's no cursing, anger, or frustration. I try it out. I blow hot air onto my cold fingertips and smile. I think, *I am in Tokyo, playing with salarymen, on top of a skyscraper.*

But I also think about the tryout. In one fast go, I filled out the player application form for the newly revived U.S. pro league and pressed Submit before I could change my mind.

The idea of a tryout feels a little counterintuitive, regressive, and shameful: I've spent two years meeting people who are playing for no other reason than to play, people who don't need a league . . . and now I'm going to go tryout for one? It seems undignified; there are stay-too-long-at-the-party undertones. But, if I don't go, I worry that I'll look back on it as a chickenshit move. I don't want to quit without having tried.

I'd received the e-mailed invitation: "Congratulations on your selection to participate in the Women's Professional Soccer Player Combine at the U.S. Olympic Training Center. This event provides general managers, coaches, and scouts an opportunity to evaluate your talent before the Women's Professional Soccer Draft." It's one more chance to play with my heart in my throat.

THE LAUGHTER ON the courts in Tokyo doesn't mean the game matters less. "I work all day long, from seven A.M. to nine P.M. Sometimes I sleep at the office," Kenji says to the camera once our game is over. "So the time I spend here is all I've got."

While the men shower in the locker room, I sit on a bench between the courts. I can hear the faint sound of an automated voice: "Thank you for visiting Mitsukoshi Department Store." The smell of beef wafts up from the food court. Two benches down, a man wearing a heavy wool topcoat over a suit and tie smokes a cigar, briefcase in his lap as he looks out at the courts. He's a little older than the guys we are playing with, maybe fifty. His face is serious. I catch eyes with him as he exhales, smoke puffing out from his mouth. Something about him is compelling.

When I ask if we can talk to him about what the game means to him, he nods, face still solemn.

"To play in Tokyo, you must pay money in places like this. It is expensive," he says slowly. He puts his hands in his coat pockets and looks down, comes back up smiling. "I work. To earn money. Only so that I can kick a ball. Soccer is the center of my life."

AFTER WE LEAVE the court, Ryan, Ferg, Luke, and I drink warm sake and eat rice with Kenji and Hiroki, who stare at my hands as I maul my chopsticks. This apparently is very funny. Hiroki tries to fix my fingers. My rice chunk splashes down into soy sauce. "But it's easy," he says, out of breath. "So easy."

Later that night Luke and I wander off on our own, arms linked as we stare up at neon lights. At the subway station, I follow Luke through the turnstile and wait on the platform for him to tell me where to go. "Why don't *you* figure it out this time," he says. I slow up, smile, try to make myself look lovable.

"Do it," he says.

I stare at the sign and pick at my mittens. I have no idea where we're staying.

"Just tell me," I say.

"No," Luke says. "You can figure it out." He thinks I self-handicap. I guess I probably do. But I'd have a hard time with a subway map in

New York City, let alone a subway map written in a script that looks to me like squiggly lines and houses. There's not going to be any "figuring it out."

Train after train comes and we just stand there, watching them leave.

"You have a fifty-fifty chance," Luke says. "Which side of the platform do we belong on?"

Finally I just point at one side.

"No," he says, leading me over to the other.

Can't learn new languages, understand directions, or maneuver two wooden sticks . . . but I'm excellent with the ball at my feet.

THE FUTURE

AK IS A twenty-eight-year-old Chinese man who gave up a highly paid, highly respected job as a banker so that he could have more time to work on his football tricks. I want to say that while I watch him juggle the ball on his shins, it's hard for me to imagine him wearing a business suit and sitting at a desk, but that's not true—I can easily imagine it. Maybe he could, too: like us, he's at that age where you can be funneled in directions you're not sure you want to go. Maybe that's part of what led him to tell a disbelieving father that his adult son wanted to become a street soccer player.

Several years ago, AK saw a YouTube video of various freestylers. He enjoyed watching them so much that he started trying tricks himself. Every day he spent hours mastering the moves he saw on the computer screen and then inventing his own. He became arguably the best street-baller in China. I came across his homemade video when I googled "Asia + street soccer." I e-mailed his YouTube account and had a response one hour later: "Come! I will show you street soccer!"

We land in Shanghai in the middle of a record-setting stretch of rain. Men use brooms to sweep the water off sidewalks. It's the dead of winter, though we haven't planned or packed much differently than we did for summertime. In Tokyo, we were American ragamuffins—layering our T-shirts, each wearing our one packed sweatshirt over and over again. In Shanghai, we're wet, all layers soaked.

Playing in the warm rain of summertime is different than playing in the rain when it's thirty-five degrees outside. Ferg and I buy tights, and Luke and Ryan wear jeans beneath their warm-up pants. The four of us huddle beneath the umbrella we check out from our hotel. (Ryan believes umbrellas bring out the worst in people: you see selfishness loud and clear as you're jabbed in the eye, doused with repelled water, or nudged off the sidewalk. Being tall, Ryan is especially susceptible to the hazards of oncoming umbrellas.)

AK—who is five feet seven, stocky, and dressed in a black hoodie splattered with neon flecks—takes us to his favorite spots to play across Shanghai. He does tricks in the center of People's Square; in front of the Mao statue at East China Normal University; on the psychology building's pyramid-shaped stairs; inside the pagoda of a traditional Chinese garden while an old man fishes with a bamboo stick in the neighboring lily pond. Some people stop to watch, and some avoid him like one might avoid a bird lady.

The kaleidoscope of scenery and motion, the sweat on his face, his hot breath in the cold air—it all reminds me of a sequence from *Rocky*. Except AK isn't training for anything: there is no fight or game to win. He pushes himself for the sole sake of artistry. "It is very fun to get better," he says, which is finally something I can understand.

AK HAS A small following of guys who meet him in public places— anywhere they think people will see—and perform tricks. On Saturday, we meet at the small amphitheater outside the downtown metro station. (They know all the spots in the city where they can play without hassle from the police.)

Every freestyler has his own style: one guy's specialty is a kung-fu infused ball dance; another guy's a master of the "around-the-world," in which the foot somehow makes a full circle around the ball while it stays up in the air. He used the trick to woo his wife; she told him she'd marry him if he could do ten in a row. A small sixteen-year-old wearing a black I ♥ SHANGHAI T-shirt and baggy jeans is a relative beginner and has not mastered a full range of tricks, but his around-the-worlds are tight and clean. He and his friend wear earbuds and periodically trace out dance moves. In order to improve their streetballing rhythm, they've taken up Crip Walking. In the same way the Brazilians wove the hip sway of the samba into their *futebol,* they want Crip Walking to inflect their tricks. It's a funny thing to stand in Shanghai, watching a sixteen-year-old try a dance that originated from a 1970s Los Angeles gang.

Of course, I can't do their tricks. I can't do half a trick. Even Luke is floundering, and he at least knows how to do things like the around-the-world, even though he wouldn't call it that because he doesn't believe in naming moves. When I say things like "scissors" and "foundation," he makes a face. He doesn't like the idea of learning a prescribed set of movements. He thinks every move should be unique and unpredictable, not something you can fit into a word. Luke has a similar approach to driving: he knows where he has to go and takes a new route to get there every time, following instincts. I only trust instincts if they've been honed by experience.

I stand behind AK as he does his move again in slow motion. "Try," he says. "You can do it."

It's been a solid ten years since I've set out to learn a move. I vaguely remember a Sunday-afternoon practice and a circle, the fear of something I didn't know how to do but dribbling into the middle and doing it anyway. Maybe as we get older and rule out what we're not good at, there are fewer face-to-face encounters with looking stupid.

Inside the Shanghai amphitheater, moving my legs in awkward, unfamiliar patterns—and invariably getting it wrong—looking stupid is hard to avoid. I wait it out until it's time to go to the neighboring park and play for real . . . and see if their juggling moves can translate to the game, to the kind of soccer I know how to play.

WE WALK IN a pack to a cement courtyard in front of a statue. AK asks the man reading his newspaper on the bench if he wouldn't mind moving to a different bench so that we can make a goal under the one he's sitting on. AK fishes juice bottles out of the garbage can and sets them up a couple feet apart. "Now we play two-v-two."

I'm good at two-v-twos. I am as tricky with the ball on the ground as they are with it in the air. I have twenty years of practice, twenty years of ritual. Everything comes out of me on its own.

I figure that a freestyler's focus on making pretty dollops with the ball would mean they weren't competitors. I set out for hard tackles, cold-blooded finishes, and redemption. Watching YouTube videos isn't a recipe for winning.

Luke too is playing for his injured pride. We felt for a second like fakes, people who'd talked our whole lives about game dedication, yet had nothing to offer in that amphitheater.

When our game begins, a guy with one sweatpants leg pushed up comes at me. I strip the ball off him, do a cap move around his teammate, and slide the ball to Luke, who taps it home. We dispatch the first pair in fifteen seconds. When the next set comes on, Luke pretends he's going to wail it through the juice bottles, making the kid slide across the cement, sprawling out to cover the goal, only Luke doesn't shoot it—it's still at his feet. He taps it in.

There's the laughter again—thunderous. All the freestylers are sitting on the steps. They've told us that they're as keen for the meg as they are for a goal, so Luke megs guy after guy. He's making up moves. He stands one-footed on top of the ball, and when the guy goes to kick it out from under him, he slips it between the gap in the guy's legs. It's pretty incredible.

Luke and I hold the court, beating pair after pair until AK and the wife-wooing juggler are up. I guess I should've realized a guy who skips class and spends eight hours playing in the rain isn't going to be bad with the ball. His feet are faster than the Brazilians', maybe faster than the kid's in Marseille. It's still mostly performance: he pulls the ball back and forth, back and forth, without really going anywhere. (Having spent years dribbling nowhere, I can't pass judgment.) He megs me twice. "Yes!" he cries, unabashedly joyful. He roars, each puff of laughter visible in the cold air. He laughs so hard I laugh, too.

Families watch us, not with the passive expression we've seen in most places—people watching the sport they've watched their whole lives—but with surprise, delight: What is this? What is happening? A cluster of old men, probably card players who have just finished their game on the tables on the other side of the park, smoke cigarettes and watch with their hands behind their backs, their mouths gaping open any time they see a trick. There's a gray-haired woman wearing a turtleneck whose eyes dart from the game to the row of guys laughing; she can't stop smiling, can't quit watching, even though you can tell she was on her way to somewhere. One father holds the hand of a son who is young enough to still be a little unstable on his feet. The kid wears a red Manchester United hat, and the dad looks exuberant, shocked to stumble, right here in his own park, upon the game he's trying to show his son.

THAT NIGHT, AK takes us to a dark pool hall near his house to celebrate Luke's twenty-seventh birthday. We shoot pool, drink rice liquor, and get philosophical. About the comparative politics of the United States and China, AK says, "It's not that different. We don't like our government. You don't like the other party. Everyone blames someone." About the difference between his street game and a full game: "Why on earth would I want to run all over the field when I can just do tricks? Be happy?" About getting older: "To be honest, I am twenty-eight. It's probably time for me to get a new job, to start a family."

Luke and AK lean against pool cues, both looking broodingly into the space in front of them. "You two will get married?" AK asks.

"No," Luke says, smiling at me.

I hit him. AK laughs.

"What about you, AK?" I ask. "Will you marry your girlfriend?"

He frowns. "We are in a fight. She is angry. She does not like my street soccer. She ask me to choose. You are very lucky, Luke, very lucky to have soccer girlfriend."

We sometimes forget about the grace of sharing soccer, as unlikely as that sounds. Even though we met on a field, soccer somehow feels entirely peripheral.

"Maybe I will go to Canada, to learn English better. Maybe I will do accounting," AK says, grinding his cue tip into chalk.

Luke sips rice liquor and nods supportively. He peppers AK with follow-up questions: Why Canada? How will you get there? Will you keep freestyling? Luke says nothing about his own map for the future.

I know he's thinking law school. He bought a book called the *LSAT Logic Games Bible*. Before we left for Asia, he set his alarm for 6 A.M. and sat at his cousin's breakfast table for three hours every morning, tackling studying with an athlete's discipline. I drank out of my huge coffee cup and stared at him from the armchair on the other side of the room, resisting the urge to tease him, to make fun of his thick lawyer bible, his heavy breathing, the way his whole forehead creased as he scribbled answers in margins.

I'd never want to be lawyer, not ever. So it's hard for me to believe that's what he really wants. I've grilled him about this, rolled over in bed and said, "Are you *sure*?" I don't want him shriveling up on me. I worry that a desk strewn with cases he doesn't believe in will kill off the intangible thing I love about him.

He's not planning to practice the kind of law he doesn't believe in. He's self-conscious about his idealism and won't talk about his intentions. And he still has the parable of the two sons ingrained in him: if he talks about all he's going to do, he might not actually do it.

At midnight, we hold up our cups of rice liquor, sing "Happy Birthday" to Luke, and say, "To the future. . . ."

WELCOME TO IRAN*

A WEEK LATER, we are back in California, sitting at an In-N-Out Burger, eating Double-Doubles and drinking sodas out of cups rimmed with palm trees. Ali, pronounced like the fighter, not like the girl's name, had Facebooked Luke several weeks earlier: "I hear you're going to play in Iran! We Iranians are such football lovers! I will tell you everything you should look for!" Now he sits across from us, wearing a shark-tooth necklace and running his hands through long wavy hair.

He's only been in the United States a year, but he speaks perfect English. "Satellite TV—*Friends,* Chandler, Monica—that's how we all learn English," Ali explains matter-of-factly. "Now, on to the football!" He scribbles Farsi soccer terms and the phonetic equivalents into my notebook. "You must look for a 'dough-lay-year.' It is a ball special to Iran. Children buy twenty-five-cent rubber balls from drugstores and rip them open, then stuff them inside each other so the rubber gets thicker and the ball gets heavier." He draws a picture of a ball next to the word. Then he writes out a list of phonetic sentences that we can use later: "Do you

* *Some names in this chapter have been changed.*

know where we can find soccer?" "Can I play with you guys?" "Is it OK if she plays, too?"

When I tell my mom we're going to Iran, she says, "No you are not." Luke's grandma says, "Turkey's a beautiful country—why don't you go there?" And Luke's aunt tells me over the dinner table, "You know, over there, they stone women for adultery. When you try to play, what do you think they will do to you?"

We never really expected to be able to go. We made a few phone calls just to see, just to rule it out so we wouldn't always wonder if we could've gone to Iran. The first two tour groups that came up after we googled "Iran + travel + agency" told us no right away. They could take us to museums, to the Towers of Silence and the Zoroastrian Fire Temple, but they could not let us wander the streets filming pickup games. For that, we would need a press visa. Rick Steves—travel writer / TV personality extraordinaire—barely got approved for a press visa. There was no way the Iranian government would give them to four kids who'd only made school documentaries about ferret-lover clubs and college sports teams.

The last company we called wasn't really a company. It was just a guy, an anthropology professor in San Francisco who helped people get to Iran because he wanted them to know the country the way he did. "Excuse me, Gwendolyn," he said, saying my name right away, as though he'd known me forever. He sneezed hard into the receiver. "I have a horrible cold, but please tell me what I can do for you."

Jerry said, "Sure, sure" and "Of course" as I explained our film and what we wanted to do. "Well, you know," he sniffed, "the people of Iran love their football." And, yes, we would have to go with a tour guide, and, yes, we had to have a set itinerary approved by the government . . . but one does not always have to follow the itinerary. "I will call Ahmadreza—he is the head of an Iranian tour company. I will see. . . ."

ONE MONTH LATER we land in the Tehran Imam Khomeini International Airport. Ahmadreza, as it turns out, has a son who considers himself Manchester United's number-one fan. A series of e-mails with the subject line "The Sports Enthusiasts" ended in a visa approval and the implicit understanding that these four Americans were coming to look for soccer. There would be the appearance of a tour, and we would be assigned a guide. "Everything depends on whom you get as your guide," Jerry said. "Not only must you trust him but he must trust you."

Like every other female on the flight, I'd wrapped my hair in a hijab fifteen minutes before touchdown. (Rebekah and I had watched how-to-wear-a-hijab videos on YouTube.) My hijab is actually a pashmina, normally worn over the shoulders, but wrapped around my head, it looks the same as any other scarf. Over jeans, I'm wearing a long-sleeve shirtdress I bought at Target. Ferg is wearing a fitted navy blue trench coat. We feel rather impressed with ourselves by how much we've managed to look like everyone else. Somehow, this is important to us—we always want to belong.

Standing in line at customs, I'm nervous. When it's my turn in front of the glass booth to face the officer, I smile up at him, even though this is exactly what I told myself not to do: *Persian Odyssey,* the book I'd read on Iranian culture, said women aren't supposed to make eye contact with strangers. I quickly look down at my feet . . . until he begins to speak, and then I forget again and look right into his surprisingly apologetic face. "I am very sorry but we must take your fingerprints," he says. "It is stupid, I know, but your country does it to us, so we must do it to you."

He ushers us—Ferg, Ryan, Luke, and me—over to a holding area where we wait to be fingerprinted with the other Americans. Everyone back home treated us like we were leaving for a distant, dark corner of the earth, so we feel melodramatic as we sit on the airport floor with fifty-five-year-old tourists going on adventure sports tours. A burly man with a twitchy face and hairy forearms tells me, "I've heard the hiking here is out of this world." He begins to speak "backpacker," something about trailheads and river rapids. I wonder why he is here: surely he didn't need to come to Iran to go hiking. Is he an adrenaline junkie looking for a new kind of high, or someone with a true desire to see a place for himself? It's a question I guess I should ask myself.

Then I'm called into an office where a woman in chador—the long black robe that covers a woman's body from head to toe—grabs my hand and pries apart my fingers, placing each one firmly down upon a glasslike plate. My sweaty fingers elude the print receptor, so she repeats each hand several times. I'm the last in our group to be released. When I come out, the other three hop up from their sprawling floor positions. Together we ride the escalator to the bottom floor, where our bags and guide are waiting.

BEFORE WE LEFT, I imagined our guide—the man who'd be helping us skirt Iranian law—as a roguish rule-breaker with a provocative grin and stance. He'd grab our bags from the carousel with an authoritative, casual swoop. A buzzed head, old faded T-shirt, you'd be able to see right away that he was a player, good on the field.

But the man standing before us, with four roses and a clipboard, is thin and rather frail looking. His shoulders are narrow. He's wearing a Tommy Hilfiger polo shirt and designer jeans, and, to be honest, he looks like somebody who'd scare easily. He has wavy brown hair, big green eyes, a big nose, and expensive eyeglasses. I smile at him, feeling guilty for my disappointment. He waltzes toward us, bent slightly forward, arms crossed in front of his chest, fingers grasping the sides of his arms. His chin moves side to side as he talks, an involuntary no: "Welcome to Iran. I am Atef."

Atef leads us over to a man standing on the curb. "This will be our driver, Saeed." Ryan and Luke shake his hand, and Ferg and I wave. Saeed has the kind of face you trust—gray eyebrows and mustache, brown eyes, bashful smile. He hurries off to retrieve his taxi, and we wave good-bye to the adventure-tour Americans. Then Atef asks, "So, what would you like to do while you are here?"

I study his face, looking for football, for some awareness that that is why we are here. I'm thinking of the San Fran professor, how he repeatedly urged us to follow the unspoken way of doing things in Iran. Maybe what Atef wants is a conversational commitment to an itinerary none of us intend to follow.

"Football," I say, casually, quickly, lobbing out the word.

"Football?" he says with a half laugh, a polite sort of bluff—unsure, it seems, if the American is making a joke that doesn't translate.

Atef knows nothing about any football.

Ryan, Ferg, and Luke turn and look at me. I am the one who set this up; I am the one whose fault it will be if we spend the week inside museums.

"Ahmadreza, Ahmadreza," I say. "The head of the tour company—he knows about the football."

"Ahmadreza? I do not know any Ahmadreza."

I pull out the chart of phone numbers we'd made for ourselves and point to his name, hoping I'm just butchering the pronunciation so badly he can't recognize it. He shakes his head and looks up at me. "I do not think this person exists."

OUR TAXI IS a slime green VW van with big rectangular windows. There's great light coming in on all sides, reflecting off the white vinyl seats. Over the past three years, the four of us have reversed down a main highway in both Trinidad and Peru, wrecked a taxi in China, and hydroplaned during a violent storm across a mud road in the Amazon, but we've never seen anything like the scene on the streets of Tehran. It's a kind of communal dance: an old woman walks into the center of the road and holds up her hand with the authority of a traffic cop, cars screeching to a halt in front of her; motorcycles cant like sailboats in high wind as they zoom in between the taxis; wide boulevards converge upon one another, old Peugeots all going in different directions. Tehran has fourteen million people, and it feels like they are all out on the street.

Drivers move at the same speed as those on foot, and everyone talks to one another, screaming over the loud sounds of construction. There are tall buildings the same color as the heavy smog that blocks the view of the Alborz Mountains. I keep my window down, wanting to hear everything, but the pollution that Tehran is famous for is very real. My eyes burn as I stare out at the women who pass by, some clad in the full

chador, some wearing skimpy, brightly colored scarves that seem provocative, accessories to brightly colored faces, rouge streaked across cheeks,
thick liner defining red lips. I see some of the thinnest, most aggresively
plucked eyebrows I've seen in my life. Even more startling are the bandaged noses that keep passing by. Luke, keeper of a wide collection of
random facts, told me Iran was the nose-job capital of the world, but I
hadn't really believed him. But the bandaged noses, which, according to
Luke, are status symbols for the wealthy, are as frequent as the police. I
see a female officer in a long robe usher a woman wearing high heels into
the back of a green-and-white squad car. "That's the 'morality police,'"
Atef tells us. The morality police is the arm of the Islamic Revolutionary
Guard Corps that patrols the streets, enforcing the Islamic code of behavior, cracking down on Western-style clothing and hairdos. But the
Tehran youth, like youth everywhere, risk the crackdowns, attempting
to get away with as much as they can.

I brace my knees against the seat in front of me. Our *Iran* guidebook warned that visible signs of Iranian football fever were almost
nonexistent—because the government puts the fields behind brick walls.
So every time we drive by a wall, I sit up very straight and try to see, annoyed that we might be zooming past games, people I'll never know
playing behind walls I can't get through.

Iranians have a reputation as the most courteous people in the world,
never wanting to disappoint a guest, never wanting to tell you no; maybe
this is why Atef decides he's willing to let us look for games. It helps that
Saeed was a player. From the driver's seat he speaks in fast, enthusiastic
Farsi, which Atef translates: "Saeed grew up playing in the streets. He
loves football."

Saeed tells us that nowadays, the alley games are dying out, traffic and
construction eliminating the small safe places you could play. In nearly
every country we go to we hear this—people frowning, voices thickly nostalgic, speaking of old ways and games that disappear. But there are still
fields, and after twenty years of driving the city, Saeed knows where to find
them.

• • •

ON THE FIRST field he shows us, there are some young kids practicing. This is not the kind of soccer we are looking for, but we get out and watch anyway. The boys wear their shorts very high, shirts tucked in, and for some reason this makes them look innocent, swaddled. Saeed frowns, knowing this isn't what we're after. He taps Luke on the shoulder and points to a gym abutting the field. We follow him inside a great brick building.

Men, presumably dads, stand in the entrance, watching young boys dribble soccer balls around cones. The cavernous ceilings echo the sound of feet drumming against wooden floor. One of the onlookers—he reminds me of Jack Arnold, Kevin's dad from *The Wonder Years*—eyes us with interest and then speaks to Atef, who does not translate the conversation.

Mr. Arnold comes and stands beside me. "My English is no good," he says shyly, waving his hands. "But it is an honor to have you in our gym."

"Thank you," I say, my mind racing with possibility. I struggle to come up with the Farsi word Ali had taught us for "pickup." Cringing, knowing my pronunciation will be terrible, I ask, "Do you know where we can find 'gol-koo-chik'?"

His head jerks back in surprise. "No, no one plays on the street anymore—we scoop them off the streets and teach them here." He says this with a frown, like he's feeling a little embarrassed, even though he's never been embarrassed of this before. He doesn't like not being able to help us. He stands there, eyebrows furrowed, trying to think if there is anything he has forgotten. "There is a game—in southern Tehran, around midnight. Unbelievable stuff, tricks you haven't seen anywhere."

"It is too late," Atef's voice says from behind me. "As your host, I cannot permit you to go there."

Once Atef has walked away, the man scratches behind his ear and we stand together in silence. Then he says, "Of all the gyms in all the world, I find it incredible that you have walked into ours." It sounds like *Casa-*

blanca and gin joints and fate. I lean my head against the brick wall of the gym and think about that. Probably, I'll never see him again, and probably, this meeting changes nothing. I don't like it when you can only know someone for ten minutes.

As we leave the gym, I catch the end of a conversation between Ryan and Ferg and one of the dads. "You come to my home—I will give you special alcohol," he tells them. He glances around and whispers, "Iran is the largest prison on earth . . . please tell the world."

OUR NEXT STOP is a fake-grass field made from nylon and synthetic-rubber pebbles in the center of Tehran. I feel disappointed seeing the turf, perfect and flat. Coming to Iran, I imagined sand-swept desert terrain, goalposts rising out of dust, alone on the horizon. Instead, it's the same artificial crap replacing real fields everywhere. I could be in Plano, Texas, or Orange County, California. It's like books going on Kindle e-readers: there's no reason to resist, except that I miss the smell and feel of the real thing.

Luke doesn't want me to play. We've been having this fight for the past two weeks and he continues it now. "They've already come to a decision on this," he says. "Are you going to try to change national policy this week?"

"But they haven't come to a decision—it's against the law for women to wear toenail polish, but women still do wear toenail polish."

"It's against the law for you to play—it's illegal."

He's right; it's against the law. But there's a giant fissure between the government's laws and people's actions and beliefs, and not every law is enforced.

A policeman walks up behind us, so I don't push it, and Luke is the only one who tries to get on.

It's a game of teenage boys, same as any group of teenage boys—a little arrogant, a little thrilled with their sudden independence. One kid's T-shirt has a Star of David stitched next to a swastika. Part of me thinks,

Holy shit. But the other part of me thinks he's just a fourteen-year-old kid trying to show how cool and defiant he is, not unlike an American teenager who stitches an ANARCHY patch on his backpack.

Joining a game is about picking your moment. You don't want to go up to them when they're in the middle of the action. You wait for a window of opportunity—when teams are switching halves or taking a break or when someone's just skyrocketed the ball and is now off to chase it. When Luke sees two kids sit down, jiggling their calves and gulping down water, he takes off, jogging up to the game and climbing through the hole in the netting that surrounds the field. He's learned how to say "Can I play?" in fifteen languages, but the boys know what he wants before he asks, grabbing his shoulder, introducing themselves, and sticking him on a team, all without a word from Luke.

Ryan films the game, while Ferg films me watching the game from the sidelines. They goof around—not great soccer players, just happy ones. Watching them play, I don't see any staunch adherence to rules; I don't think they'd care if I play.

Luke blasts a shot and the keeper deflects it away, right to the feet of another guy, who finishes it soundly into the back of the net. The guy sprints at Luke, jumping onto his back and celebrating wildly, legs wrapped around Luke's waist, arms flying high in the air.

WHEN WE ARE back in the van, Luke sits next to me, loose and relaxed as the smoggy Tehran air blows in through the windows. Iran, for Luke, is a changed place. When you play, you get to know people in a way that isn't possible from the sideline. His blond hair, damp from effort, sticks straight up, and his face is red and sweaty: he's happy. And in this state of happiness, I know he's less convinced the world's going to end if I try to play.

When we arrive at a field on the eastern side of Tehran, close to the neighborhood Saeed grew up in, I stand next to Luke and say, "I could try to play."

He doesn't flinch. "We can ask," he concedes.

We begin to walk up to the gate, but I hesitate at the last second and stride as fast as I can back to Atef, who hasn't gotten out of the van: "Do you think it's OK if I ask if I can play?"

"Why are you asking *me*?" he says, smiling.

I laugh uncomfortably and stammer, "I mean, will I offend them if I ask to play?"

"Sure you may ask, but I do not know what they will say. Maybe they say no, maybe they say yes," he says, shrugging, not getting out, as though staying in the car might ward off implication.

Holding on to my hijab, I run to catch up with Luke, who is standing outside the fence. He looks nervous. It's not easy to approach strangers in a foreign language.

When the ball goes out of play, he speaks his learned sentence: "Can I play?"

The players, a mix of old and young, welcome him to the field, their hands waving him forward. He walks halfway out and says, flustered, in English, as though he's forgotten they speak Farsi, "Can she play, too?"

His question is swallowed by a general excitement. Men from both teams are hanging on to Luke's arm, and kids along the sideline are yelling what we'll find out later means "Golden-haired man!"

He tries again, this time pointing at me: "Can she play, too?" I shuffle forward.

"Yes, yes," they answer, but I hang back, waiting to make sure they understand.

An old man wearing a matching nylon warm-up suit jogs up to me and hands me a green pinny. (Funny how all over the world, in every country we visit, teams are divided with these same silly pinnies, little shrunken basketball jerseys.) I'm nervous putting it on. I pull it over my head, imagining myself accidentally pulling down the hijab and my hair spilling out. So worried about the head hole, I manage to overlook the armholes. A man strides over to me and lifts the pinny so that my left arm goes through the appropriate hole. *An Iranian man just helped me get dressed,* I think to myself as the game begins.

Ryan's in the center of the field, crouched down over the camera. In Trinidad he'd stayed along the sideline, not wanting to get in the way, but sometime in the middle of our month in Brazil, he'd ventured onto the field, whimpering slightly but holding the camera steady as players and the ball flew directly at him and the lens, allowing the viewer to see what the game looks like from the inside. Now, he walks toward me and waits for me to say something to the camera, some interesting observation. I have no idea what to tell him. "It's so hard to keep the head scarf on," I say. "And it's impossible to see out your sides—no peripheral vision." He lowers the camera, looks at me like, *You're playing in Iran and that's all you can come up with?*

In many ways, it feels like any game—familiar, easy. The players grew up on neighboring alleys and have played together for twenty-five years. Everywhere we travel, the field seems to be the place where people are most themselves, and here, on the eastern side of Tehran, this feels especially true. When a man on my team scores a diving header, he sprints around the field, miming the celebrations of the professional players, pretending that he is going to take off his shirt. Of course, he doesn't. He jumps into the arms of a teammate, who then falls down. I didn't expect horseplay; I don't know why not.

I'm careful not to touch anybody. Normally, when I go in for a tackle, I'm physical: my hand is on the back and my body is aligned so I can react quickly in any direction. But here, I'm conscious of avoiding touch. I fish for the ball, extending my reach the way you might angle for an object in a river while keeping one foot on the bank. Against Luke, though, I'm not careful. When the ball shoots out toward us, we both accelerate forward; he turns left and I turn right, and my body hits his hard. It's contact I never would have noticed, but now it feels electric.

The Iranians pass the ball to me more than anyone had in any other country. Even when I make no attempt to put myself in any sort of advantageous position, still, they pass it to me. If they are scandalized by my presence, they're careful not to show it. The old man in the nylon jumpsuit who helped me with my pinny appears delighted by me, like I'm the most interesting teammate he's had since the revolution, as if this game and my presence remind him of the past. I imagine him in the park, playing with his daughters. If he lived in the United States, he'd be the kind of dad who did not miss a single game. He'd be in the bleachers, clapping until his hands hurt, walking out of the stadium holding his daughter's shoulder. He cheers whenever I do something good or even when I try and fail to find him with a pass. He seems to be wanting this for me, happy at the chance to see an exercise of freedom that, in his lifetime, had been taken away.

When the game ends, the players take a picture. They don't ask me to be a part of it. I watch from a few feet away as the Iranians wrap their arms around Luke's neck, joking with him, smiling for the camera. After-ward, they smile, nod in my direction, and say something to me, although Atef doesn't translate. He is rigid along the sideline, arms crossed in front of his chest. It's raining and he is cold, wet, and distinctly uncomfortable with our cameras and my presence on the field.

Later that night, while I'm lying in bed in the hotel room trying to sleep, I think about a woman in full chador who walked by the field at the end of the game. What did she think, seeing me? She was definitely look-ing; I thought I saw a smile. But maybe I didn't. Maybe she was thinking, *Who does that American think she is, coming into my country and brazenly joining in, breaking the laws that prevent me from playing?* The chasm be-tween these two possibilities bothers me. It feels wrong to play with men when it's not OK for the Iranian women to do the same; it feels like an unfair privilege. I don't want to play just because Iranians can't say no.

THE NEXT MORNING we visit the main bazaar in the center of Teh-ran. Beneath a vaulted stone ceiling, vendors pedal hand-knotted rugs, exotic spices, electronics, and copper hookahs. We follow behind Atef. There are benefits to a guide: he is able to tell us that the electronic sign flashing Farsi script advertises bridal gowns for sale, and that's the kind of detail we miss while we're roaming other countries on our own. But I don't like being led around. Maybe I get it from my dad, who disappeared during trips to the grocery store, wandering aisles alone. As a kid, this was exasperating—standing with Mom at the checkout counter, Dad nowhere to be found—but now I adopt this approach, drifting as far as possible away from our guide, out on my own.

In the rug alley, vendors attempt to seduce us into their shops. Not wanting to lead anybody on, I leave and lean over the railing of the balcony, staring down below at the wave of people drifting through the corridor.

A handsome man with wavy hair, brown eyes, and a stubbled face strolls up to me. In English, he says, "Soccer—it is soccer you want, correct?"

I nod, my hands rapping against the ball I'm holding, worried that this will somehow end with rugs.

He leans down on the rail, pointing across the way. "There—there is a fire station," he says, exhaling cigarette smoke. "In the afternoons, they play until there is a fire." He smiles at me. "Follow me," he says, as Atef comes darting up, panicked.

"You . . . I always lose you!"

STANDING IN THE opening of the station, I'm again a bystander as the firemen talk to Luke. In Italy, this also happened, but while the Italians treated me like the destroyer-of-man-space, the Iranians seem only shy, respectful. I am not their wife or sister, so they have no right to talk to me. They glance briefly at me before their gazes flutter away. Luke and the firemen talk Champions League and hand balls and goals of the century, acting it all out in what looks like an enthusiastic game of charades, when Atef, who'd been talking on the cell phone in the corner, comes walking back toward us. I can see from the hang of his face that something in that phone call has made things change.

Before the call, I'd go as far as to say he was buoyant; the mixture of indifference and anxiety that had plagued him since we'd arrived and inquired about soccer had momentarily lifted. Atef didn't like soccer; he'd told us that on the first day, when he'd crossed his legs like an academic, pushed his glasses up on his nose, and frowned at the game. I'd thought to myself, *Great. We managed to land the one twenty-six-year-old in the country who doesn't like football.*

But the firehouse was different for him. In Iran, Atef had explained, it is an honor to receive the fireman position. The majority of them are former professional athletes who, once past their prime, receive the position as a gift from the government. So there Atef was, hanging out with the gods of his country. Huge men, men out of fables. And you could tell he thought it was cool.

Now Atef is walking toward us incredibly slowly, as though he is making giant decisions over the course of his twenty-five-yard walk, trying to figure out what he will tell us and how much he will tell us. He's got doom on his face.

"You have been reported to the government," he says.

ATEF, SAEED, AND I sit down together on the bench. Atef is clammy, wiped out. He doesn't know what to do. He doesn't want to ruin this for us. So he just sits with his legs crossed, biting his fingernails, as Luke and the firemen begin to play.

Firemen are government officials, so there's no chance I could play with them, but sitting on a bench outside the station, I don't even feel like trying. Atef's not sure what happened or why we got in trouble. It could be because of our cameras; it could be because I played. I feel naive, like I may have ruined the trip for everyone. We spent ten thousand dollars we didn't have in order to come here, and Atef's face says we aren't taking our footage with us. Maybe he's just letting us film now because he knows we won't get to keep the tapes anyway. Everybody told us not to come, and we didn't care. We didn't believe them. But I never really understood that we could end up with nothing.

I sit on the sideline in the courtyard, sipping tea, watching the light bend down the narrow alleyway, breaking against a gold mosque. Two 1940s-style Mercedes fire trucks are parked behind the goal. A row of lockers line the wall; red helmets and black jackets with iridescent stripes

"Gol-koo-chik" in the fire station at the Tehran bazaar (Courtesy: author)

around the sleeves are hung on hooks, boots scattered below. On the other side of the field, men in old-fashioned leather jackets lean against tilted motorcycles, smoking cigarettes, eyes tracking the ball.

They are playing with the *dough-lay-year,* the ball Ali told us about in the very beginning, when Iran was still a distant idea. It is purple, tiny, and light, and I only see how difficult it is to control when it is in front of Luke. While his touch is normally perfect, he struggles with the mini-balloon.

When shots fly high, they land on top of the fire trucks. The men heave themselves up the ladders with the speed and familiarity of any fireman, tossing the ball back down to the game.

When Luke has the ball, one guy calls for a pass: "George Bush! George Bush!"

Luke, startled, sends it to him, a smiling guy who is big and bulky, brimming with muscles and jokes.

The next time the bulky man has the ball, Luke, with the same casual grace with which he'd serve a through-ball, calls out, "Ahmadinejad, Ahmadinejad."

Loud, loud laughter sounds across the field. The bulky guy slaps his hand against his leg, grinning hugely and pointing at Luke as if to say, *Touché, touché.*

The station chief watches the action from the doorway of his office. He has the face and composure of Mikhail Baryshnikov. (My mind keeps doing this, assigning each face an equivalent, so that there's a familiar feel, like I'm meeting people I've known all along.) The fire chief places his thumb under his chin, his index finger against his lips, his other arm folded in front of him. Although he has consented to the game, you can tell he's not a man who lets things slip by.

Luke blasts a shot, which deflects off a defender's leg and rockets into the fire station window, which shatters loudly. We've made it to twenty-three countries without breaking anything, and I regret that this first happens on the property of the Iranian government. I look straight to the chief to gauge his reaction. I don't know what I expected, maybe a frown, a flash of regret for allowing us to play. I didn't expect him to be looking back at me, face full of pleasure as he studies the worry on mine. When our eyes meet, he glances away and walks back into his office with his hands in his pockets, clearly unbothered about the window.

Several plays later, the ball flies out of bounds and I am the closest person. Eager, I trot off after it, holding onto my hijab. I scoop it out of the gutter and volley it, excited to at least show them I know how to kick the ball. I kick it straight into a bush.

Dusk sneaks in and I know our time is limited. Our cameras can't cope with the dark, and Atef can't cope with us being out in the dark. I sit on the bench, itching for interviews but afraid that this will be too much for Atef.

"Atef," I say, voice meek, "do you think we could do just a couple interviews? Just soccer questions?"

While Ferg films the game and Luke plays, Ryan and I nab one of the guys on the bench and take him to a quiet spot behind the fire trucks. We ask him nothing about Iran or the United States, only what soccer means to him. He's an animated guy, open and nostalgic; he grew up playing with his brothers, and he wants to play forever. As he speaks, Atef turns to me. "You know, I must tell them that the government will be reviewing your tapes."

I nod, knowing this is the end of it.

Atef walks over to the office. I watch the chief stand up and wave his hands—the international sign to stop. The game ends. The chief whistles over the man we've been talking to. He's silhouetted from the light of the office, and I can see his arms flail as he talks frantically to Atef. They call Ryan into the office; I follow. "The man wants you to erase the interview tape," Atef explains. "He fears he will lose his job. A fireman is a government official, you know. You are American. It is not good." We erase the tapes, Ryan doing it as quickly as he can, hands fumbling.

On the court, Luke stands in the dark with the other firemen, laughing, clasping each other's arms. I stare at them from the side, leaning my head against the wall next to the broken window. None of the Iranians speak English, and Luke cannot speak Farsi, but you would never know it. This is what the game can do; this is why we're making our movie.

By now it is dark and Atef's distress is at its peak. In the van, he gets phone call after phone call, and we lean over the seats and listen. We're so used to listening to languages we can't understand that we've developed a habit of guessing, almost believing we know what's being said from the rush of words and the flinch of the face.

"What's happening?" I ask.

His eyes dart toward mine as he lets out a disbelieving laugh and then sits quietly, as though I have not asked him anything.

Finally he says, "We will have to go to the government. They want to see your tapes. I fear they will take them."

The rest of the drive home Atef stares out the window. I feel awful about what we've put him through. At one point, he smiles. "I did not want to be a tour guide forever. It is fine."

BACK AT THE hotel, we are planning to meet Bahram, a friend of Ali, our friend in Southern California. Though meeting him is outside the standard tour-group itinerary, it pales so much in comparison to our illicit soccer games that Atef seems fine with it, too wasted to protest. He eyes Bahram, as though assessing whether this is someone who might help him control us. As he leans against the reception desk, he seems relieved to have someone to dish us off on.

Bahram looks like a mad scientist, a young Iranian Einstein—black hair in cottonball-like poofs, wild and enthusiastic hands, round eyeglasses. It is easy to see why Ali and Bahram are friends. Both have a strange mix of rocket-scientist intelligence and surfer cool. Both give off the distinct feeling of happiness: they are keen to see, to hear, to taste, to live.

In English as perfect as Ali's, Bahram tells us, "Atef told me not to tell you, but you're not going to be allowed to film anymore. And he said I'm not to let you leave the hotel." Bahram just waves his hands, unfazed. I'll learn that Bahram loves Tehran, the hulking puzzle of a city, and that these occasional blockades that pop up are nothing more than small obstacles, annoyances he manages to skirt, almost enjoying the maze as he navigates the ins, outs, shortcuts, and ways around.

He sits down on the couch. "I will make you a dough-lay-year," he says. "It has been a long time. To tell the truth, Ali was always the one who made the ball."

TEN MINUTES LATER, Bahram, Ryan, and I are walking through the streets of Tehran. Ryan and Bahram will head to a drugstore in search of the twenty-five-cent balls and then to Bahram's house to make the ball. At the corner of the main intersection, Bahram gives me directions to an Internet café, where I can buy a phone card so that I can attempt to call Jerry, the San Fran professor.

I'm not sure I've ever felt more exhilarated, walking down the sidewalk by myself in Tehran, which, as an American, I'm not allowed to do. The cars are everywhere, a seething, charging mass, and venturing into a crosswalk is no easy matter. I glue myself to two bold women who charge out into the street as though there aren't cars racing at them with no indication of stopping. As I walk, I repeat in my head *right, left, left,* over and over, scared I will forget. I always forget. Here, I know I can't let that happen. I cannot mix up the wide boulevards. My heart thunders. Before he and Bahram had turned off, Ryan had said, "You can do this, can't you? You won't get lost?" He said this at the last second, sort of a joke, and I laughed, as though it were a joke, but it's not a joke, because nine times out of ten, I will get lost.

I find the café easily enough, and buy a card as several people sitting at computers eye me curiously. I hold up my bills, and the guy takes what I assume is the correct amount. I nod, say "Merci," and head back to the hotel.

I don't turn down a wrong street, but it looks as unfamiliar as if I had. I stare at the storefronts, trying and failing to recognize the awnings, the medicine, spices, and appliances in the windows, the slanted Farsi script. I keep walking, knowing my tendency to give up too early. I'm too entrenched in this inner dialogue—*This is the wrong street; no, it's not the wrong street*—to notice that I've passed the hotel, until I see the sunglasses store with sleek, fancy glasses that I've stared at for the last couple of days, fascinated by the posters of suntanned men with windblown hair who look more Californian than Iranian.

I turn around and walk through the glass doors to the hotel, smiling quickly at the hotel man behind the desk but not meeting his eye, afraid he knows I'm not supposed to leave the hotel. I charge up the stairs and plop down on the hotel bed next to Luke, feeling envious as I imagine Ryan inside Bahram's home, drinking tea with his mother as the rest of us sit in our sterile hotel rooms. Luke watches an Iranian soccer game on the TV, captivated and impressed, but my head is out on the street. I get up from the bed and go into Ryan and Ferg's room, where Ferg sorts tapes as she listens to the news. We'd packed double the number of tapes we thought we'd need. The rest of the trip, Ferg makes backup copies in case the government takes the originals.

I lay on the bed, watching the news ticker on the bottom of the screen. Every second piece of news is about the United States. In the van, while we'd driven past murals that said things like DEATH TO THE USA, we'd talked to Atef about U.S.-Iran tensions, about all that was at the root of it—the oil, the U.S. Embassy hostage crisis, nuclear energy, Israel. He told us about the airplane crash of 1988, when a U.S. missile brought down a plane of 290 Iranian civilians. We'd heard of this, just barely, but we understood it as a terrible accident. Atef turned back in the van toward us: "It was *not* an accident."

When we drove by a mural of the United States flag, the fifty stars replaced with fifty skulls, we wanted to turn back and drive by it again so that we could film this symbol of the tension between our two countries. Saeed would not turn back. He spoke in fast, emotional Farsi, and Atef translated: "That mural is not how we feel. If you film that, people will think we do not like America. The government paints that, not us. And the men you see who chant 'Death to the U.S.,' they are scooped up from the poor neighborhoods and paid to chant it—it is not real. It is not how *we* feel. Please, I beg of you, do not film that sign." We didn't film the sign.

AROUND 8 P.M., Bahram and Ryan arrive back at the hotel. Anxious to see beyond the tour-guide-approved Iran, we ask him where we should eat. It is risky to go out, to walk by the man sitting behind the hotel desk, and, in retrospect, it seems brash and arrogant to disobey Atef's do-not-go-out mandate. But we do go, Bahram dropping us off at his favorite restaurant before racing off to chemistry cram sessions. "You will like this place," he says, waving his frenetic hands and darting off into the night.

The restaurant is a tiny room lit by candles. The Italian menu is scrawled onto a chalkboard, and the plates of lasagna and bowls of minestrone are passed down a staircase from a woman in a floral smock. There are four or five tables, occupied by groups of friends, men with Latin-lover hair and women with red lipstick, whose scarves fall lower and lower as the night goes on. In the two weeks before we left, I read *Persepolis, Lipstick Jihad,* and *Reading "Lolita" in Tehran,* books about Iranian lives that unfolded away from the streets, in the privacy of homes. Seeing these dashes of hair as the women lean forward across the table—they are little glimpses into the world I know I will not see.

When we get back to the hotel room, I call Jerry, the professor, for the third straight night. He does not answer. Hanging up the phone, I am frustrated but unsurprised. All along he had warned me of this: once we got to Iran, it was up to us.

THE NEXT MORNING, we take off for Yazd, two days ahead of our itinerary. Atef is anxious to get us out of Tehran. Saeed drops us all off at the local airport, where we'll catch a short flight to what is likely the second oldest city in the world. Atef, Luke, and Ryan head to men's security, while Rebekah and I branch off to the women's. We stick our camera bags and the soccer ball on the conveyer belt, experiencing the familiar airport-security nerves: will they open our camera bags? Will they see our tapes, and if they do, will they care? We've each got several tapes crammed into our pockets as we walk through the X-ray machine, hoping we won't beep. A woman in a chador summons us through, and there is no blaring sound of alert like the one I hear in my imagination. The conveyer belt spits out our bags and ball. I pick up our gear and am starting to feel the relief of having once again made it through security, when the officer walks up to me and reaches for the ball.

She spins the ball in her hands and I wait to hear what we've done wrong. She walks briskly around the side of the X-ray machine—and then tosses the ball to the other security guard, who attempts to trap it with her chador-engulfed thigh. Here we are in the Tehran airport, and two fifty-year-old women, government security officials, are juggling the ball and giggling. I feel like I'm in a surreal version of that Nike commercial where the Brazilian national team does tricks through the terminal. All over the world, from the ghettos of Argentina to the border control in Togo, the ball has done this. It has the magnetizing effect of a cute puppy, people stopping to touch it, to play with it, to smile at you as if you are lucky.

As we wait at the gate, a very old woman walks toward us. Hunched over at the waist, one foot moving at a time, she comes right up to me, and her stoop puts her eyes an inch from my own. Breathing heavily, she says, "Where are you from?"

"The United States," I say, my smile unsure.

"Ah!" she says, smiling. Grasping my hands between hers, she says, "Welcome to our country."

Welcome to our country. People keep telling us this, and it's no flimsy welcome-to-our-country, no polite offering. They absolutely mean it.

YAZD IS IN the middle of nowhere. Desert stretches out in all directions. Except for the slow whistle of the wind towers—*badgirs* they are called, and they look like bell towers without the bell; they catch hold of the wind and keep the buildings cool—Yazd is incredibly quiet. The Old City is one color, a sand castle come to life, buildings made of mud bricks bleached by the sun. The buildings have thick wooden doors with two ancient iron knockers, one for women, one for men, the shape of each knocker making a slightly different sound so those inside know which sex is calling. There are narrow alleys and arches and old bicycles propped against clay walls. We drift into mosques as cool as caves. We pay two dollars to go inside a sprawling historical home that's being restored, just to see a sand castle from the inside. There are narrow, meandering staircases, sometimes leading nowhere, sometimes leading to rooms that feel like surprises. All the rooms are empty—no beds or dressers or closets or clothes. Ancient mirrors are recessed inside the clay walls, framed by a wandering mosaic of turquoise stones. Some of the mirrors have fallen, and they lay jagged and broken along the floor, refracting light that

Old City, Yazd (Courtesy: author)

makes the arched doorways glow. "I love it here," I keep saying to Luke. Luke and I never hold hands and rarely show affection in public, only mushy when we are alone. But here, where I know I can't, I want to touch him. I come up behind him, talk into his neck. "This place," I say, "is my favorite."

THAT NIGHT WE sleep in a palace—domed ceilings, stained glass windows, ornate stonework. It's very different than the floors we normally crash on. Feigning exhaustion (and harboring ambitions of going out again on our own), we get Atef to drop us off early. Inside the hotel courtyard, we walk beneath mosaic arches, past the lush green gardens I'd read about—the green that Iranian-Americans now long for. Deep benches draped with Persian carpets line stone sidewalks; sitting Indian-style, both locals and Europeans sip their tea as thunderclouds roll in.

The storm is violent and short. After, the clouds are still there but only faintly, like the imprints of recent fireworks. We have maybe half an hour before it's dark. We are both too nervous and too full of guilt to take our nice cameras with us. It's one thing to wander out onto the streets on our own; it's another to wander out onto the streets on our own while carrying the camera that might've gotten us in trouble in the first place. Ferg packs the small, more tourist-looking camera in her purse, and we set out, walking the dirt alleys neighboring the hotel.

A kid, maybe four years old, kicks a ball against the wall. Two teen-agers, barefoot on a motorcycle, draw aimless figure eights in the dust. I call out "football" and tap my knuckles against the ball. They slow, standing up on the pegs. The kid in an orange T-shirt and MC Hammer pants dismounts, grabs two bricks from the rubble on a nearby lot, and begins to make goals. I lean against the wall and watch Luke and the guys play until dark.

An alley in Yazd (Courtesy: author)

. . .

THE NEXT MORNING we go again to the Old City. For the past two days Atef has only allowed us to film from the safety of the car. Ferg propped the camera up on a pillow, shooting tracking shots out the window as we drove by sand buildings. But now Atef says, "It is the Old City. It is very quiet. I suppose it is OK to film." I'm surprised by this change but I don't ask any questions. It's drizzling lightly and the narrow sand lanes are empty. Every few feet an arch spans the lane, light coming through on both sides of it. Ryan films and Ferg walks in step with him, covering the camera with an umbrella. Luke and I are a couple hundred yards ahead. They film us walking: it's one of those shots you get in every country, just in case it will somehow help in the editing room. Most likely, it will never be used.

"OK," Ryan calls out. "Can one of you talk about soccer in the alleys?"

"I've got something," Luke says. I look at him, surprised, as he's usually resistant to talking to the camera. He only likes to say something if it's completely spontaneous, a thought that comes to him naturally, without prompting. Anytime we try to get him to say some skeletal line of setup, he clams up completely.

"This trip, it's been great . . ." he says, talking in a strange voice. Even after two years of filming, we both still have a hard time being natural on camera. I frown, hoping he'll sort it out and start talking normal.

Then I hear him say my name: "Gwendolyn, you are the . . ."—and I understand what's happening, why his voice sounds like that. It's not camera-voice—it's shaky, emotional, a tone I've never heard from him before.

He sinks down to one knee, still speaking. I try to say yes, but my voice gets stuck, so I just start nodding, vigorously nodding.

Still down on his knee, he holds up both hands. "Uh, I don't have a ring. I thought I might lose it if I brought it to Iran."

I nod, laugh, reach for him and then halt—remembering where I am—but he pulls me toward him and kisses me anyway.

Atef, Ryan, Ferg, and the camera are fifty yards back, and I'm grateful for the separation. We walk slowly toward them, and I feel massively shy.

All three congratulate us. The camera is still on, and I know we're supposed to say something, but I just burrow my face into Luke's shoulder.

"That was the most romantic thing I've seen in my whole life," Atef says, his voice cracking.

I smile back at him, still wordless.

"Why don't we give you guys some time to yourselves," Ryan suggests.

We drive to the Zoroastrian Fire Temple, home to a flame that has burned for more than 1,500 years. While the others go inside, Luke and I sit close together on a bench in the garden.

"I messed it up," he says. "I meant to say, 'Traveling around the world has been incredible, but what I really want is to be with you.' But instead I said, 'Traveling around the world *with you* has been incredible but . . .' Those two tiny words—'with you'—they changed the whole meaning."

I laugh, tell him I loved it. I hadn't heard any of it, anyway. As soon as I realized what was happening, I stopped processing in any normal kind of way.

While I'd imagined a roaring fire, when Luke and I go inside the temple, we see only a small flame, not much bigger than that of a candle. With fifteen or twenty other people, we watch it flicker and continue.

TWO DAYS LATER, after we have wandered the insides of mosques and castles, watched a green man make hemp, and walked through wide-open space in the foreground of the Towers of Silence, we drive back to Tehran, miles of sand shooting by our open windows. We listen to music, first Atef's ("It is Western music—it is forbidden," he boasts), and then ours, because Atef tells us, "I want to hear young American music—my Western songs are from my other guests . . . but they are, well, older." We play our favorite, The National, and all five of us are quiet as we listen to the lyrics and watch the small, ancient towns, appear on the horizon and then pass.

It takes seven hours to cover the three hundred kilometers back to Tehran. As we enter the outskirts of the city, all along the grassy banks and sandy medians of the main highway, every fifteen yards or so, there are families, eating cheese and sitting on blankets with legs folded beneath them. "On Fridays, we take our picnics," Atef explains. We pass one family after another. The sun is 5 p.m. soft and the city feels calm. I hang on to this calm, even as my mind starts moving toward tomorrow, toward our meeting with the Iranian government.

That night I meet Bahram and his friend in the lobby of our hotel. Ferg has stayed up the past three nights, setting her alarm to go off every hour, dubbing tape after tape: our plan is to leave a copy of the footage with Bahram, in case our meeting with the government does not go well.

"Hi," I say, as I reach for my new friend's hand and then stop, hand freezing midair as I remember the no-touching policy in Iran. I sway awkwardly, hand now embracing my other arm. (I also keep giving people the thumbs-up, which in Iran is the equivalent of flicking people off, but we have twenty-three countries of habit to break: *I cannot speak your language, so I can't tell you, but I like you, I like this place, and I want you to know it*—thumbs-up.)

"OK, should we go up?" I say, meaning to my room to get the tapes. Bahram and his friends look briefly at one another and start to follow me upstairs until the desk manager surges up from his chair and around the counter, face red, head shaking violently from side to side: "I am sorry. It is impossible. Room, no. I am sorry."

"Sorry," I echo. "So sorry." I get up from the couch and run up the stairs, taking them two at a time, face burning as I realize the implications. *I am an American hussy who just tried to take two men up to my room.*

After retrieving the tapes, I give them over to Bahram, my hands clumsy, guilty. I've never been a troublemaker. I've never flirted with danger. I can still remember the time I let Tiffany Long copy my sixth-grade grammar homework—indescribable panic. So now, here, shanghaiing my new Iranian friend, planning subterfuge, I am jumpy. I feel like a drug smuggler. I worry that the man behind the desk will report us. I imagine two men banging at Bahram's front door, raiding his home, tearing at his stacks of chemistry papers in search of contraband.

Bahram stuffs the tapes into his satchel, and we bow awkwardly toward each other, standing on the steps of the entrance. Ferg comes down the stairs as they are about to leave and, without thinking, reaches toward Bahram for a hug. He looks miserably uncomfortable with his head smushed against her chest. "Uh, I'm sorry," he says, "but this is illegal in our country." Red patches creep up Ferg's neck.

"Tell Ali I say hello—and to come back to Iran," Bahram calls out as he heads down the street with our dubs.

Bahram gone, the desk manager stops us before we can get upstairs. He says, "There is a field, a few streets away. They play late into the night—one or two A.M."

I'm moved by this but also confused. Does he know what we are doing? That we are filming soccer? We won't go out and play tonight—there's too much at risk—but his willingness to let us go makes it clear that he has no plans to turn us in. Like everyone else, he just wants to help.

"Thank you," I say.

Later, Luke and I sit in the lobby with the man from behind the desk and the two guys who wait the tables at breakfast, watching Barcelona play Real Madrid.

PACKING OUR TAPES the next morning, Ryan, Ferg, Luke, and I eat flatbread and prep each other on what to say. "We are twenty-something-year-olds, making a small college documentary. We want to show our pictures of Iran to our friends."

An hour later, we enter the tour agency office. Old posters of China and India are tacked to the walls. "Who is Gwendolyn?" asks a man sitting at the corner desk.

I raise my hand. "So you are the one I have been e-mailing with," he says. "I am Ahmadreza." Ahmadreza—the head of the tour company that Atef professed no knowledge of.

I look to Atef.

"Ah, Ahmadreza . . . I knew only his last name."

"How have you liked your time in Iran?" Ahmadreza continues.

Luke, Ryan, and Ferg speak up, helping me gush. We talk about the civilizations scattered across the desert, stuff out of the imagination. About the dolmas Atef's mother made for us and the beautiful arches and sideways light of Yazd. Then we are out of chatter and wait to see what's going to happen to us.

"It was a misunderstanding," Ahmadreza says.

He shakes our hands and walks out of the office. Soon we are exiting the building, silent and hesitantly excited, walking fast down the tree-lined boulevards until we are far enough away from the office to feel safe enough to ask, "Atef, was that *it*?"

He smiles his first big smile all week—we can see his gums—and says, "That was it. We shall go for ice cream."

TWO DAYS EARLIER, while we sat in an Internet café, I received an e-mail from a friend of a friend of a friend, a woman named Niloofar who used to play for the Iranian national team. I'd e-mailed her on the off chance she could meet us for a game before we had to leave her country.

We are licking nutmeg ice cream when I bring it up to Atef, hopeful that because the meeting—the review of tapes, the assessment of the Americans—passed without incident, he will be OK with this idea. But when he nods his head and says, "All right," it is more like we have just broken him down so completely he can no longer muster any resistance.

The field where Niloofar asks us to meet her, the last we'll see in Iran, is an elevated chunk of Tehran with a hazy skyline backdrop. We arrive before Niloofar and climb up on a wall with a vantage point of all of the city. Three young guys stand nonchalantly on the overhang, hands in their pockets, backs to the city, ignoring the straight drop behind them.

Ferg spots two women approaching, one carrying a ball in her arms. We wave to one another from across the square. Niloofar has green eyes, long eyelashes, and boyish mannerisms (a wide stance, hand fiddling with her wristwatch). Her friend is stunning—bright purple head scarf, highly arched eyebrows, delicate cheekbones, bright red lipstick, long manicured fingernails. "This is my best friend," Niloofar says of the woman whose features are so striking it's as if her face breaks the rules. And it does—the plucked eyebrows, the bronzer, the lipstick, the purple hijab worn far enough back to reveal a few inches of shiny hair; none of it is allowed.

"Will you play?" I ask.

Niloofar laughs and translates, and the woman in purple shakes her finger. "She likes to watch," Niloofar says.

As two other girls approach, Atef stands fifteen yards away, his arms around his binder. There are still men playing on the field, and I know we won't have much time, so I ask to start the interviews right away. It's reverse order: normally we play and then talk, and once we've played, the word "interview" doesn't feel right; you're just talking to another player. But if we wait until after the game, I worry we won't be able to talk to them at all.

Atef is disapproving and miserable as he translates our questions, saying, "OK, is that all?" after every question. We learn that Niloofar got her moves from watching YouTube videos of Ronaldinho; that David Beckham is her favorite player, that she grew up playing in the streets with her brothers; that all she wants is to play.

WHEN THE MEN finish their game, we take over the field. The guys linger outside the chain-link fence and watch.

"We must wait until they go away," Niloofar says as we make a goal out of shopping bags. No matter how slow we go, the men will not leave, so Niloofar explains that we will pretend to leave. We exit the field as though we have decided not to play after all and wait around the corner until the men disappear. Then we head back onto the field.

The women undo their manteaus, but the field owner comes out, shaking his head and finger. They rebutton their manteaus, reluctant, as though they know the billowing long shirtdresses will make them look different from the other players around the world.

I didn't really think they would be good. Two of them played on the

Game with Niloofar and friends on a court overlooking the
Tehran skyline (Courtesy: Luke Boughen)

Iranian national team, but in a country where women's soccer seems
barely allowed, I didn't think that would mean much.

But, again, I'm wrong. They juggle the ball without spin; they go for
the meg; they send through-balls. Every touch is clean. One way or another, they've found a way not only to play but to play well.

When the game ends, it begins to pour, lightning bolts sharp and dramatic across the top of Tehran. We hug good-bye and exchange e-mail
addresses. I feel strange and sad as I walk back to the car. Even if we
shared this game, I'm going back to the United States and these women
will stay in Iran.

In the van, Atef asks if I had a good time.

"Yes," I answer, grateful. "Thank you so much."

"I would've been too nervous and ruined your fun," he says shrugging, smiling bashfully. "So I waited here."

OUR FINAL MORNING we pack our belongings, spreading the tapes
between us, stuffing them in underwear side pockets and the insides of
running shoes. We drift through security. I am pent up with nerves as I
watch careful inspections of bags, but no one examines the inside of ours.

An hour later, we board our plane and the women begin removing their hijabs as they walk down the aisle, hair spilling out over shoulders.

Fifteen hours later, we pick up our bags and head for United States Customs.

Reaching the front of the line, the security guy looks down at our passports and our tickets and makes a choking sound. "Iran?" he says. "Why in hell would you want to go there?"

"Tourism?" Ryan says.

He snorts. "Go to line six."

So we walk to line 6 to join dark-skinned people with darker beards waiting for American officials to press their fingers against glass.

A TRYOUT

WE'D BEEN SITTING in an Internet café in Tehran when we got the news. The results from the MelroseMac contest were in: we got nine hundred more votes than second place. We could buy editing equipment: we had a way of finishing the movie. (Ferg and I jumped and gasped like *The Price Is Right* contestants, while Ryan and Luke pulled us back down to our chairs and whispered, "Shh. . . .")

For the next six months we cart our new Macs between apartments. (Luke: "My cousin's out of town this week—we can work at her place." Ryan: "Maisie said she didn't care if you guys slept over again." Ferg: "As long as we're quiet, I think it's fine to work in my room.") We shape our footage into stories, some puzzles harder than others. We watch clips over and over, gazing at faces we know. We yell about what *must* go in, attached to moments we feel we cannot part with. All of us know every word by heart; sometimes we speak only in movie lines.

On Facebook, we post "Seeking Farsi, Quechua, Sheng, Arabic, Japanese, French, and Chinese translators" and call up college language programs, hunting for students willing to do it for free. We gnaw on highlighters and study transcripts. On weekends, we go to concerts of obscure bands in search of songs. We send long-shot e-mails to our favorites. Kasey Truman, a Duke teammate who now works for Chop Shop Music, slides us tracks from small great bands who are willing to give us rights for free or cheap. Young the Giant, Nico Stai, Takénobu, Ceci Bastida, We Were Promised Jetpacks, Anya Marina—great indie artists' songs soundtrack our film.

I EDIT IN the morning and at night and train in the afternoon.

I work out at Luke's cousin's apartment-garage gym in Koreatown, doing sprints on the treadmill, really pounding, making the whole weight room shake. I run up and down the seven flights of stairs that no one else in the building seems to use. I do interval sprints down Wilshire, breaking at the stoplights, weaving around traffic. The two fields closest to the apartment stay locked. Our attempts to climb the fences go poorly. The nearest park is strewn with signs that say NO SOCCER HERE. (Nowhere in the world have we encountered anything like it. Luke, incredulous, takes a picture and posts it on his Facebook wall.) MacArthur Park's a mile and a half away. Luke and I do one-v-ones in the dirt area, shooting on heavy trash cans that remind me of how much I wanted it when I was twelve. After games, we run home with dusty shins, listening to the car horns and breathing in fumes.

A fancy synthetic field in El Segundo is open during the daytime. A group of local players at various stages in their careers—a few, like me, headed for the West Coast Combine—play pickup during lunch breaks.

Two weeks before the tryout, I'm out in El Segundo working on my stride, trying to kick it out, make it longer, raising my knees, reaching with my toes. Right when I think I've got it, when I'm really flying, running in a way I never have before—track-star-like form—I feel a twig-snap in the back of my leg. It's hot and tearing and I sink down, light-headed with disgust and disbelief, black balls of turf sticking to my wet legs. My hamstring—it's pulled, all the way. It's spasming and twitching and I'm trying to control my face because other people can see me and I hate the indignity of injury. No matter how real it is, it still feels like an excuse.

In the car Luke keeps his hand on mine. My foot up on the dashboard, ice wrapped around my hamstring, I'm doing the math. The tryout is fourteen days away. If I ice and heat and ice and heat, and maybe find one of those portable electrical stimulation machines to pulsate the hell out of it, could I be healthy in time for the tryout? Even if I do recover enough to go, I won't be fit. Fitness is something I'm good at. I came in as a sixteen-year-old freshman and won the two-mile Cooper Test by a hundred yards. I can outrun anyone. But now I'll have to rest the leg and do arm weights and pool laps, when I should be doing ball sprints, working on my first step, my explosion. I wanted to be at the top of my game. I wanted to play my best and be chosen or turned down so that all the wondering could stop.

I STAY OFF the leg for a week and then I start jogging, careful not to push it. Two days before the tryout, I test the hamstring, doing some 70-percent sprints and then eighty- . The leg feels shaky but handles it. It's close, too close not to go.

On December 14, we drive down to Chula Vista, site of the United States Olympic Training Center. We pull into the parking lot. I look at the sign with the Olympic rings.

I've been here twice before, once when I was fourteen, then again at seventeen. Now I am here again, nine years later. I get out of the car, press myself against Luke for a second, and then wave good-bye, swinging my bag up on my shoulder. I follow paper signs with arrows to check in. I breathe deeply, fake-smile at the person behind the counter, and pick up my kit and room key.

Unlocking my door, my hand shakes stupidly. Someone opens it mid-lock-fiddle. Katie, a brunette from Denver, and Sarah, a blonde from Seattle, arrived before me; their room shares a living room with mine. We shake hands and ask one another where we've played and what year we graduated and who plays which position. All of us are midfielders.

I tear open the plastic bag and take out my numbered tryout jersey and tiny white shorts. "We think the league must be going for a sexpot angle," Katie says as I hold up the scrap of see-through white fabric.

Chioma, my roommate, arrives an hour later. She is young and funny and knows everyone, and this makes me feel intimidated and quiet and too shy for all this. (I'm not afraid of prisoners, but put me in a group of girls and I shrink inside myself.)

All the players I know from college who are still playing go to the East Coast Combine next week. I know almost no one here, which is just like when I tried out for the Florida Olympic team as a twelve-year-old: Pensacola, the northwest part of the state, was an eight-to-twelve-hour drive away from the other players trying out. I arrived in the dorm room I was assigned and saw that all four beds were taken. A boom box was playing, it smelled like Sun-Ripened Raspberry Body Splash, and four girls with Clearwater Chargers T-shirts, bumblebee socks, and Princess Leia buns stared at me. I smiled and introduced myself, and they said, "We moved you to another room." So I left the loud room and went into an empty room, crawling into the bottom bunk, listening to my music, imagining myself on the field.

Now, on the other side of the country, I say good night to Sarah and Katie and lie down on my bed with my headphones in the same way I did at twelve. Maybe I'm not tough enough for this anymore. How brave you are as a kid—to pack a suitcase and go out on your own to try your hardest and wait for people to say yes or no.

THE UNIFORMS, OUR identical ponytails, the pristine fields, the orange cones—it seems so sterile. Is this the same game I've been playing? The first morning, we jog across the grass in one straight line. We are friendly to and afraid of one another. We stretch in silence.

My combine coach is Albertin Montoya, a regal-looking Argentinean with slicked-down curls, a handsome face, and a long neck. He talks in a smooth voice that makes me uneasy. He brings us together in a huddle, holds his hands behind his back, and says, "Play with confidence. Separate yourself from the rest."

We start with a small-sided game. All chasing good first impressions, we sprint the field wildly. I win two balls right away, picking them off somebody, and while a train of self-doubt hits me every time I'm about to do anything (*Will I screw up my touch? Is there someone sprinting I didn't see?*), I connect both passes. Two minutes in I'm heaving and light-headed, feeling more out of shape than I've felt in my life. I lose one ball but win two others, dribble past someone, and connect a through-ball. As I sprint, I can feel my hamstring hanging on, hanging on, and then the hot ripping as I repull it. It held up for ten minutes. I keep playing, trying to use the adrenaline to keep me from feeling.

FULL-FIELD, ELEVEN-a-side games are scheduled for the afternoon. I consider not playing, but I can hear my dad's voice telling me one of the main lessons of childhood: Never ask to sub out. No matter what, you don't choose to come off the field.

My roommates and I walk out to the game, each wearing headphones, trying to tune out the rest of the world, including one another. I listen to "About Today" by The National. It's a sad song. Probably no one else would listen to it to get psyched up. But when the chorus comes on—"How close am I to losing you"—it fills me with feeling, chokes me up right there on the sideline. I bend down, tape my shinguards to my calves, and think, *This is all you've got left, right here.*

We do high-knees across the field. I find a ball and go through a series of touches until Albertin pulls us together.

"Who is the best team in the world?" he asks, in a voice that expects a definitive answer.

No one says anything, each of us afraid of being wrong, aware that we don't watch as much soccer as we should. I don't have cable, don't know the latest. But I do know he's probably looking for Barcelona or Manchester United. My heart pounds as I consider whether or not to speak. I break the silence: "Manchester United?"

"No," he says, like I'm definitely wrong. (Even though Manchester United won the most recent Champions League.)

"Barcelona?" Chioma says.

"Good," he says, hands behind back, legs spread a foot apart, that body positioning that conveys *I am the dispenser of answers.* "Lionel Messi. Best player on Barcelona, best player out there. The pride of all of Argentina. This is the weakness of women. You know nothing about the soccer happening around the world."

He speaks so knowingly that I want to tell him what he does not know—that if you go into Villa 31 or any of the other ghettos around Argentina, they won't tell you Messi is the pride of Argentina. He's the best, but he was off to Spain at fourteen. Tévez is the hero: "He's one of us," Gustavo, a villa player, had said. "He comes from a place like this. He always played in poor neighborhoods like we do now. And on the field, you can see he hasn't forgotten. He still plays like he's in the ghetto."

"Our game kicks off in ten minutes," Albertin says. "Make sure you're ready."

I start the game on the bench and go in for the second half. I'm an outside midfielder, but Montoya isn't using outside midfielders, so he puts me into the center. The game thunders around me.

Girls wilt my composure, deflate my ego. Playing all the time against guys is a little bit gutless. When I beat out a guy who is faster and stronger than me, I feel good. And when he beats me, I don't dwell on it; he's faster, he's stronger. They're the ones with something to lose, which means I've got the reckless confidence you need to be good.

I take a couple terrible touches, the kind you see on TV that make you say, *Are you kidding me?* I hang in there the rest of the time. I feel like a one-legged hack, an ogre with a bandage falling down my leg. It's disgusting to me not to be in shape, to be a step late, to get beat to the ball.

After the game, you can see which ones of us Albertin's interested in, and I'm not one of them. I don't blame him—I wouldn't like me either. Still, it's hard to like a coach who doesn't like you.

THAT FIRST DAY of play, we all looked the same. We canceled one another out. Lots of trying hard, not much flair. When I watched the other two teams play, I saw only one standout: Tina DiMartino, a UCLA kid who's five feet two but smooth. She glided across the field, everyone else's effort emphasizing her ease.

In the second game, Albertin Montoya decides to switch formations and use outside mids. I'm standing on the left wing when I see DiMartino lining up across from me, the other coach wanting to test her playing ability out wide. She doesn't look happy about it.

Outside mid is what I know how to do. A one-v-one battle where I am playing against someone better than me: that may be my favorite scenario. We are right in front of the bleachers full of coaches when she tries to dribble. I read her cut and take it, dribbling forward, slotting it to the center mid. DiMartino gets the ball again a minute later (this is one of the great parts about being a star—people play you the ball a lot), and again tries to go by me. Even though my hamstring screeches and I can't breathe, when I strip it off her, there's that world-washed-out feeling of being fully inside the game.

I receive a cross on my chest, play it down to my feet, thread it to the center mid, and take off. She finds me again deep up the wing. I get end-line and serve in the cross to the forward streaking into the box, putting the ball on her feet. She finishes it into the side netting. It's the only goal scored in the run of play the entire weekend.

"Now *that* was soccer," Albertin says at halftime. "I can't remember who played the cross—Sarah maybe? But that was strong. *Now* we are playing."

I notice him not notice me, but I also notice it doesn't bother me. It wasn't for him; that moment was mine.

THE FINAL DAY, I am very, very bad. My leg is shot. I limp like a drama queen, and I keep getting run by. I look flustered and disoriented out there. I get subbed out fifteen minutes into the half.

When the game ends, I walk fast back to my room. I cry in the shower.

I throw on sweats, pack up my bag, and strap it across my shoulder. I want out of there. I get to the parking lot, and there's Ferg, with the camera, wanting me to talk. Which is pretty much the last thing I want to do right now. I can still feel the lump in my throat, and I know that if I try to talk, I'm going to cry, and there's no way I'm going to cry on camera.

I pull my wet hair off my neck and feel hard and cold, unwilling to play along. Luke is next to Ferg and he has a sweet, pitying expression, and even that I don't want to see.

"Hey," Luke says, pulling my face into his chest.

When I resurface, I am calmer, able to say some of what I'm thinking. The first English class I took in college was during my freshman season, and even though it was the best collegiate season I would end up having—five goals, five assists, All-ACC—I was still frustrated; I wrote my English 90 paper about perseverance. No matter what, you just keep persevering: that was the crux of it. It dripped with hope. My professor, an old man, wrote in sloppy cursive at the end of the paper: *Of course, sometimes it's just better to give up.*

When you're sixteen, eyes moving down your paper anxiously for the comments of your all-knowing professor, that sentence is a shocker. I sat there in the back row with the other athletes and gaped at him shuffling in front of the chalkboard, his tired voice calling on the raised hands of students trying to come up with answers.

As I got older, I wondered: Maybe he wasn't being a bastard. Maybe he was just worried I didn't know. It's OK to let go of a dream.

I throw my bag into the trunk of our deer-dented Camry and drive away from the U.S. training center, knowing I didn't make it and that I'm not going to try again.

I'm embarrassed of how sad I feel. There are bigger deals than not making a professional league. And even though it didn't turn out like I'd planned, the game gave me my whole life.

There's a line from a Jonathan Franzen essay that's been banging around in my head: what you begin "as a bid for . . . attention, eventually invites you to pursue it for its own sake, with a seriousness that redeems and is redeemed by its fundamental uselessness."

Most players want the stage—we want to enthrall. But one day we realize that even in the quiet, with no one watching, it feels very good to try very hard and play very well.

Maybe, like Luke says, the game does beckon us, calling us beyond what we had imagined, offering us more than we knew how to ask for when we were kids. The dream, it turns out, isn't the national team or a professional league. The dream is playing; playing is the dream.

THE HOMESTRETCH

PELADA—NAKED, THE barest form of the game. We think the idea is beautiful. This, we say, is the essence of our film. This is our title. (Never mind that no one knows what it means, that no one will be able to pronounce it or remember it, that it doesn't let anybody know the film is about soccer. We don't care, we name it *Pelada* anyway.)

We throw ourselves into editing, racing to meet the film-festival entry deadlines. Between odd jobs and a night shift bagging groceries at Trader Joe's, Ferg saves up enough to rent a bedroom in an apartment advertised on Craigslist. It's big enough to fit a computer in the corner, so we sit on her bed, eating trail mix.

During one of our editing marathons—working until four in the morning, passing out on Ferg's bed, waking up again at eight—we hear a knock on the front door. Ferg goes to answer it and comes back holding an eviction notice. She sits down on the bed. "It says three months' unpaid rent."

Ryan and I watch the red spreading up Ferg's neck and across her cheeks. "I've written my roommate a check every month. Where the hell has it been going?"

Pink notice in hand, she knocks on his bedroom door. Ryan and I listen as their voices get louder:

"That was the landlord. Why are we getting an eviction notice?" She tries to keep her voice calm, but we can hear it tremble.

"What are you doing with my mail?" he asks, emerging from his room and shutting the door tightly behind him. (He always keeps it shut and enters the room from the balcony; although we'd gossiped about this routine, developing wild theories of out-of-control drug habits, we ultimately ignored it.)

"Where has my rent money been going?" Ferg asks.

"You need to mind your fucking business."

"It is my business. I need to know if I'm still going to have a place to live."

"Listen, bitch, my check is going to get here tomorrow. You're making a big deal out of nothing."

"How do I know that?"

"Are you calling me a liar? Get out—get out now."

"What do you mean 'get out'?"

"You have one hour. Pack your shit and get the fuck out of here."

You can't just throw your roommate out without warning, so we sort of ignore him, Ryan and I continuing to edit as Ferg sits back down on the bed, fuming. Then the roommate comes in. He stands just past the doorway. "I want you out."

Ryan, maybe because he's slightly older than we are, is better at arguing. "You can't do that," he says, fully composed. "You have no right to throw her out." He turns away from him and continues to edit.

Ten minutes later, as we trim final shots and adjust subtitles, our computers go dead. From behind us, we hear a sinister voice: "Yep, I turned off the power." He cackles, arms folded in front of his chest. "Now get the hell out of my apartment."

In the kitchen, he throws Ferg's pots and pans off the shelves. Then he goes bigger: he opens the windows and chucks her groceries out to the sidewalk.

"OK!" Ferg shouts. "I'll leave, I'm leaving."

Even though after more than two years, we are only about an hour away from finishing the first full cut of our film, we start helping Ferg pack. We stuff her things into garbage bags and make trips out to the street, filling our cars with her life.

My Camry is a solid eight hundred yards away. When I go to try to find a closer spot, it doesn't start. It's made it through 190,000 miles; surely it won't quit now. I jiggle the steering wheel, as though I can jiggle it awake. Luke, who knows the trick for getting it to kick up, is at a law school orientation. I call him and he walks me through it—still nothing.

Ferg and I fill up the Camry anyway, not knowing where else to stick her stuff. Dripping wet with sweat, we weave down the sidewalk, arms full of clothes, toiletries, and MiniDV tapes.

Two hours later, while Ryan drops off a carload at his friend's house, Ferg and I sit on the curb next to her dresser. Her arms draped over her knees, she looks defeated. "Do I make bad decisions?" she asks, more unsure than I'd ever heard her sound.

"You couldn't have known he'd be a crack addict," I joke, putting my hand on her arm.

We sit, sweating, listening to the rev of car engines. Three years ago, we were in a library, hatching a plan; now we're here, on the curb.

When Ryan pulls back up, we wedge Ferg's dresser into his backseat.

We give my car one last go. Ferg guns the engine and throws it into drive: the Camry's rolling down the hill, Ferg's hopping out of it, Ryan's yelling at me to get in. I jog after it, jump into the seat, and get my foot on the brake right as the car reaches the stop sign. I yell good-bye and accelerate down the road, on a weird adrenaline high: it feels good to pursue what you believe in even after you've literally been kicked to the curb.

I pass four streets before I realize I don't know where I'm going. I forgot to arm myself with directions. Normally I write my steps down on a napkin or a receipt, my thumb pinning them against the steering wheel. Without a planned route, my tendency is to assume I'm lost, even when I'm not.

I make it to the 405, cars zooming by on all sides of me, feeling relatively unfazed. I think, *Well, here goes.*

WE FINISH THE final edit (now based in Ryan's bedroom) and hunt for guys who will do our sound mix and color correct on the cheap. We charge expense after expense on the credit card. We can only afford two days in the narration studio. Narration is frightening—I've made fun of enough movie narration to know what's at stake. Until now, we just recorded lines on Luke's iPod mic again and again until we were satisfied with the pitch and the tone and the feel. But in the studio, you enter that glass room, put on headphones, lose complete control of what you sound like. Monotone and bored or dripping with cheese—it's hard to find the in-between. Morgan Freeman we are not.

Even though I'm never hoarse, I am hoarse our first day in the studio. Everything I record is useless, which means I have only one day to get it right.

They give us a CD with our recordings, and I spend Saturday in Ryan's bedroom plunking lines into the editing timeline. We have to ship the film off by Monday, so Ferg is sitting over my shoulder and telling me to hurry. We recorded ten to eleven takes of each line, and I want to pick the best version, which means I keep listening to them over and over again and saying, "Do you like this one . . . or this one?"

"They all sound the same!" she says, but she's not the one who's going to have to listen to the sound of her own voice filling a theater. I don't even like hearing my voice on an answering machine.

Sometimes I can't find a single read I like. For the next three weeks, the narration lines swim around in my head, waking me up at night. I fantasize about one more day in the recording studio. I sit up in bed, repeating words aloud the way I wished I said them, the way I know they're meant to be said: *I wanted to be the best player in the world. But that never happened.* "But that never happened" should be matter-of-fact; instead my voice is breathy and sentimental, like I forgot for a second that I am totally fine with that.

Luke opens his eyes, brushes my hair off my neck, and sleep-smiles at me.

ON MARCH 14, 2010, after spending months huddled around the bed, editing four hundred hours of footage into ninety minutes, we premiere at South by Southwest in Austin, Texas. Five hundred people fill the theater. We sit together in a middle row and watch the faces in the audience, waiting to see if they'll smile where we do, if they'll laugh at the parts we think are funny, if witnessing the stories of the people who play will move them the way it does us.

We set up screenings across the country, filling theaters, high school auditoriums, community churches, any place we can afford. On September 21, we have our New York premiere. Not at a theater—which would've cost thirty-five hundred dollars we didn't have—but at Legends bar, a three-story venue with a projector screen, a dozen-odd flat screens, and a Scottish lady named Geraldine who's willing to let us take over for a night. The soccer bloggers are massively helpful, embracing our film. From Minneapolis to Los Angeles, from New York to Fort Lauderdale, the writers play a huge part in getting people out to the shows. We also cold-call soccer clubs: "Hi," I say. "We made this movie about pickup. . . . You guys should come." Sometimes coaches are enthusiastic; sometimes they rebuff me in the same way you'd get rid of someone trying to sell you insurance.

We get strong reviews in *The New York Times, Variety, ESPN The Magazine,* and papers across the country. (The *Variety* review does include a narration barb: ". . . delivered in the cadence of a 'how I spent my summer vacation' presentation.") About four hundred people show up in New York, another four hundred in Los Angeles. Six hundred people come to our outdoor screening in Durham, North Carolina. Four hundred and fifty–plus people watch in D.C. and Irvine, California (some people sitting on the floor). We sell out fourteen cities, from Kansas City to Seattle. In Sarasota, Florida, two old ladies with walkers approach Ryan after the show and say, "We came last night on accident—

wrong theater door. But we loved it so much we came back tonight." In Portland, Oregon, we have a weeklong theater run: while there are only thirty people at the first screening, by the end of the week, *Pelada* is the theater's highest-grossing film. In Mathare Valley, Kenya, we screen against the brick wall at Austin's Field. After a screening in Vail, Colorado, one hundred–plus people walk to the neighboring field and play in pickup games until midnight.

ON JUNE 5, 2010, Luke and I get married in Six Mile, South Carolina. A storm comes in a couple hours before the ceremony, while I'm washing dishes instead of painting my toes or curling my hair or doing any of the things I should be doing, because all I can think is that I need for a second to just wash dishes. I rinse a plate and think about how the storm will cool the weather off, but it doesn't cool it off: the water hangs in the air. By 5 P.M., it's the hottest day of most of our guests' lives. The heat hits me at first, but then it is gone.

I hold on to my dad's arm as he speed-walks us down the aisle, my heels plugging into the grass. *Fast, fast, we're going fast,* I try to say, but he doesn't hear me, and I'm feeling sort of touched by his swiftness, like he's trying to outpace the chance for tears.

Then I am in front of Luke, my hands in his.

Leah, my maid of honor—the one who gave me the planner when we were fourteen—sings "Sideways," by Citizen Cope: "These feelings won't go away/They've been knockin' me sideways."

Luke's friend Matt reads our favorite lines from *A Farewell to Arms:* "Often a man wishes to be alone and a girl wishes to be alone too and if they love each other they are jealous of that in each other, but I can truly say we never felt that. We could feel alone when we were together, alone against the others. It has only happened to me like that once."

Standing beneath the stick arbor we made ourselves, when our officiant asks for the rings, I realize we forgot about rings. I hold up my hands and laugh, this moment distinctly ours. We borrow my grandma's and the one

on Luke's best man's finger, and then I say I take this man to be my husband and he says, I take this woman to be my wife.

We drink margaritas and eat barbecue and I pull Luke's tie on the dance floor while my nieces and nephews break-dance around us.

PICKUP

A YEAR AFTER our Austin premiere, we've paid off the credit card bills, no more threatening messages on Ryan's voice mail—although it'll probably be another ten years before we can pay back our investor. Ferg and Ryan are pursuing film careers: Ferg freelances in San Francisco; Ryan's at work on a documentary centered on the stories of Freda Kelly, longtime secretary of the Beatles.

Luke's a law student at the University of California, Irvine. He runs the environmental and international law societies and received the award for most pro bono projects. In the mornings on his way to school, he drops me off at Orange Coast College, where I teach English classes. I throw my favorites at them—Junot Diaz, Denis Johnson, David Foster Wallace, Aimee Bender, Hunter S. Thompson, Lorrie Moore, T. C. Boyle. My hands wave violently. I want my students to love reading like I do.

In the summer, a stack of half-graded papers on my lap, Luke and I drive across the country to Chapel Hill, North Carolina. Luke has an internship at the Southern Environmental Law Center, where he'll work on saving rivers and trees from suburban sprawl and toll roads.

At 6 P.M. on our first day there, I kick what look like gumball-size brown sandspurs down the brick sidewalk, walking from our apartment on Hillsborough Street to the turf in front of Fetzer Field, looking for a game I can play in every night.

CHAPEL HILL FEELS like home—twenty minutes from the place I spent four years of college—but also like enemy territory, domain of the Tar Heels, the team that beat me every time I played them. (After each game, the PA system blasted James Taylor's "Carolina on My Mind." That can really kill a song when you are the loser.)

I'm wearing a Duke soccer T-shirt. As I get to the field, a frat boy with his torso stuck out his car window yells, "DUKE SUCKS."

Walking across hot turf, I hold up my hand, marveling at the sweat that's found its way into the webbing between my fingers. I tell myself, *This is the wet-blanket air you said you missed,* California air so light it doesn't feel real. I look past the Ultimate Frisbee players to the soccer game happening on the other side of the field. Luke bikes up to me, unbuttoned work shirt blowing backward. As he changes, I tinker with the ball and survey twenty guys playing against twenty others.

Any eyes watching that game land on one kid: fro, oversized purple T-shirt, gold chain necklace, superstar speed. He's nineteen, maybe twenty. He walks like he's aiming for thug, but he's got these big Bambi eyes that make him look like someone you want to protect. When he calls for the ball, people give it to him. He takes on so many people, I expect to hear someone yell *Play it, pass the ball, get rid of it,* which is what they yell at everyone else. But they never yell that at him. People seem glad just to witness him. He looks like footage I saw of Allen Iverson playing high school basketball: he's flying while everybody else is running.

The game is so big it's easy for us to drift into. I figure it will take a while to get the ball—in games this big you're vying against your own team as much as the opposing one—but right away a skirmish spits it out to my feet. I Cruyff it away from the pack and dish it off. My next three plays are more or less the same: take a touch and pass it quickly, part of my campaign to earn trust.

The purple shirt, a guy they call Champe—you learn the best players' names the fastest because their names are the ones in everyone's mouths—takes interest in me. He tests me out. Every time he gets the ball, I'm nervous because I know it's coming to me. They aren't easy balls. I'm having to amp up my level of vision to keep up with him. He pings hard, tight passes to me even when I'm surrounded, which means I've got to one-time it into the space in front of him. I'm high on it—his expectation and my effort to meet it.

The ball sharing continues the next four days at the field: he gives it to me, I give it back. This reading-each-other feels personal. We don't talk, don't meet eyes. I remember a similar connected feeling in Santos—all those weeks playing together without speaking, until it felt like I knew my team better because we weren't able to talk. You know the way each other moves; you know how each other reacts to loss and surprise; you see the fifty-fifty chances, the mistakes, the small wins. When I'm at a dinner or a cocktail party or a conference or anything that is not a field, all the chatting, the conversation-making—none of it feels as honest as when I am playing.

I don't want to ruin our silent passing, plus I'm still new to the game and I don't like talking when I'm new. And I'm not sure he speaks English. But eventually I risk it at the water fountain, because I've got to know: "Did you play somewhere?"

"No papers," he says, wiping his mouth, his brown eyes catching mine.

No papers? Papers were stopping him? A gift like that? We were the only ones who'd get to see?

Jose, an El Salvadorean with a curly mop of hair who passes the ball with me before our games start, tells me Champe got offered a tryout with Chelsea but that his mom didn't want him to go: if he didn't make the team, he'd have no way back into the country. He's already been deported once.

One day Champe's face gets stomped on in La Liga. Even though for a month he can only watch, he still comes to the field, sitting in the shade behind the goal. He wears a hard-brimmed Yankees baseball cap over a white towel that hangs down on both sides of his face like Dumbo ears. He pulls the towel over his wired-shut jaw whenever he speaks. Sometimes guys carry kids across the field and drop them with Champe. Surrounded by eight-year-olds, he keeps his eyes on the game.

THEY CALL THE Japanese guy Japan, the Guatamelan guy Guatamala, the Jamaican guy Jamaica, the Cameroonian guy Cameroon (and sometimes Eto'o), the Uruguayan guy Uruguay (and sometimes Forlán). They call one guy Pacquiao after the Filipino fighter, even though the soccer player is Malaysian. Pepperoni is the guy who runs the pizzeria. The Saudi Arabian—short, stocky, olive skin, yellow-brown eyes—they call Arabia (and sometimes Allah). In return, he calls everyone Mexico. For farce value, he occasionally takes off his T-shirt and wraps it turban-style around his head.

I get my name after I'm hit so hard I somehow end up doing a backward summersault. There's a lot of yelling but I keep playing. I hear someone say, "See? She ain't no trouble." (It's stupid how proud this makes me.) Champe laughs and says, "That dude wanted to *kill* you." He starts calling me Flaca, "Skinny Girl," I guess because I fly easily. By the end of the game, everyone calls me that.

Flaca, pelota, cojones, mierda, sin camisa, pinche—I'm up to about ten words. (A Belarusian twenty-year-old says to me, "I'm signed up for Spanish next semester. I can't stand it anymore. I've got to know what's going on.") There's some English yelled out, too: "Let me get my dribble on." "My minutes-to-ball ratio is thirteen-to-one." "Get Hope Solo on that shit." "Ain't this hot in Jamaica." "The ball never lies." Arabia's shit-talking starts in Spanish, moves into English, and finishes in Arabic that is only for himself. When someone dribbles, he yells, "He's going to lose it, he's going to lose it." Or, "She's going to lose it, she's going to lose it." Never saying the phrase once, always twice, like a nursery rhyme.

Often people watch. A middle-aged Hispanic lady sits on a boulder off to the side. I don't know if she's someone's mother or wife or just likes to stop on her way home from work. Twice, I see a white guy with white hair and spectacles standing up on the parking deck, hiding behind a tree, watching us from above. We respond to having a spectator, everyone playing a little harder.

I LEARN THE game regulars, start picking up on the details you miss when you only get to go to a game once. Jeffrey—lanky, twenty-five-ish, good—wears diamond studs in both ears and goes for the meg every one in three times. Champe has a tattoo on his forearm of two hands praying to God. Malik, a Tanzanian, wears a red Iniesta jersey every day, dribbles in circles, and laughs as everyone yells at him. Angelo has a mohawk and wears green Nike sneakers, which he says feel better than cleats on his flat feet. Two teenagers with long noses and shaggy haircuts wear gray Triangle United club T-shirts; they're twins or brothers or such good friends they've started to look and move the same. A Puerto Rican named Monique, who they sometimes call Monique-ah, can hit the trash can from twenty yards out. "What, you too busy looking at her sports bra to remember to defend her?" someone yells after she scores her second.

Maybe Pane (pronounced Paw-nay) is the game's heart. He doesn't miss a day. He wears long-sleeve jerseys, as though it's cool outside. Probably in his forties, he has a Lionel Messi half shag, half mullet, a clipped running style, and a face so fierce I'm afraid to look in it. Arabia calls him El Capitan. He's short, five-four or five-five, but it's hard to notice that. When people don't know what to do with the ball, they look for him. Occasionally he torpedoes up the center. While he teases back and forth with Arabia and Champe and Jose, and will once in a while start laughing wildly, he is not like that with me.

One day I run at him. My right foot pushes the ball to my left foot, drawing a greater-than sign around him. My timing is perfect—the best I've ever done it—but he reads it completely and strips the ball off me, connecting with so much force he lays me out flat. There'd been noise on the field, guys responding to the move I was making, but the rising-in-pitch *ohs* morph into descending *oohs*. It's the worst I've ever been stuffed. It may be the worst I've seen someone stuffed.

Having found the satisfaction of rivalry, I hover close to him the next day. We go in for a fifty-fifty. This, two players cracking the same ball at the same time, is how I tore my MCL in college. But if you're tentative, if he's hitting you at full power while you're only going in at half, that's when you tear it. I try to match his strength. We crush each other. The bones in my leg vibrate. *Jesus,* I think. *Does he hate me?* (It will take me a few weeks to see he is just paying me the respect of going at me with the same psychotic force that he uses on everyone.)

Then the ball is under him and he's holding me off, and in a streak of instincts, I grab on to his waist with both hands (a tactic I usually only use against Luke). This is partly out of frustration and, I guess, partly out of affection. It's me asking him to like me.

Spanish ricochets across the field, guys teasing Pane. I want Luke to be there so that he can tell me what everyone's saying, but his knee's been bothering him, which means I'll come home and sit on the stool in the kitchen and tell him how I finally broke Pane down and made him laugh. This is what I do every day—walk home, peel off my wet T-shirt, guzzle water, and tell him about the game I found.

YOU CAN GO to the same field at the same time, drag the same trash cans into the same spots, kick and dribble the ball in essentially the same way you've kicked and dribbled it for the past twenty years, and there's always still a surprise. On Monday, after months of wearing nothing but long-sleeve, Pane comes to the field in a short-sleeve jersey. On Tuesday, Monique wears giant pink clown glasses and tries to play with them on for the first ten minutes. She dribbles snazzily in the back and loses it. "Monique, what the hell?" one guy yells. "You roll in with gangster glasses and dribble in the box and then *lose* the ball?" On Wednesday, it's raining. I stand under the overhang of our apartment and watch the drops pummel everything, but I go to the field at six anyway, feeling ridiculous, figuring it will be me on the turf, standing alone in the downpour. But when I get there and lean over the brick wall and look down—men, running on the field.

The sun sets around 8:30, and we linger, talking about whatever game was on yesterday and whatever game's on tonight. No one talks about work more specifically than "work." It's just a job, while this game is what we do.

All day I wait for 5:30, and then I take off on my walk to the field, hungry to get there, to see everyone, to play.

I'm learning to appreciate the education of twenty against twenty. You have to figure out how to get the ball. One tactic is to develop alliances: when I get the ball, I look for them; when they get the ball, they look for me.

Sometimes we pretend like we are Barcelona, playing one-time small balls, our passes making stars on the field. We run across the turf, silently calling for it. We all want the ball.

ACKNOWLEDGMENTS

Grateful thanks to Luke for his patience, thoughtfulness, and insight; Ryan and Ferg for their creativity, drive, wisdom, and street smarts; Les Allan, Francis Gasparini, Peter Lange, Tom Rankin, and the Center for Documentary Studies at Duke for making this story possible; Allen Creech, Alexa Dilworth, Thomas Ferraro, Brad Hammer, Gary Hawkins, Donna Lisker, William O'Rourke, Courtney Reid-Eaton, Valerie Sayers, and Peter Stephens for inspiring and encouraging me; and Evelyn Boria-Rivera, Lee Ellis, Alexandra Katona-Carroll, Casey McCluskey, Matt McGowan, Jeff Rusnak, Yaniv Soha, Allison Strobel, Joey Yenne, and my family for their input and support.